MUSEUM STUDIES IN MATERIAL CULTURE

Museum Studies in Material Culture

EDITED BY SUSAN M. PEARCE

LEICESTER UNIVERSITY PRESS
(a division of Pinter Publishers) London and New York

First published in 1989 by Leicester University Press
(a division of Pinter Publishers)

Editorial offices
Fielding Johnson Building, University of Leicester,
University Road, Leicester LE1 7RH.

Trade and other enquiries
25 Floral Street, London WC2E 9DS.

British Library Cataloguing in Publication Data
Museum studies in material culture.
1. Museology
I. Pearce, Susan M. (Susan Mary), *1942–*
069

ISBN 0–7185–1288–X

Typeset by J&L Composition Ltd, Filey, North Yorkshire.
Printed and bound in Great Britain by Billing and Sons Ltd, Worcester.

Contents

List of figures

List of tables

Acknowledgments

Many people have worked hard to bring this book into being, and to produce the anniversary Conference which preceded it. Singling out individuals is always difficult, but I should like to record my thanks to all those who have contributed to the discussions and to the final papers, to Eilean Hooper-Greenhill and Gaynor Kavanagh for much encouragement, to Jim Roberts for valuable assistance during the Conference, and to Jacky Smith who helped to prepare the typescript. I am grateful to Geoffrey Lewis, Director of the Department of Museum Studies, for his support, and to Leicester University Press for the interest which they are showing in Museum Studies. Finally, as always, my grateful thanks go to my husband.

SUSAN M. PEARCE
January 1989

Acknowledgments

Preface

The conference *Museum studies and material culture* marked the 21st anniversary of the Department of Museum Studies in the University of Leicester: as the first university department in Western Europe specifically concerned with this area of study, its establishment in 1966 was a significant event in the history of museums and museology. As befitted such an occasion, a number of key contributions were presented and this volume now makes some of them more widely available.

These papers embrace a number of issues of critical concern to museology and therefore to all involved with museums today. There are here contributions to the development and the intellectual base of this relatively neglected subject. Among them will be found, sometimes implicitly, reflections of the considerable societal and economic change of our times. Where do museums stand today and, more importantly, what impact should such change have on their aesthetic and intellectual role?

Clearly the fundamentals of museums do not change: they are concerned with objects and with people, and the papers in this volume indicate this. But the nature of museum collections, their significance in contemporary perceptions of the museum's function, their potential contribution to knowledge and their role as interpretative media are influenced by such change. If the fundamentals are justified, then this brings with it a need to ensure their continuity and stability but at the same time to exploit the considerable new opportunities.

At no time have there been so many museums or visitors to them. These changes too present challenges as museums attract new audiences. But what is the public's perception of museum visiting? Is there a conflict of purpose between provider and customer? The apparent success of museums may be illusory and it should be asked whether the prime reasons for the museum's existence are themselves being eroded.

The Conference was attended by some 130 people, among whom we particularly welcomed our chief guest, Raymond Singleton, the Department's first Director of Museum Studies. No less than 34 overseas institutions were represented for the occasion. For the conception and organization of the Conference and now the preparation of this volume we record our deep gratitude to Susan Pearce.

GEOFFREY LEWIS

1 *Museum Studies in Material Culture*

SUSAN M. PEARCE

In recent years, after some decades in the doldrums, the interpretation of material culture has become a major academic preoccupation. One reason for this is the fact that museum collections represent the stored material culture of the past, while museum exhibitions are the principal medium through which that past is publicly presented; museums move steadily into the forefront of the picture as the past, and its tangible memorials, become increasingly a political issue in the broadest sense. A second reason is the style of much post-war thinking which shows interest in the idea of universally applicable concepts in ways in which the earlier generation of students did not, and which tends to see objects, with language, as the principal medium through which human relationships are created, expressed and validated. These impulses have come together to stimulate a range of endeavours. Courses in material culture interpretation are given at a number of British universities including Southampton, London, Durham and Leicester; a substantial body of literature is beginning to develop (e.g. Miller 1985 and 1987; Pearce 1986b,c; Deetz 1977; Kristiansen 1984; Schlereth 1985), a number of models for artefact study have been published (Prowne 1982; Elliot 1985; Pearce 1986a); and several international gatherings have been organized, including that by the Department of Museum Studies at Leicester University in 1987, of which this volume is the outcome.

The subject is a large one, but we may begin by suggesting three areas where the thinking which is applied to material culture in museums needs to be developed. The first concerns the interpretation of objects in a formal sense and the identification and development of philosophical approaches which may be fruitfully brought to bear on this process. It includes the hope, not yet realized but beckoning from afar, of drawing on a range of disciplines and schools to create broad principles for artefact interpretation which will be applicable to all objects, and which will increase our understanding of them and our pleasure in them. The second revolves around an understanding of the nature of collections, of what they are, of why they are so, and of what they may become. The third brings these two together with the curator and the public, and considers the nature, actual and potential, of this interaction.

So far in this discussion the words 'material culture', 'object', and 'artefact' have been used as interchangeable synonyms, but this needs amplification. Definitions of material culture and of the purposes of its study have proliferated recently, a natural development in a relatively new enterprise. In North America 'material culture' tends to mean what in Britain would be called 'social history', although it usually includes a considerable input from the applied arts; in chapter 2 Thomas Schlereth gives an overview of the relationship between North American social history and material culture. In Britain, the term has been used for a considerable time by anthropologists and archaeologists, and more recently by sociologists and social historians, and normally they have considered it to mean artefacts constructed by human beings through a combination of raw material and technology, which for practical purposes can be distinguished from fixed structures because they can be moved from place to place. This would of course include the fine and applied arts, although in the past art curators have been less than grateful for this hospitality. To this definition much has recently been added, particularly in North America, and, in the words of James Deetz, material culture is 'that section of our physical environment that we modify through culturally determined behaviour' (Deetz 1977). A definition of this scope would include houses and gardens, towns and fields, and even dance and song, all of them areas in which museums have been showing an interest for some decades now, usually as part of an effort to place their collections in contexts which make them more intelligible and more interesting to the public. Deetz's definition also takes in animals and plants whose genetic constitutions or life patterns have been affected by man, and the meals which can be prepared from them. More pertinent for many existing musems, it would also include all natural science specimens which have been selected and organized into collections, a process which turns them into constructs of the human mind. All this is obviously important for the development of philosophical approaches and for the collecting and exhibition policies which follow from them. For this volume, however, it was decided to include papers which concentrate upon the traditional areas of material culture because, in Britain at the moment, this is where most of the relevant work is being done. The principle, in any case, remains the same across the field: material culture is studied because it can make a unique contribution to our understanding of the workings of individuals and societies – because, in short, it can tell us more about ourselves.

Bearing these points in mind, we may turn to the first of the suggested areas of study, that of the formal (as opposed to the ideological) interpretation of objects. In essence, this means the development of philosophical positions and techniques of analysis which may be brought to bear upon individual objects (or groups of objects) so that their role in the operation of society (their own and that of others) may be illuminated and our perceptions of them sharpened. Object interpretation has had a long and complicated history. The collections of material culture which had arrived in musems both public and private by the 1850s tended to fall into two broad groups: on the one hand, there were the collections of fine art, including not only paintings and sculpture but also ceramics, fine metalwork and coins; on the other, there were the accumulations of 'artificial curiosities', to use the eighteenth-century phrase, and it is interesting to note that both these two words have declined from their original sense of 'strange things made by human artifice' and acquired a distinctly pejorative tone when applied to objects or books – a sour comment, presumably, on the contents and motives of this kind of collecting made by a generation for whom it had become unfashionable. These collections were generally of material which we would call archaeological or ethnographic, like the Pacific artefacts acquired on the Cook voyages which were dispersed after the sale of Sir Ashton Lever's museum in 1786, and found their way into a number of British musems.

The guiding principle behind most of these collections was 'high quality'. Their accumulation was in no sense systematic, but involved the choice of 'good' pieces which were considered to embody the finest design and craftsmanship of their kind. The late eighteenth and nineteenth centuries saw the development of connoisseurship into a full theory of aesthetics, backed up by the very considerable effort expended by the art historians to put the history of artists, studios, patrons and art styles on to a proper footing; the implications of this legacy in the light of the more recent history of design for mass production and consumption are explored here by Wolfenden. The traditional aesthetic and historical considerations were applied chiefly to the fine and applied arts and to the material of classical, and to a limited extent, British archaeology which seemed to justify them. Those curiosities which could not creep into the criteria of the nineteenth- and early twentieth-century art historians remained just that: objects which might, from their bizarre or barbaric form, excite interest and a range of gratifying emotions, but which were, essentially, of limited significance.

From the 1850s onwards much fundamental scholarship in all fields was being completed and published, but the interpretation of material culture remained shallow, and this, perhaps, for two main causes. Firstly, most interpretative work was tied to the fine art ethic of the day, which, as we have seen, had little to offer for much material. Secondly, and perhaps more importantly, the real mid-Victorian preoccupation lay elsewhere, with the true age of the world and the *Origin of Species*, and these focussed attention upon the natural science collections, for which interpretative methods of study and museum display were greatly elaborated as the century proceeded. But in

1880 General Pitt Rivers inherited the estate at Cranbourne Chase where he was to conduct archaeological work up to his death in 1900, and three years later, in 1883, he gave his existing collection, which embraced most kinds of human history artefacts, to Oxford University for permanent display in what became the Pitt Rivers Museum (Chapman 1985). The collections were arranged not geographically or by find site, but typologically, with objects of the same type from many places grouped in sequences which were intended to show how the complexities and the different designs which they exhibited could be related to each other, and to a common ancestor. Pitt Rivers's debt to Darwinian ideas of evolution is obvious, but equally clearly the concept also holds the germ of functionalist ideas about adaptation to circumstances which were later to dominate British anthropology. The gulf between him and earlier collectors is demonstrated by his remark that his material was 'not for the purpose of surprising anyone, either by the beauty or the value of the objects exhibited, but solely with a view to instruction. For this purpose ordinary and typical specimens rather than rare objects have been selected and arranged in sequence' (Daniel 1950: 171).

Pitt Rivers had explained these ideas rather earlier in lectures and papers, notably in his lectures on *The Principles of Classification* given to the Anthropological Institution in 1874 and *The Evolution of Culture* to the Royal Institution in 1875, although probably the full impact of his ideas was not felt until his collections went on display in Oxford. Pitt Rivers offered, for the first time, a theory of material culture interpretation, an intellectual concept which, whatever weaknesses or limitations it was subsequently shown to have, could be applied to *all* artefacts and render them intelligible within the wider scheme. His ideas, correspondingly, were enormously influential, in Britain and North America, as the many exhibitions which survived into the 1950s or even 1960s demonstrate (the author, for example, dismantled just such an ethnography display in Exeter City Museum in 1969). Pitt Rivers's notions dominated museum work, especially in the ethnography field; but academic anthropology in the period between 1914 and 1950, through the influence of Radcliffe-Brown and Malinowski, took a different turn, and the functionalist approach – which both men, very broadly, shared – concentrated upon the detailed studies of single societies through which all aspects of that society could be understood as a self-supporting whole. This approach tended to dismiss artefacts as simply the outcome of social processes and gave them little significance in their own right, a view which devalued museum collections of all kinds, and the study of material culture in general.

Meanwhile, the historical approach, traditional among art curators, was being applied to material culture of the kind which in British museums is usually called 'social history', and which concentrated originally upon the artefacts of nineteenth-century rural and industrial Britain, which by the 1920s were beginning to disappear. This recording of the immediate past, sometimes by photograph and by personal accounts as well as by material culture, used the normal methods of the historian in conjunction with those of the person-to-person recorder and depended in essence upon what, drawing upon the language of the psychologist, may be called behavioural history, where interest concentrates upon the events generated by inter-reaction between individuals, and their physical and social environments (Pearce 1986b). Academic historians showed as little interest in these bygones as anthropologists were showing in museum ethnography, and the ways in which the methods of historical research can be brought to bear on the interpretation of artefacts as such is today a subject of continuing debate among museum historians.

The mid-century intellectual climate of material culture studies in archaeology was markedly brighter. The scene was dominated by Gordon Childe, who interpreted artefacts in terms of their typology, a refined version of Pitt Rivers's ideas, in order to produce a relative dating, and in terms of their spatial distribution; he used this data in conjunction with similar study of fixed structures to define 'cultures' which were perceived as historical realities coming and going across the face of Europe. This approach gave a high priority to the study of museum collections and resulted, if rather infrequently, in corresponding museum displays.

So matters stood at the beginning of the post-war period, with art curators concerned with the provenances of their works and the value judgments relating to their collections, ethnographic artefacts largely neglected and despised while functionalist principles were taught in the universities, social history material culture divorced from the academic historians but looking tentatively towards the broader fields of social science and popular history, and archaeologists alone finding a wider interpretative significance in the study of material culture, a process reviewed here by Crowther. The different disciplines did not work in harmony but it is interesting to see that their various points of view showed a fundamental common stance: all believed that their material was valuable because it was unique in its own way and whether as a picture, a craft work or a cultural assemblage, it owned a particular position in social time and space, a stance which is at the heart of the historical studies from which all these approaches had developed, and still do develop. The post-war decades, with their interest in the universal rather than the particular, were to look rather different.

Before this is discussed, however, it is important to mention two crucial post 1950 advances in artefact study, both of which have in the past had their primary impact upon archaeological material, but which would be capable of adding to our interpretation of more recent material. The first of these are the scientific techniques, which include dating, where Carbon 14 and dendrochronology are perhaps the most useful, and characterization, the techniques of material analysis like petrology or metallurgy, which give much information about sources of raw materials and technology and so about social processes (for a recent overview see Phillips 1985). The second involves learning from the advances made by the 'new' historical geographers, especially Lösch and Christaller, and applying to artefact distributions the analytical techniques of location analysis, place hierarchy and dispersal modes (see Haggett 1956). All these analyses, which are capable of being handled very usefully on a large scale by computer programmes, have been common curency now in archaeology for two or three decades, and experimentation with them in other fields seems overdue.

Fresh intellectual scope for artefact interpretation has come from the French and German-speaking philosophers, sociologists and social anthropologists, like de Saussure, Jacobsen, Barthes and Lévi-Strauss, whose books were translated into English in the years either side of 1960, and whose ideas have been disseminated into the English-speaking world by writers like Leach (1976) and Hawkes (1977). The semiological and structuralist concepts associated with these thinkers do not form a unified school, and each proposition has had its own long history of orthodoxy and heresy giving, among others distractions, a proliferation of terms. Nevertheless, some common ground can be identified. The field of study is taken as synchronic, as a slice of social action frozen at a moment, rather than as diachronic; it is, that is to say, essentially a-historical, a position it shares with the earlier functionalists. Within this social slice can be perceived the operation of communication in the form of words, kinship systems, myth and ritual, material culture, and so on, and these embody distinct individual or collective roles, by creating categories of relationships which are either metonomic, that is involving members of the same set, or metaphoric, that is the relationship with another set (or several others) which is opposite and equivalent (for specific examples taken from dress and pottery see Pearce 1986c).

These principles are regarded as universally valid, and the grid charts which such analysis produces are seen as specific manifestations, or individual figures in a universal dance (to use an image which appears a good deal in the relevant literature), deriving their character from specific times and places but conforming to the underlying human pattern. Lévi-Strauss and his followers developed the notion of opposed sets, or binary pairs, into a technique for analysing the underlying structure of societies, and some of the implications which this can have for material culture interpretation are explored in this volume in the paper by Pearce: it can offer a way of understanding why objects carry the symbolic weight, first discussed by Freud and his followers, which we experience them as carrying. One of the chief difficulties in these ideas lies precisely in their a-historicism, which is another way of saying that they find it difficult to explain why societies change and what part individual men and women play in bringing change about. Explanations of social change have tended to revolve around the application of ideas from systems theory (see, for example, some of the papers in Friedman and Rowlands 1977) to societies on the assumption that human culture can be divided up into different, although related, spheres of activity, known as sub-systems, one of which is usually material culture. Anthony Giddens's (1979) concept of 'structuration' which suggests that the actions of individuals in their ordinary lives produce and reproduce the characteristic structural features of those actions so that the sum of the actions continually re-produces the social organization concerned. It is clear from this brief sketch that the contemporary scene in formal material culture interpretation offers a wide field of possibilities, ranging from the historical and quality-judging approach of the traditional art-curators, concerned as they are with the recording and understanding of context and process, the analytical techniques of the archaeologists, the functionalist inheritance of the social anthropologists, and the potential offered by the structuralists and systems analysts. All of these traditions have approaches of great value to the material culture specialist, and there is no reason why they should not be used in harness.

We may turn now to the second area for discussion suggested at the beginning, that of the nature of human history collections. The tradition of analysis here is as slender as it is as yet in most fields of museum study, but a start has been made by Stewart (1984). Much material culture seems to arrive in museum collections as the result of three processes, giving groups of objects which may be described as souvenirs, fetishes, and collections properly speaking. Needless to say, in practice the motives behind their accumulation are frequently mixed, but the underlying strands may be distinguished. Souvenirs may be defined as those artefacts which have been preserved because they represent for the individual concerned the tangible essence of a past experience. They are objects which form the starting point for a personal narrative and which demonstrate the truth of the story. Like the preserved silver decorations from a wedding cake, they are nostalgic and backward-looking, romantic in their suggestion that the past was better than the present, and bitter-sweet in emotional tone. Like war mementoes from the trenches or the Western Desert, they make intelligible and personal experiences which, in any wider view, are beyond a single individual's comprehension. Much of the material in museum social history and military collections, and in ethnographic collections also, has arrived by this route, and its intensely personal character means that the separate pieces tend to remain separate and are very difficult to display successfully.

Both Marx and Freud used the word 'fetish' to describe material goods, meaning, with rather different shades of emphasis, that artefacts are given meanings beyond their original ones by individuals or societies, who pass their own emotional needs over to the objects concerned. Accumulations formed in this style are essentially different from souvenirs, in that fetishes do not have an historical but more-or-less fortuitous link with a personal experience, but rather are deliberately acquired by somebody who already knows that something in his nature will respond to them. The cabinets of material collected during the Renaissance and post-Renaissance may have been organized according to the scientific and philosophical ideas of the day, strange as these were to seem to a later generation (see Hooper-Greenhill, this volume), but this tradition of accumulation continued in a degenerate form after its intellectual basis had been discredited. These groups are random and mixed in character because their common thread is a single human personality, and only death, or bankruptcy, or a sudden switch in interest puts an end to the accumulation, because its aim is to acquire as many samples of the admired material as possible. This is not to deny that many great collections have been formed on this basis, particularly in the arts where a cultivated taste can operate in many directions and impart its own stamp. Particular ways in which the fetishism of artefacts can operate are explored by Gathercole.

Both souvenirs and fetishes are, of course, still collected and still presented to museums, but in terms of collecting history, their mode belongs to the archaic phase, which arguably came to an end about 1850 with the formation of the Pitt Rivers collection. What distinguished this from the majority of its predecessors was the way in which it was gathered and arranged to bear out an intellectual proposition. The collection had an internal coherence which went beyond the accumulation of samples to become a demonstration by example, and it was not complete until it included an example of each of its main types, a cast of mind now engrained in curators, who habitually talk of 'filling a gap in the collections'. The underlying concept is now often that of a cultural assemblage which would record life in a specific time and place, and this notion is the premise upon which many of the best of the more recent social history and ethnographical collections have been made, while archaeological excavation and field techniques have been refined to produce the closest possible approach to this criterion for material from the more distant past. The definition of valid collecting policies in these disciplines, however, now looks a more daunting task than it did a generation or so ago, partly because we must recognize that the collectable material culture of past societies is finite and should sometimes be left undisturbed for those who will come after with their superior techniques, and partly because the ways in which objects may relate to perceived realities in the past is seen now to involve the wide range of historiographical problems about bias and representation, problems to which we must now turn.

So far, the modes of object interpretation and the nature of collections have been discussed from a formal or 'objective' stance, but there remains a further crucial dimension which brings together interpreters, collectors, curators and the general public and takes us back to the word 'political' used in the first paragraph of this discussion. As we have come to realise, societies are not neutral and objects are not innocent; on the contrary they weave a web of dominance and exploitation which it is the student's business to expose. While nobody can doubt the 'truth' of objective facts (King Charles was executed; bronze is an alloy of copper and tin) the working of these facts in society can be seen, equally 'truly', as knowledge manipulated in order to serve ideological interests which are helpful to some and oppressive to others. A keyword in this kind of thinking is 'critical' in the specific sense associated with the Frankfurt School of German social philosophy which sees all social study as an enterprize, like those of Marx or Freud, dedicated to freeing individuals from the ideological conditions which have formed their beliefs and ideals, and so their actions (see, for example, Geuss 1981). All this tends to bring morality back onto the scene and to involve subjective ideas about 'good' and 'bad' societies, judgements not much relished by traditional workers who have been accustomed to think that all human manifestations are equally 'valid'; perhaps for 'valid' we should now substitute 'interesting'. Since, as Marx demonstrated, the production and distribution of material culture lies at the heart of ideological process, there is clearly considerable scope here for the artefact analyst.

The same considerations apply to the production of knowledge, particularly the production of knowledge about the past. All the material in our museum collections has been selected from the large range of possible choices by individuals who acted in the light of their own ideologies, conscious and unconscious, and is, accordingly, flawed as an historical record. The curator who works on this material is inevitably similarly biased, even though s/he may strive for a better self-understanding than used to be required. The standing of curatorship as a profession and the ways in which the professional operates within a museum also has an important bearing on all these issues. Problems like these are approached by a number of contributors to this volume including Kaeppler, Fürst, Reynolds, and Jenkins, while Hooper-Greenhill shows how the post-structuralist ideas of Foucault can be applied very illuminatingly to museum history. The relationship of the professional curator to the public, and the balance of power within such a relationship raises questions about 'whose history?' and 'produced for whom?' which are of particular significance to ethnographers and social historians and are pursued here by Kavanagh and Jenkinson, but which are also bound up in the reasons why people do, and do not, visit museums, issues explored here by Merriman.

One final point must be made with emphasis. Material culture as a specific field of study is still relatively new, and although in some areas, conspicuously that of archaeology, it has made considerable progress (see Shennan 1986 for a critical review of current thinking), in others it has started only recently. The study of material culture in its museum aspect, embracing not only the formal interpretation of artefacts, but also the analysis of collections and their history, and that of the museum as a cultural phenomenon is only just starting. This volume is part of that beginning and even within its limited scope a number of possible patterns begin to show themselves. Will the study of objects and collections share some of the experience which has befallen language and literature in the recent past? Will the 'poverty of theory' referred to by Jenkinson be enriched by the new schools of social study, with their clearer appreciation of the working of ideology in history? Will a more detailed application of systems theories improve our understanding of the role of material culture? We shall see.

BIBLIOGRAPHY

Chapman, W., 1985. 'Arranging ethnology: A. H. L. F. Pitt Rivers and the typological tradition', in Stocking G. (ed.), *Objects and Others: Essays on Museums and Material Culture*: 15–48.

Daniel, G., 1950. *A Hundred Years of Archaeology*.

Deetz, J., 1977. *In Small Things Forgotten: The Archaeology of Early American Life*.

Elliott, R., *et al.*, 1985. 'Towards a material history methodology', *Material History Bulletin, 22* (Fall): 31–40.

Friedman, J. and Rowlands, M. (eds), 1977. *The Evolution of Social Systems*.

Geuss, R., 1981. *The Idea of a Critical Theory*.

Giddens, A., 1979. *Studies in Social and Political Theory*.

Haggett, P., 1956. *Locational Analysis in Human Geography*.

Hawkes, T., 1977. *Structuralism and Semiotics*.

Kristiansen, K., 1984. 'Ideology and material culture: an archaeological perspective', in Spriggs M. (ed.), *Marxist Perspectives in Archaeology*: 72–100.

Leach, E., 1976. *Culture and Communication*.

Miller, D., 1985. *Artefacts as Categories*.

Miller, D., 1987. *Material Culture and Mass Consumption*.

Pearce, S., 1986a. 'Thinking about things: approaches to the study of artefacts', *Museums Journal, 85, 4*: 198–201.

Pearce, S., 1986b. 'Objects high and low', *Museums Journal, 86, 2*: 79–82.

Pearce, S., 1986c. 'Objects as signs and symbols', *Museums Journal, 86, 3*: 131–15.

Phillips, P., 1985. *The Archaeologist and The Laboratory*, Council for British Archaeology Research Report, No. 58.

Prowne, J., 1982. 'Mind in matter: an introduction to material culture theory and method', *Winterthur Portfolio, 17.1*: 1–19.

Rahtz, P., 1982. 'The Dark Ages', in Aston, M. and Burrow, I. (eds), *The Archaeology of Somerset*: 98–107.

Renfrew, C., 1979. 'Systems Collapse as social transformation: catastrophe and anastrophe in early societies', in Renfrew, C. and Cooke, K. (eds), *Transformations: Mathematical Approaches to Culture Change*: 48 1–506.

Schlereth, T. J. (ed.), 1985. *Material Culture: A Research Guide*.

Shennan, S., 1986. 'Towards a critical archaeology?', *Procs. of the Prehistoric Society, 52*: 327–338.

Stewart, S., 1984. *On Longing: Narratives of the Miniature, the Gigantic, the Souvenir, the Collection*.

2 *Material Culture Research and North American Social History*

THOMAS J. SCHLERETH

A generation ago only a few North American scholars would have recognized or have been interested in either social history or material culture research. In the past two decades, however, both forms of scholarship have gained supporters. More significantly, students in these two subject areas have become increasingly interested in one another's work. With this trend in mind, I would like to assess three principal issues: what has been the import of North American social history for material culture research? how have material culture studies contributed to social history? and, what ramifications does the interaction, past and present, between students of material culture and social historians have for history museum interpretation and museum studies?

I would begin with a brief analysis of several definitions presently current in North American artefact studies as well as changing conceptions of social history. In the twentieth century, the meaning of material culture has undergone various redefinitions and reformulations (see, for example, Schlereth 1985: 2–5). Perhaps the most striking is that in the past decade, the term has gained growing currency among researchers in the arts and humanities. Its diverse North American advocates now include Jules Prown, Henry Glassie, Brooke Hindle, Kenneth Ames, and James Deetz. In the latter's estimate material culture can be briefly defined as 'that segment of man's physical environment which is purposely shaped by him according to culturally dictated plans' (Deetz 1977a: 10).

Two other nomenclatures now appear in North American discussions about object research. Canadians prefer the term 'material history', as in the title of the *Material History Bulletin*, a journal published by the National Museum of Man in Ottawa, or in the new Master's degree programme (Diploma in Material History) now offered by the University of New

Brunswick in St John (Turner 1984; Finley 1985). To complicate things a bit more, a third phrase, 'material life', or its sometime synonym 'material civilization', has recently received some attention. French economic historian Fernand Braudel's stated attempt to devise a label that would be an alternative to 'technology' but 'maintain a bridge to the material culture of anthropology and archaeology' and yet still convey an overview of 'an economic culture of everyday life' is one source of this term (see Dupree 1981: 585). Another is the work of American social historian Cary Carson. In Carson's estimate, the study of material life entails object research into social institutions and social relations because 'artifacts serve on one level as the devices that men and women have always used to mediate their relationships with one another and with the physical world' (1984: 6, 9).

Elsewhere I have assessed the assets and liabilities of these three terms (Schlereth forthcoming). For the purpose of this argument, I prefer the label 'material culture' for several reasons: its common use in several disciplines in both the humanities and social sciences; its historical lineage of scholarship dating back to the middle of the nineteenth century, beginning among British anthropologists such as Pitt-Rivers (see Myers 1906: 6); its embodiment of the culture concept; and its increasingly widespread usage, at least in the United States, among those who E. McClung Fleming identifies as 'museum historians' and 'academic historians' (1969).

While North American social historians have not been as prone to debate their nomenclature, they certainly have contended the purpose and practice of their approach to the past. In the past decade sides have been drawn on a number of important philosophical and methodological questions. For example, there have been debates about the neglect of political issues and ideological concerns in the writing of much American social history. Other practitioners have worried over the tendency to concentrate on the private, rather than the public, aspects of human experience. Finally, still other social historians have taken their comrades to task for failing to account for issues of power and conflict between social classes and social structures (Vesey 1979; Genovese and Fox-Genovese 1976).

Despite the debates currently taking place among both social historians and material culture researchers – debates I take to be more creative than contentious – one can point to several affinities between these two students of the past. There are several areas of common ground between the two. For example, both social history and material culture studies challenge the older view of history as only past politics, and both have sought to demonstrate the great diversity of the North American people and their lifestyles (Stearns 1980; Carson 1969).

Students of material culture and social historians tend to agree that most individuals in the past left few literary records. For the majority of people, the primary historical evidence of their lives is not written but survives as data gathered about them or, as happens even more frequently, as objects made and used and finally discarded by them. Material culture, claim its advocates, is more democratic than literary or statistical documents as well as less sensitive to the subjectivity which every person brought, however unconsciously, to his or her written or oral accounting of peoples and events. Such an assertion concurs with social history's concern for a higher degree of representativeness in the evidential basis of all historical explanation (Vesey 1979: 7; Carson 1969: 48–61).

Among historians working with objects and among some North American social historians, there is a growing mutual commitment regarding formats of communicating historical information and insight other than the history establishment's traditional rhetorical mode of presentation. As James Henretta has pointed out, social historians have proposed various new presentation techniques (for example, quantification, conceptual models, phenomenological analyses) as alternatives to the traditional linear narrative approach (1979: 1314–1321); material culturists in their work with extant three-dimensional evidence have likewise sought innovative formats (for example, participatory exhibits, experimental archaeology, outdoor living history musems).

Despite these several convergent interests, a number of issues separate social historians and historians who have sought to use artefacts as a primary database. One difference has been their respective publics. Academic social historians have tended to write only for other fellow-specialists. Material culturists, on the other hand, have usually worked in a more diverse and decentralized institutional structure composed of museums, government agencies and state historical societies as well as colleges and universities. With a few exceptions, most material culturists have not shared the enthusiasm of those in social history who see quantification as the principal salvation of historical studies. Finally, it must be acknowledged that material culture studies, despite all the methodological creativity demonstrated by some of its most pioneering proponents, are still only beginning to explore the conceptual and analytical potential of this approach to historical studies. Traditionally content to collect and describe objects, many material culturists still resist the methodological necessity of extracting and synthesizing social behaviour from such three-dimensional data. Or, to put it another way, many resist the imperative to deduce, wherever possible, the culture behind the material (typical examples of the debate may be found in Prown 1982, Bronner 1979 and Schlereth 1982: 1–75).

In several topical areas, however, the scholars in material culture research have made both methodological advances and substantive contributions to contemporary knowledge about American social history. I would like to note, and briefly describe, six such areas: residential spaces, domestic life, women's history, working and workers, life-cycle experiences, and community landscapes.

When John Demos devoted Part I, 'The Physical Setting', of his *A Little*

Commonwealth: Family Life in the Plymouth Colony (1970) to the domestic shelter and artefacts of the seventeenth-century Pilgrim community, he was recognizing a fact crucial to much material culture research: as the elementary unit of humankind is the individual, the elementary artefact on the landscape is the dwelling. Demos went on the explore the societal implications of architectural evidence (for example, status, privacy, social segregation, repression of familial anger and aggression, child-rearing practices) in his pioneering application of social and behavioural concepts to the houses of seventeenth-century Massachusetts.

Other North American scholars have done similar studies, with particular emphasis on the nineteenth century. Here one thinks of Gwendolyn Wright's *Building The Dream: A Social History of Housing in America* (1981); George McDaniel's *Hearth and Home: Preserving a People's Culture* (1981) and David Handlin's *The American Home, Architecture and Society* (1980) and, more recently, Clifford Clark's *The American Family Home* (1986) and Alan Gowan's *The Comfortable House: North American Suburban Architecture* (1986). Such research eschews the usual approach of the traditional architectural historian in that it avoids mere 'façadism' (for instance, interpreting the structure primarily through its front elevation and aesthetic style) as well as elitism (for example, researching only structures designed by professional architects) (Maass 1969).

This is not to say that contemporary material culturists are totally uninterested in architecture or in style as historical evidence. In fact, it can be argued that style is currently very much back in vogue among students of the artefact. Nonetheless, current interest is more in typology than in style, with vernacular forms rather than academic idioms (Upton 1985a). The quest for the meaning of vernacular housing has, of course, received a large part of its inspiration from a coterie of British scholars, particularly those who form the core of the Vernacular Architecture Society.

Popular housing is now being studied from numerous perspectives. For example, ever since Herbert Gans's work on *The Levittowners* (1967), an interest in the material culture of the Anglo-American suburb has steadily increased, due to the work of individuals such as architect Robert Venturi (1976), and social historian Kenneth Jackson (1985). Now the history of urban middle- and lower-class neighbourhoods has also been examined through their extant housing stock. Tenement districts, slums, and even alleys are receiving attention, as are issues such as the social meaning of home-ownership, housing and property controls, and residential class segregation (see, for example, Borchert 1980; Luria 1976).

A last group of material culturists who work with housing do so in more piecemeal fashion. They are interested in the various elements of the house and how such artefacts may have shaped human behaviour and attitudes over a period of time. For example, they have studied the domestication of the garage, the historical role of residential gardens and landscaping, the rise and fall of the porch and its evolution into the patio, as well as the significance of a home's front and bank entrances as social spaces (Jackson B. 1976; West 1976; Welsh 1979; Constantine 1981). Works in contemporary environmental psychology like Robert Sommer's *Personal Space: The Behavioural Basis of Design* (1969), have frequently informed these analyses. And in keeping with the folk proverb that claims a house is not a home, scholars have long researched the material life of North Americans as revealed in the patterns of domestic furnishings and the organization of domestic spaces as ways of gaining insight into the social past of middle-class and working-class culture (Shammas 1980; Cohen 1980).

Material culture in the decorative arts (the North American preferred term for the applied arts) have been intrigued by a wide range of domesticity. In addition to several innovative cultural history surveys, we now have work being done on parlour furniture, mourning pictures, hallway stands, eating utensils, cleaning devices, family photograph albums and kitchen appliances. Whereas previous work focussed on the eighteenth century, current research is largely directed at the patterning of material artefacts in nineteenth- and twentiety-century households (Ames 1978, 1980; de Bretteville, 1979). The photograph (an artefact first created in the nineteenth-century,) has been of immense interest to historians exploring North American domestic life. Historical photography, when examined closely and in sufficient quantity to insure a representative evidential sample, has often provided valuable inferences as to how occupants organized and used space as well as how they interacted with one another. Through photography we now know more about family life as lived in residential spaces such as nurseries, kitchens, bedrooms, hall passages, pantries, ingle-nooks and servant's quarters as well as in parlours, living rooms, front porches and dining rooms (Schlereth 1980; 11–49; Bogardus 1981).

Until recently North American social historians and material culture students have paid scant attention to eating, assuredly one of humankind's most common necessities. The exception is the research of folklorists, and their work tends to concentrate primarily on rural and pre-industrial communities. Only in recent years has some limited attention been given to the artefacts of twentieth-century food preparation, service and disposal (Champ 1979; Jones *et al.* 1980). In calling for the integration of foodways (and all other appropriate material, statistical and documentary data) into his cultural history approach, James Deetz has argued for a research paradigm that seeks 'the detection and explication of apparently unrelated changes in all aspects of a people's culture, material and otherwise'. Although not directly influenced by the devotees of a *mentalité* approach to the past, he shares this school's interest in the study of popular beliefs, customs and modes of behaviour as well as its commitment to 'thick description'. The Deetz argument is an excellent example of historical revisionism on the basis of material culture evidence. Deetz's interpretation challenges the traditional political and diplomatic interpretation that claims that the American independence movement was the major cultural watershed of American colonial history: the documentary and material data that Deetz integrated suggests that the Revolution actually had little impact; in fact, the general American pattern of cultural involvement with British material culture, both before and after the war (Stuart and Georgian periods in his chronology), remained remarkably constant (Deetz 1977b; 1981).

Historians interested in women's history and the history of childhood have increasingly turned to using artefacts to interpret the social experience of these two heretofore largely neglected groups of actors in the past. It is often argued, for example, that public documents and private correspondence rarely make mention of the tasks of housewifery, tasks which consumed so much of the time, energy and creativity of women in the past. The work has sought, through the interpretation of common household utensils, furnishings and interior décor, answers to a number of questions: what were the tasks of housewives? how did they adapt to changing economic patterns? what were their responses to technological innovations? how did the more functional divisions of various rooms affect women's relations with others in the family? what impact did household chores have on women's self-perceptions? Such questions have led to historical studies of women's role in household production and processing, servant management and social control, and the design, manufacture and social role of clothing (Cowan 1979; Carrell 1979).

The most generic female function is, of course, the bearing of children. While this uniquely female experience has prompted a wide range of material culture, its social history has only begun to be explored (Bullough 1981). While the technology of contraception has received some attention, we know little about the social and cultural impact of bottle sterilizers, baby pacifiers, or pasteurized and condensed milks. As Ruth Cowan points out, none of the standard histories or bibliographies of North American technology contains extensive reference to such a significant cultural artefact as the baby bottle (Cowan 1979; Drachman 1980): yet here is a simple implement which, along with its attendant delivery systems, has revolutionized a basic biological process, transformed a fundamental human experience for vast numbers of infants and mothers, and served as one of the more controversial exports of Western technology to underdeveloped countries.

Modern material culture students have, perhaps understandably, focussed their research on child play rather than child nurture (Mergen 1980). Playthings, for instancc, arc perhaps the principal artefact focus of object-based studies of childhood. So far, students of toys have been struck by two obvious facts: first, that in the selection of toys, children have been encouraged to follow the scientific and technological fads of their elders; and second, that these toys were often advertised as being more appropriate for one sex than the other (Bale 1967; Marchese 1980).

Products for one individual's play are, of course, the products of another individual's work. North American historians have begun to study seriously material culture of American working-places as well as their products. Some of this research has taken the form of town or community studies, some has focussed primarily on working conditions within mines, mills, shops and factories, and some has primarily investigated workers' housing (Warner 1981; Lubar 1986). In an attempt to move beyond the traditional subjects of labour history – unionization, strikes, the personalities of labour leaders – these scholars have probed both the specialized work *processes* of American labourers and the total historical experience of such workers as individuals in a wider society. Whereas much previous material culture study, especially in art and decorative arts history, tended to concentrate its research efforts solely on the objects produced by a worker, now more scholars consider such artefacts in a wider social and economic context (Hindle 1981b). Likewise there is growing interest in the study not only of an artefact's maker but also of its user. Interest in the cognitive processes involved in the production of past material culture has intrigued a group of scholars who sometimes call themselves 'experimental archaeologists': the history of their approach has been discussed by John Coles in his primer *Archaeology by Experiment* (1973). In North America most experimental archaeology has focussed on tool manufacture, industrial processes, house-building and food preparation.

While most students of material culture evidence are interested to some degree with inferring human behaviour from objects, a particular group of folklorists and other more behaviourial-minded researchers seek to understand life experiences from life's objects. Although these interpreters begin their historical analyses with artefacts such as country furniture, musical instruments, vernacular houses or common tools, these things are but a means to an end: the objective is to understand and explain personal creativity, aesthetic individuality or collective social psychology. Michael Owen Jones, a folklife scholar, has been one of the major practitioners of this orientation in North American material culture studies. In his major book, *The Handmade Object and Its Maker*, Jones concentrated his research primarily on one man, an Upland South chairmaker who simply went by the name of 'Charley'. Jones did this for two reasons. First, he insists that 'an object cannot be fully understood or appreciated without knowledge of the man who made it, and the traits of one object cannot be explained by reference only to the antecedent works of an earlier period from which later qualities allegedly evolved.' Second, 'a researcher cannot divorce what he calls artistic or creative processes from technological ones' (1975: vii–viii).

However, by no means all behaviouristic studies follow the Jones model. In a manifesto, 'Toward a behavioural history' (1980), Jones singled out Alan Ludwig's *Graven Images, New England Stonecarving and its Symbols* (1966) as a model application of the life experience perspective to material culture evidence. Ludwig's research into the symbolism, rituals and forms of funerary art in colonial Massachusetts and Connecticut reveals a story different from conventional histories of New England Puritanism based solely on written sources. The strictly verbal evidence depicted the Puritans as an iconophobic, non-mystical people whose piety, while once pronounced, declined dramatically near the end of the seventeenth century. Not so, suggests the cross-section of New England gravestones that Ludwig documented, analysed and interpreted. The material culture evidence examined appears to lead to at least three other conclusions: (1) that a very strong religious sentiment flourished until well into the nineteenth-century; (2) that America had an art tradition emphasizing abstraction, simplicity and purity of line; and (3) that the Puritans in America created much figurative as well as religious art, despite the inference to the contrary that has usually been drawn from official written sources.

Among those scholars interested in the behavioural approach, analysis of material culture data from the distant North American past remains the exception rather than the rule. Most research deals with contemporary persons, processes and products, and in order to conduct such research, field work is essential. A number of such workers are to apply performance theory to material culture study. For example, researchers such as Dell Upton (1979) and Thomas Adler (Adler 1985) argue that the human processes involved in conceiving, making, perceiving, using, adapting, decorating, exalting, loathing and discarding objects are intrinsic elements of human experience. Such experiences, not just the objects involved in them, are what the material culture student should strive to comprehend. Adler, for example, suggests the necessity of personal experience with the artefacts that the researcher studies in order to understand more fully how earlier people actually experienced those objects. In making this claim the performance theorist is akin to the experimental archaeologist. Thus, in addition to the usual referential knowledge of an object (for example, seeing a banjo in a mail order catalogue or reading a description of it in a nineteenth-century diary) and mediated knowledge (for example, hearing banjo music played over the radio or at a folk music concert), a material culture student must also, whenever possible, acquire experiential knowledge (in this case, by playing the banjo). It is only possible to understand performers of the past by becoming performers in the present.

A final category, community landscapes, has also been of interest of material culture students and social historians. Here the work of British scholars such as H. J. Dyos in urban history and W. G. Hoskins in landscape history has influenced different aspects of North American research. In this context, one would cite the publications of urbanists such as Sam Bass Warner (1972), Blaine Brownell (Brownell and Goldfield 1979) and Richard Wade (Wade and Meyer 1968) who have used material culture (for example, public transportation patterns, housing, public works, cartography, urban photography, landscape architecture) in their historical interpretation of American cities; geographers and landscape historians such as Peirce Lewis

(1976; 1979), David Ward (1971), John Stilgoe (1982), Grady Clay (1979), and S. B. Jackson (1972) have paid attention to rural and suburban sites.

Public structures comprise the most obvious element for probing the city as a historic site. Yet the topographical and geographical features of an urban area (particularly as parks, public squares, recreational facilities, waterfronts and open spaces) have also provided historians with indices for measuring social change. Fortunately there is some work now being done in exploring the interconnections between politics and urban design. For example, the editors of the *Radical History Review* devoted their entire (1979) issue to the 'Spatial dimension of history', featuring research on class recreation, industrial archaeology, housing and property relations, the evolution of charity hospitals and the development of the American department store and the shopping mall.

Despite the great hopes for continued collaboration by social historians and material culture researchers, it must be openly admitted that there are methodological difficulties involved in using artefacts as cultural explanation. In addition to the difficulties of inadequate data survival and the problem of accessibility and verification (Washburn 1984), three obstacles are especially problematic: (1) the exaggeration of human efficacy; (2) a penchant toward progressive determinism; and (3) a proclivity for synchronic interpretation. The exhibition of artefacts in musems often promotes a view of social history as a story of success and achievement. Such exhibits usually neglect the downside of human history, common to us all but not commonly depicted. For example, in many living history farms in North America there is little material culture that helps a visitor experience anything of the isolation, monotony, or high mortality rate of a frontier prairie existence. Where are the instances of insanity, personal depression, chronic loneliness, or the anxiety over mortage foreclosure or frequent childbirth? In these contexts, the documentary and statistical records (rather than the artefactual) may prove more helpful to the researcher since people could and did write about the dark and unpleasant side of their existence – the uncertainties, the false starts, the half-way measures, the intentions that failed.

Nonetheless, in object study we also need analyses of material culture pathology so that we may know more about what things, in various historical periods, did not work, what consistently broke down or was quickly junked in favour of other products. Inasmuch as much of the North American material culture history studied to date has been, like so much of North American written history, the history of winners, a greater appreciation of the losers (people and products) might be a valuable corrective. John Demos, in a review of *New England Begins: the Seventeenth-Century* (1983), an exhibition and catalogue produced by the Department of American Decorative Arts and Sculpture of the Boston Museum of Fine Arts, suggests as much in his recognition here of the possibly exaggerated human efficacy. Demos notes

that both the material culture exhibit and its impressive three-volume catalogue depict New England settlers as uncommonly active, effective and forceful in coping with the circumstances of their lives. This viewpoint contrasts sharply with a generation of scholarly opinion on seventeenth-century New England life that emphasizes the unanticipated and the unwelcome aspects and effects of life in a new environment. Colonists arrived with plans, expectations and assumptions as to what they were about, but environmental circumstances transformed most of these (Bailyn 1960). The artefacts analysed by the BMFA research team of archaeologists, decorative arts specialists and social historians leads to quite another conclusion. New Englanders were in control of their lives and their actions: artifice, and artefacts, show them so.

A belief in progress has been enormously influential in both American social history and material culture research. The latter has often seen the American past as one material success after another in an ever-upward ascent of increased goods and services for all the nation's citizens. George Basalla has traced this tendency in the history of technology and in technical museums. Such museums, notes Basalla, are often dominated by a 'technological cornucopia' mentality in their celebration of North American progress (1974: 360). Michael Ettema (1982) sees the same problem in the North American decorative arts as does Dell Upton in North American vernacular architecture (1985a: 72).

In opposition to the tendency to progressive determinism is the proclivity towards synchronic method in material culture research. Some cultural anthropologists, literary critics, folklorists and art historians, for example, have been prone to this approach to the artefact. Synchronic analysis I take to mean simply a descriptive study of objects without reference to time duration or cultural change. Its antonym, diachronic analysis, is a comparative study of objects as historical data – that is, as resources that can be considered as both effects and causes in history (Eighmy 1981). The synchronic syndrome also expresses itself in a perennial quest for aesthetic uniqueness, special artistic achievement, and a Procrustean stylistic periodization. These tendencies manifest themselves in many temporary and permanent museum exhibitions as well as catalogues and monographs.

The tendency towards a synchronic approach to the past often neglects the causes and consequences of human conflict. Most North American history museums, as well as material culture students, have yet to offer convincing explanations regarding conflict. To be sure, military conflict is well represented in museum material culture collections, exhibits and battlefield sites, but domestic conflict and violence in the North American past still receive little notice. Court rooms, city halls, police stations, factory gates, prisons, town squares and historic house museums have been artefacts for both individual and group conflicts such as Indian-white confrontations, ethnic rivalries, religious vendettas, clan feuds, urban riots, agrarian uprisings, and

labour struggles. So far, only a few museums and scholars have collected and interpreted this material culture (Baker and Leon 1986). There are several reasons for this. One is professional: social, as opposed to political, conflict has only been a topic of interest to North American historians for a few decades. Some are practical: many museum staff members and their boards of trustees worry how visitors will react to presentations on ethnic tensions or religious conflicts. Some are political: many museum historians, like social historians, avoid issues of conflict because they are uncomfortable with questions of power. Here the broader criticism levelled against social history by Eugene Genovese and others may also apply; that is, while social history focuses on group behaviour, social historians have often ignored political relationships between groups. Like much social history writing, social history as presented in North American museums is often depoliticized. We may learn much about the details of everyday life but not 'who rides whom and how' in the political and economic arena (Genovese and Fox-Genovese 1976: 205–20).

This critique notwithstanding, it must be admitted that the social history approach to material culture research, particularly in North American history museums, is the dominant theoretical model. Whole other paradigms – art historical, functionalist, environmentalist, structuralist – influence material culture research in art museums, museums of natural history and anthropology as well as technical museums, a social history perspective has enjoyed an increasingly acceptance in history museums. Young scholars trained in the 1960s and 1970s are particularly attracted to its explanatory potential. Many of these took advanced degrees in social history and, instead of pursuing careers in academic institutions, joined the staffs of North American history museums. The full impact of this important occupational shift and intellectual reorientation will probably not be known for another decade or so; I would suggest, however, that its ramifications for more sophisticated museum interpretation and more rigorous artifact study are auspicious.

To conclude, what else might be ventured as to the future of material culture and social history in the North American history museum? With regard to topics that might provide opportunities for further studies, I would propose that consumerism, foodways, childhood (already in vogue), recreation and creativity will be subjects of growing interest. On the last topic, the historical origins, dimensions and ramifications of human innovation and invention, we are already seeing research combining social history documentation and material culture evidence (e.g. Hindle 1981a, 1981b). If the current arguments of Jules Prown and Dell Upton are heeded, there will also be a return – despite the influence of the social history juggernaut – to elite material culture, particularly high-style decorative arts, architecture and fine arts. The strategy suggested here (at least by Upton) is to study high-style objects along with common material culture in a 'total landscape approach' to artefact research (Upton 1985b).

Although there is renewed interest in material culture scholarship among some anthropologists, especially in consumerism, it remains to be seen whether or not the founders of the movement (or their museums) will make any serious claims to take over as its institutional or intellectual home base. It is also difficult to predict the institutional future of the North American material culture movement. Some, like James Deetz, anticipate that it could be lodged in multi-disciplinary programmes (like American Studies) called Departments of Material Culture. Others argue for its reorganization through a new consortium of history museums (with university affiliations), perhaps concentrating their efforts regionally or chronologically. If history museums are to play a larger role in material culture research, they need to amplify their voice in the scholarly forums that cover the field. For example, peer review of exhibits is an absolute necessity if material culture research in North American museums is to advance. Finally, we need more careful exploration of the theory and practice of the history museum exhibition as a type of publication. We need to realize that the selective arrangement for artefacts and other related information in a public display is a history museum's special mode of communication and that such displays are one of the mediums for exploring the intersections of material culture and its larger social context of meaning. As Harold Skramstad observes: 'Perhaps more than anything else a museum's exhibition environment is an accurate index of its attitude toward material culture' (1969: 175–6).

The history exhibit as a distinct form of culture discourse has already been touched upon. A number of North American scholars have suggested the complexities of the exhibit process. Fath Davis Ruffins (1985) argues that we need to think of every exhibition as a special, often non-linear, interactive, visual form, a complicated material culture assemblage that is more than the sum of its parts. In her estimate, every exhibition is an approximation of the past, and therefore ought be best thought of as a 'metaphor about the past' but also a 'cultural argument' in the present. Finally, as Barbara and Cary Carson have proposed, one might think of the historic house, site, or setting as a material culture theatre, a stage furnished with appropriate and accurate artefacts and where historical dramaturgy might be enacted either by visitors or for them (Carson and Carson 1983).

These ideas regard the history museum environment as a public form where the exploration and evaluation of material culture can be presented in a manner both intellectually stimulating and visually comprehensible to a wide audience. Each sees exhibits as cultural arguments that grow out of and are the vehicles for communicating the best insights of material culture research. Each recognizes that those who study material culture have a mission that includes but also extends beyond the marshalling of objects or the description of artefacts. This mission – to integrate the three-dimensional remnants of our past with appropriate documentary, oral and statistical resources – remains an engaging task for both museum and academic historians in North America.

The growth of social history has aided greatly in this enterprise. And, in fact, perhaps the strongest bonds between current material culture studies and social history research are mutual interests in the vernacular, the typical, the commonplace of the past; a desire to make history, as William Makepeace Thackeray once hoped, 'more familiar than heroic'; and perhaps, most importantly, the common concern to bring a wider socio-historical understanding, as Peirce Lewis put it, to 'the way ordinary North Americans behave most of the time' (1979).

Bibliography

Adler, T. A., 1985. 'Musical instruments, tools, and the experience of control', in Bronner S. J., *American Material Culture and Folklife; A Prologue and Dialogue*: 103–11.

Ames, K., 1978. 'Meaning in artifacts: hall furnishings in Victorian America', *Journal of Interdisciplinary History, 9.1*: 19–46.

Ames, K., 1980. 'Material culture as non-verbal communication: a historical case study', *Journal of American Culture, 3.4*: 6 19–41.

Bailyn, B., 1960. *Education in the Forming of American Society: Needs and Opportunities for Study*.

Baker, A. and Leon, W., 1986. 'Conflict and community at Old Sturbridge Village', *History News, 41.2*: 6–11.

Bale, D. W., 1967. 'Toward a sociology of toys, inanimate objects, socialization and the demongraphy of the doll world', *Sociological Quarterly, 8*: 447–58.

Basalla, G., 1974. 'Museums and technological utopianism', in Quimby I. M. G. and Early, P. A. (eds), *Technological Innovation and the Decorative Arts*: 355–71.

Bogardus, R., 1981. 'The "Carte de visite to posterity": a family's snapshots as autobiography and art', *Journal of American Culture, 4*: 114–22.

Borchert, J., 1980. *Alley Life in Washington, D.C.; Family, Community, Religion and Folklore in the City, 1860–1970*.

de Bretteville, S. L., 1979. 'The "parlorization" of our homes and ourselves', *Chrysalis: A Magazine of Woman's Culture, 4*: 22–9.

Bronner, S., 1979. 'Concepts in the study of material aspects of American folk culture', *Folklore Forum, 12, 2 13*: 133–72.

Brownell, B. and Goldfield D., 1979. *Urban Americans from Downtown to No Town*.

Bullough, V. L., 1981. 'A brief note on rubber technology and contraception: the diaphragm and the condom', *Technology and Culture, 22.1*: 104–11.

Carrell, K. W., 1979. 'The Industrial Revolution comes to the home: kitchen design reform and middle class women', *Journal of American Culture, 2.3*: 488–99.

Carson, B. G. and Carson, C., 1983. 'Things unspoken: learning social history through artifacts', in Gardner, J. B. and Adams, G. R. (eds), *Ordinary People and Everyday Life*: 185–6.

Carson, C., 1969. 'Doing history with material culture', in Quimby, I. (ed.), *Material Culture and the Study of American Life*: 41–9.

Carson, C., 1984. *Chesapeake Themes in the History of Early American Material Life*. Unpublished paper presented at Conference 'Maryland, A Product of Two Worlds', St Mary's City, Maryland, 19 May 1984.

Champ, C., 1979. 'Food in American culture: a bibliographical essay', *Journal of American Culture, 2*, 559–70.

Clark, C., 1986. *The American Family Home*.

Clay, G., 1979. *How to Read the American city*.

Cohen, L. A., 1980. 'Embellishing a life of labour: an interpretation of the material culture of American working-class homes, 1885–1915', *Journal of American Culture, 3.4*: 752–75.

Coles, J., 1973. *Archaeology by Experiment*.

Constantine, S., 1981. 'Amateur gardening and popular recreation in the 19th and 20th centuries', *Journal of Social History, 14*: 387–406.

Cowan, R. S., 1979. 'From Virginia Dare to Virginia Slims: women and technology in American life', *Technology and Culture, 20.1*: 51–63.

Deetz, J., 1977a. *In Small Things Forgotten: The Archaeology of North American History*.

Deetz, J., 1977b. 'Material culture and archaeology . . . What's the difference', in Leland, F. (ed.), *Historical Archaeology and the Importance of Material Things*: 9–12.

Deetz, J., 1981. *Scientific Humanism and Humanistic Science*. Unpublished paper given at the University of California at Berkeley, March 1981.

Demos, J., 1970. *A Little Commonwealth: Family Life in the Plymouth Colony*.

Demos, J., 1983. 'Words and things: a review and discussion of "New England Begins"', *William and Mary Quarterly, 40.4*: 584–97.

Drachman, V. G., 1980. 'Gynecological instruments and surgical decisions at a hospital in late nineteenth century America', *Journal of American Culture 3.4*: 660–72.

Dupree, A. H., 1981. 'Does the history of technology exist?', *Journal of Interdisciplinary History, 11.4*: 484–90.

Eighmy, J. L., 1981. 'The use of material culture in diachronic anthropology', in Gould, R. and Schiffer, M. (eds), *Modern Material Culture: The Archaeology of Us*: 31–50.

Ettema, M., 1982. 'History, nostalgia and American furniture', *Winterthur Portfolio, 17. 2/3*, 135–44.

Finley, G., 1985. 'Material history and curatorship problems and prospects', *Muse, 3.3*: 34.

Fleming, E. McC., 1969. 'The university and the museum, needs and opportunities for cooperation', *Museologist 3*: 10–18.

Gans, H., 1967. *The Levittowners*.

Genovese, E. and Fox-Genovese, E., 1976. 'The political crisis of social history: a Marxian perspective', *Journal of Social History, 10.2*: 205–20.
Gowan, A., 1986. *The Comfortable House: North American Suburban Architecture.*
Handlin, D., 1980. *The American Home, Architecture and Society.*
Henretta, J. A., 1979. 'Social history as lived and written', *American Historical Review, 84.5*: 13 14–21.
Hindle, B., 1981a. *Emulation and Invention.*
Hindle, B., (ed.) 1981b, *The Material Culture of The Wooden Age.*
Jackson, J. B., 1976. 'The domestication of the garage', *Landscape, 20.2*, 10:19.
Jackson, J. B., 1972. *American Space: The Centennial Years, 1865–1876.*
Jackson, K., 1985. *The Crabgrass Frontier: Suburbanization of the United States.*
Jones, M. O., 1975. *The Handmade Object and its Maker.*
Jones, M. O., 1980. *Bibliographic and Reference Tools: Towards a Behavioural History.* Unpublished paper presented at American Association for State and Local History Conference, New Orleans, 1980.
Jones, M. O., Guiliano, B., and Krell, R. (eds), 1980. 'Foodways and eating habits: directions for research [special issue]', *Western Folklore, 40*: 1–137.
Lewis, P., 1976. *New Orleans: The Making of an Urban Landscape.*
Lewis, P., 1979. 'Axioms for reading the landscape: some guides to the American scene', in Meinig, D. W. (ed.), *The Interpretation of Ordinary Landscapes: Geographical Essays*: 19.
Lubar, S., 1986. *Engines of Change.*
Ludwig, A., 1966. *Graven Images, New England Stonecarving and its Symbols, 1650–1815.*
Luria, D. D., 1976. 'Wealth, capital and power: the social meaning of home ownership', *Journal of Interdisciplinary History, 7*: 261–82.
McDaniel, G., 1981. *Hearth and Home: Preserving a People's Culture.*
Maass, J., 1969. 'Where architects fear to tread', *Journal of the Society of American Architectural Historians, 28*: 3–8.
Marchese, R., 1980. 'Material culture and artifact classification', *Journal of American Culture, 3.4*: 605–19.
Mergen, B., 1980. 'Toys and American culture: objects as hypotheses', *Journal of American Culture, 3.4*: 743–51.
Myers, J. L. (ed.) 1906. *The Evolution of Culture and Other Essays.*
Prown, J. D., 1982. 'Mind in matter: an introduction to material culture theory and method', *Winterthur Portfolio, 17.1*: 1–19.
Ruffins, F. D., 1985. 'The exhibition as form: an elegant metaphor', *Museum News, 64.1*: 54–9.
Schlereth, T. J., 1980. *Artifacts and the American Past.*
Schlereth, T. J., 1982. *Material Culture Studies in America.*
Schlereth, T. J., 1985. 'Material culture and cultural research', in Schlereth, T. J. (ed.), *Material Culture, A Research Guide*: 2–5.

Schlereth, T. J., forthcoming. 'Material culture or material life? Discipline or field? Theory or method', in Pocins, G. (ed.), *North American Material Culture Research: New Objectives, New Theories.*

Shammas, C., 1980. 'The domestic environment in early modern England and America', *Journal of Social History, 14*: 4–24.

Skramstad, H. K., 1969. 'Interpreting material culture: a view from the other side of the class', in Quimby, I. (ed.), *Material Culture and the Study of American Life*: 175–6.

Sommer, R., 1969. *Personal Space: The Behavioural Basis of Design.*

Stearns, P., 1980. 'Toward a wider vision: trends in social history', in Kammen, M. (ed.), *The Past Before Us: Contemporary Historical Writing in the United States*: 212–18.

Stilgoe, J., 1982. *Common Landscape.*

Turner, R., 1984. 'The limitations of material history: a museological perspective 1', *Material History Bulletin, 20*: 87–92.

Upton, D., 1979. 'Toward a performance theory of vernacular architecture: early tidewater Virginia as a case study', *Folklore Forum, 12*: 173–95.

Upton, D., 1985a. 'The power of things: recent studies in American vernacular architecture', in Schlereth, T. J. (ed.), *Material Culture, A Research Guide*: 57–78.

Upton, D., 1985b. 'Material culture studies: a symposium', *Material Culture, 17, 213*: 86.

Venturi, R., 1976. *Signs of Life: Symbols in the American City.*

Vesey, L., 1979. 'The "new" social history in the context of American history', *Reviews in American History, 7.1*: 1–12.

Wade, R. and Meyer, H., 1968. *Chicago: Growth of a Metropolis.*

Ward, D., 1971. *Cities and Immigrants: A Geography of Change in Nineteenth Century America.*

Warner, D. J., 1981. *Perfect in her Place: Women at Work in Industrial America.*

Warner, S. B., 1972. *The Urban Wilderness, A History of the American City.*

Washburn, W. E., 1984. 'Collecting information, not objects', *Museum News, 62.3*: 5–15.

Welsh, R. L., 1979. *Natural History, 88.6*: 76–82.

West, P., 1976. 'The rise and fall of the American porch', *Landscape, 20.3*, 42–7.

Wright, G., 1981. *Building the Dream: A Social History of Housing in America.*

3 *The Applied Arts in the Museum Context*

IAN WOLFENDEN

When the first public museum of applied arts was founded, in 1852, its role and the range of its collections were relatively easy to determine. The Museum of Ornamental Art, later the South Kensington Museum, collected historical and contemporary works of ornamental art, primarily as exemplars for the mid-nineteenth-century craft industries and as a means of improving public taste. At South Kensington a classification of the applied arts proposed by the German theorist, Gottfried Semper, in the 1860s, was adopted, with categories of furniture and woodwork, textiles, metalwork and ceramics and glass. That classification has been of great practical value in the study and development of applied arts collections in museums throughout Europe and North America; yet it has been open to question as a sufficient basis for applied arts museum collections since the early twentieth century, when attention first seriously turned to the aesthetics of mass-produced domestic goods. Over recent decades a history of design has emerged, concerned particularly with the phenomena of mass production and consumption but overlapping with applied arts history in many respects. Museums generally have been slow to recognize design history and applied arts museums have rarely treated it. This paper will briefly discuss the legacy of the nineteenth-century museums of applied arts and question their current role in the light of the history of design.

The mid-nineteenth-century classification of the applied arts was based on the contemporary craft industrial structure. Each craft industry was distinct in its technical as well as its material basis; some were already highly mechanized while others relied extensively on craft skills. Adequate presentation of the basic diversity of material and technique within the applied arts was quickly recognized to be difficult for a general applied arts museum to achieve. For example, the Museum of Ornamental Art was intended to 'serve to increase the means of Industrial Education, and to extend the influence of Science and Art upon Productive Industry' (quoted in Morris 1986: 18). However, after the museum moved to South Kensington the scientific, or material and technical, aspects of the applied arts came to be regarded as the province of the Science Museum. A possible solution to the difficulty, already perceived earlier in the century, was for a museum to concentrate upon just one of the applied arts: by 1809 steps had been taken towards forming what became the Musée National de Céramique de Sèvres outside Paris, and at Murano the Museo Vetrario was established in 1861, collecting Roman and Venetian glass and documents relating to the art and technique of glassmaking. However, even these specialized museums tended to emphasize art rather than technique, the museum at Murano, for example, having a school of design for glassmakers added to it in the 1860s (Barovier 1974: 113).

The specific material and technical characteristics of the applied arts were fully stressed in one great nineteenth-century museum, the Conservatoire des Arts et Métiers in Paris. Founded late in the eighteenth century, the Conservatoire was established as an institute and museum of technology. An ordinance of 1819 made provision for public displays to expound the 'application of science to art industry' (noted in Bonnefous 1980: 9). In the years around 1850, half a century before the foundation of the Musée des Arts Decoratifs in Paris, the Conservatoire began to add significant collections of applied art to its existing holdings of tools, archives and technological models. Historical and especially contemporary objects of applied art were acquired to illustrate the technical possibilities inherent in a variety of materials, and substantial sections were formed of ceramics, glass, textiles and horological items. The Conservatoire developed essentially as a museum of technology and, in this century, has reappraised its role in relation to museums of science and technology outside France. Even today, as the Musée National des Techniques, it possesses remarkable collections of applied art. It represents the nineteenth century's most positive attempt to realize within the museum context the implications of the material and technical classification of the applied arts.

Most nineteenth-century museums of applied arts adopted or modified Semper's classification but chose other themes than material or technique to unify their diverse collections. The example of South Kensington was particularly influential. That museum's aim was to educate manufacturers and the public in ornamental design, at a time of general concern over the quality of British craft industrial products. Ornamental design provided the framework within which the museum's collections were to be understood, and contemporary design theory underpinned the displays. Ralph Wornum's *Analysis of Ornament* of 1855 and Owen Jones's *Grammar of Ornament*, published in 1856, analysed the principles of ornamental design. The visitor to the original Museum of Ornamental Art was enjoined 'not to look at the articles in the Museum as mere objects "vertu" or curiosity but to examine their beauties and defects with reference to the principles laid down' (quoted in Morris 1986: 19). Even historical objects were acquired for the museum: 'First and mainly, on account of the suggestions they are calculated to afford for improving manufactures' (quoted in Wilson 1987: 18). Thus the prime objective of the Museum of Ornamental Art and its successor at South Kensington was to engage manufacturers and the general public in an issue of contemporary concern, rather than to convey the history and technical development of the various applied arts.

Despite the emphasis at South Kensington on the principles of design underlying all works of applied art, the collections were normally arranged on the basis of material and technique. An attempt had been made, in the Museum of Ornamental Art, to illustrate 'false principles' of design, but this display provoked understandable criticism from manufacturers whose products were pilloried. The central thesis of the South Kensington Museum and the many museums throughout Europe and North America which it influenced thus remained implicit. As such, it was unlikely to engage the visitor. Of the South Kensington Museum, William Morris once commented 'They talk of building museums for the public, but the South Kensington Museum was got together for about six people' (quoted in Morris 1986: 94). Morris, who was closely connected with the museum, was deeply sceptical of its potential to attract interest beyond those directly involved in the practice of design. Museums on the South Kensington model were perhaps never able to resolve the dichotomy between categorization by material and technique and the assertion of general design principles.

A quite different approach to the applied arts museum emerged under the influence of the Arts and Crafts Movement, motivated by that movement's concern for social reform. Such information as we have indicates a keen wish to make a connection with the visitor through a simple, integrated arrangement of the collections. John Ruskin's St George's Museum at Walkley in Sheffield was the prototype, although it contained little applied art, and it inspired T. C. Horsfall to found the Manchester Art Museum in 1884. This featured, in the second phase of its development, two model rooms, a bedroom and a living room, furnished in a manner appropriate for a working-class artisan earning a small weekly wage (MacDonald 1986). Items in the rooms were of good quality but of a type available from department stores rather than exclusive craft workshops. Display labelling gave prices of each object. Although based on Arts and Crafts principles of good design, and perhaps somewhat patronizing towards the working class, Horsfall's museum was, to some extent, oriented towards the consumer in the manner of a trade fair, thus differing markedly from applied arts museums on the South Kensington model.

An interesting gloss on the Manchester Art Museum is provided by a fictional Arts and Crafts museum sketched by William Morris in chapter 27 of his romance *News From Nowhere*, published in 1890. In the England of the twenty-first century, outside London in the village of Wallingford, Morris describes a 'biggish hall' with 'a large collection of manufactures and art'. The objects are of craftwork and machine manufacture, carefully selected to illustrate the immense political, social and technological changes that are the subject of the book. The hall at Wallingford, which Morris does not refer to as a museum, is readily accessible to the community. It presents, through objects from a period of civil war to the time in which the story is set, a recent history of applied arts and design, whilst offering a rigorous social critique. A single theme predominates – the nature of work. Classification systems and theories of design are at once transcended.

Emphasis on the social context of the applied arts was a new idea. In the Manchester Art Museum and in William Morris's imaginary hall, concern for social reform prevented total preoccupation with aesthetic values. By collecting items from department stores T. C. Horsfall anticipated twentieth-century interests in the mass-produced object. Machine-made objects were present in Morris's hall. Morris deprecated the machine, but it was central to his sense of a museum's purpose to juxtapose craft and machine work. Ironically, the ideas behind these Arts and Crafts museums did not survive the movement itself. Twentieth-century applied arts museums have either tended to follow the South Kensington model or have dealt with a single craft industry: the modern association of design with mass production and consumption has been difficult for applied arts museums to accommodate.

The question of the relation of mass-produced objects to the applied arts was first raised in the early 1900s. A fundamental feature of applied arts museums, the system of classification based on craft materials, was henceforward open to challenge. At the same time, the significance of ornamental design was denied, leaving the majority of applied arts museums without the framework within which their collections had been assembled. At this period Germany took a lead in design theory. The third German Applied Arts Exhibition, at Dresden in 1906, included much craftwork but also machine-made furniture for the working class and a hall dedicated to 'functional form', where motor cars, rowing boats, vending machines and kitchen and bathroom fittings were shown (Heskett 1986: 106–18). The exhibition was an instrument of propaganda for a new approach to design, in which the contemporary applied arts of the traditional craft industries were to be associated with machine-produced domestic and industrial goods. In being organized by, among others, architects and museum directors to promote a new design concept, it was also a new type of exhibition.

The ideas behind the Dresden exhibition, developed and transmitted by the Modern Movement in the 1920s and 1930s, had some impact on the museums of applied arts. In particular, exhibitions assumed importance as a means of communicating design ideology. But permanent collections altered little. The Victoria and Albert Museum began collecting from its modern design exhibitions in the 1930s but when, in the 1950s, it added a significant range of modern consumer goods, such as electrical heaters and refrigerators, these became part of the Circulation Department collections. There clearly were difficulties in integrating twentieth-century domestic products of new industries into the existing classification of the applied arts. This was, however, achieved in New York, at the Museum of Modern Art, where a collection of design was started in 1934. A system of classification emerged to embrace both the traditional craft industries and the new industries mass-producing consumer goods. Classification was into the categories of appliances and equipment, furniture, tableware, tools and textiles. A major criterion for the selection of objects for the collection was to be formal quality, reflecting Modern Movement ideals. The Museum of Modern Art, by definition, does not collect historical objects; even so, its rethinking of the classification of twentieth-century applied arts was a significant advance.

Since the 1960s and the demise of the Modern Movement, attitudes to design have changed. Also, a history of design is now well established, which explains the development of the theory and practice of design. Post-modernism is marked by an acceptance of pluralist aesthetic values, emphasizing the variety of consumer tastes. Design is now also more clearly understood as a process integral to manufacture and marketing, rather than a form- or style-giving exercise. The full significance of design can now only be conveyed in centres or museums devoted exclusively to the subject. The Centre de Création Industrielle in the Pompidou Centre in Paris is one example; the Museum of Design, shortly to be opened in London's dockland, will be another. But design history recognizes the applied arts as part of its subject matter. It remains important for the connection between applied art and design to be stressed within the context of the applied arts museums. This is necessary if they are to develop the function of relating to contemporary society and to mark the continuity between the craft industrial tradition and contemporary manufacture.

Presenting the applied arts as part of the history of design has interesting ramifications. Current design history explores not only formal aesthetic qualities but also the range of meaning attached to the visual appearance of manufactured objects. This approach involves the use of source material of a kind not always available to the applied art historian – for example, evidence from the retail trade. It may, however, be possible, as a recent account of Wedgwood ceramics by a design historian makes clear (Forty 1986: 13–28). Looking at the appearance rather than simply the style of historical applied arts helps create links with contemporary mass-produced consumer goods. Contemporary design is particularly concerned with symbolic form, with ergonomics, with achieving strong brand identity and with visual and tactile qualities which aid the consumer's use of a product. To some extent, these considerations apply to contemporary craft industrial production also.

What is implied here is a series of fresh approaches to the presentation of permanent collections of applied arts. In this century many applied arts museums felt the lack of a factor to unify their diverse collections, once ornamental design lost favour. Arrangements by period style have been chosen by several major museums, such as the Victoria and Albert, the Musée des Arts Decoratifs in Paris and the Nationalmuseet in Stockholm. While this has its merits, it ignores the technical, social and economic factors involved in the changing appearance of applied art objects. One example of an arguably more fruitful approach is the display arranged by the Council for Art and Industry in conjunction with the Victoria and Albert Museum in the late 1930s (Morris 1986: 191–2). This was only a temporary exhibition, but it could well have formed the basis of a permanent gallery. The exhibition was of domestic base metalwork and showed a range of historical implements and equipment, from toasting forks to spits, alongside their modern counterparts, such as gas and electric cookers. Labelling probably focussed on the formal qualities of the objects, but, given a broader frame of reference, such a collection would provide a valuable commentary not only on style and design but also on the social contexts of craft and mass-production industry.

There are many possible ways of presenting the applied arts in terms of design history. All involve the collecting of mass-produced objects which may not fit readily into an existing classification. An extension or rethinking of a classification could be required, even perhaps the creation of a separate department, as was done at the Museum of Modern Art in New York. That museum also adopted a dual collecting policy to cope with the special problems of collecting contemporary items. Some objects are accessed directly into a permanent collection while others are acquired for a study collection, which is reviewed periodically. De-accessioning is seen as an essential arm of the policy – something which needs serious consideration in any museum collecting contemporary design.

Only a footnote in the history of modern design but of considerable significance for the applied arts is the revival of craft since the late 1960s. Craft is developing in a number of directions, admirably discussed in two recent exhibitions, *Fast Forward*, organized by the Institute of Contemporary Arts in London, and *Craft Matters*, organized by the John Hansard Gallery, University of Southampton. Development of craft collections is an alternative to initiating a design collection for applied arts museums. However, it should be said that the most vital contemporary craft is moving far from its craft industrial origins, and some of it is frankly sculpture. In considering the museum context of contemporary craft an American example may again be instructive. Some American art museums are now acquiring pots for their ceramic departments which are then displayed by fine arts departments with paintings and sculpture (Clark 1986). A future realignment of craft with fine art is not beyond question.

Museums of the applied arts were established in the nineteenth century with the clear intention that they should relate to contemporary life. Their collections reflected the current craft industrial structure. The twentieth century development of mass-production techniques has rendered the craft industries less significant, economically and socially, than they were. In general, applied arts museums have found difficulty in adjusting to changed social conditions. They have come to seem, to a large extent, repositories of historical collections. While that is one of their essential functions, it remains important to respond to contemporary circumstances. The growth of specialized applied arts museums, dealing with technical and technological developments within a specific craft industry, has been a lively recent evolution from a type originating in the nineteenth century. For general museums of applied arts the history of design offers an approach which allows for a close connection not only with contemporary material and technical changes but also with new social attitudes. It further encourages a fresh way of looking at objects, in which visual appearance rather than style is paramount. Above all, it makes possible a full and integral presentation of the significance of the applied arts. It is perhaps ironic that such an approach is prefigured in William Morris' visionary hall at Wallingford.

BIBLIOGRAPHY

Barovier, R., 1974. 'Roman glassware in the Museum of Murano and the Muranese revival of the nineteenth century', *Journal of Glass Studies, 16*: 111–19.

Bonnefous, E., 1980. *Le Conservatoire National Des Arts Et Métiers.*

Clark, G., 1986. 'American ceramics', *Crafts, 80* (May-June): 40–7.

Forty, A., 1986. *Objects of Desire.*

Heskett, J., 1986. *Design in Germany 1870–1918.*

MacDonald, S., 1986. 'For "Swine of Discretion": design for living: 1884', *Museums Journal, 86.3*: 123–9.

Morris, B., 1986. *Inspiration for Design.*

Wilson, T., 1987. *Ceramic Art of the Italian Renaissance.*

4 *Archaeology, Material Culture and Museums*

DAVID CROWTHER

The heart of this paper, like its title, is in three parts. Firstly, it reviews some of the changing theoretical stances of archaeology, particularly prehistoric archaeology, over the last half-century in order to underline the dynamic which gives archaeology its special vitality as an especially powerful means for people to study people. Neither the subjects nor the objects of study are fixed. Secondly, it examines the particular place of material culture studies within archaeology, offering certain approaches and insights into an information resource of wide complexity and bias. Thirdly, the role of museums is discussed in terms of their contemporary functions of preservation, research and presentation of the material past in the public domain. A set of concluding remarks makes the plea for a fresh interpretive archaeology with an identity and a sense of public purpose that museums, historically, philosophically and organizationally, are well placed to provide. In examining material culture in the context of archaeology and museums, it is necessary to pay as much attention to contemporary perceptions of the past as it is to review the potential information value of its surviving physical traces, for each is a product of the other. People are, after all, studying people, albeit dead ones, and the potential for doing it well rests with the quick, not the dead.

Archaeology, like the people it studies, is in a constant state of flux, changing as practitioners' perceptions change, as information accumulates, and as new ideas emerge. So even if, in the broadest terms, the objective of archaeology remains about the same, the ways and means of getting there change with the times for, as Fowler (1977: 13) has stated, every age produces two archaeologies, one from itself to the future, and one from the past to itself.

So what is archaeology? It is a moving target, and to grasp the meaning of archaeology requires a perspective that takes into account its shifting emphases and directions. In *Archaeology and Society*, written half a century ago to describe the processes of archaeology, its aims, its limitations and its social value, Graham Clark (1939: 1) defined archaeology as follows:

> Archaeology is often defined as the study of antiquities. A better definition would be that it is the study of how men lived in the past. It is true that your archaeologist is compelled by circumstances to rely upon the material remains surviving from the people he is studying to arrive at any idea of their daily life; yet however much he may appear to be preoccupied with things, often in themselves unattractive, he is really interested all the time in people.

While few archaeologists would argue particularly fiercely against Clark's definition, in the decades following the Second World War they would have responded 'Yes, but ...'. Such an overtly humanistic stance, presenting archaeology as a pursuit dealing directly and unambiguously with people – groups of individuals – would appear to many even today as optimistic, even charming. However, in the archaeological climate of the 1930s we were, after all, in Wheeler's memorable phrase, digging up not pots but people. Jacquetta Hawkes's biography of Mortimer Wheeler shows the skilful and imaginitive use of historical expression and archaeological inference which allowed Wheeler the freedom, in discussing finds of dog figurines from a Romano-Celtic temple and bath complex of Nodens (an otherwise unknown deity) at Lydney, to comment (Hawkes J. 1982: 147):

> Now in the classical religions the dog is most widely associated with the cults of healing. At Epidaurus, dogs sacred to Asklepios were kept in the temple, and are recorded to have been instrumental in healing by licking the affected parts ... At Epidaurus also, baths were added to the temple settlement of Asklepios in Roman times, and bathing was frequently prescribed by the god as a curative measure.

The Celtic deity Nodens may have shared some of the attributes of the Greek divinity Asklepios therefore, and associated cult objects pointing to associations with sun and sea led Wheeler to conclude that: 'Fishermen from the Severn must have toiled up the narrow, rocky path to this shrine.' Such enthusiasm for populating the past with real flesh and blood based on material evidence, beefed up with history, reaches its apotheosis a few years later in Wheeler's Maiden Castle report, where he describes in blood-curdling detail the final assault by the Roman Army as evidenced by the excavations around the entrance (quoted in Hawkes J. 1982: 173).

It is difficult to see where Wheeler's Lydney fishermen, let alone his Maiden Castle slaughtered, would find a place in Christopher Hawkes's archaeology 20 years later (Hawkes C.F.C. 1954) which has a 'hierarchy of inference' for archaeological material beginning with apparently straightforward issues regarding techniques of production, and climbing largely out of reach into aspects of spiritual life. Hawkes forces the conclusion that the closer to the mind of the individual one climbs, the further one gets from the mute realities of the material evidence. This circumspection with regard to the ability or otherwise of archaeology to provide a narrative culture history can be found, at least to an extent, in Graham Clark's own rewrite of his introductory passage to *Archaeology and Society* (Clark 1957: 17):

> Archaeology may be simply defined as the systematic study of antiquities as a means of reconstructing the past. For his real contributions to be fruitful, the archaeologist has to possess a real feeling for history even though he may not have to face what is perhaps the keenest challenge of historical scholarship, the subtle play of human personality and circumstance.

Just what is meant by reconstructing the past is answered to some extent in Clark's chapters on 'Economic life' and 'Social, intellectual and spiritual life'. In the case of the latter, at least some information on the crucial matter of social organization is recoverable archaeologically, according to Clark. Specific aspects like religion are reflected in the graphic arts though hardly elsewhere (1957: 232). Cosmology, too, is potentially there in the evidence though it would be 'quite wrong to attribute to [prehistoric man] a conception of the world or of its relation to the universe' (1957: 231) based on the then barely tested megalithic surveys of the time. If social and ideological systems are obscure or even futile pursuits, aspects of economic bases may offer a more fruitful line of enquiry. It is in this context that there emerges a growing emphasis on resources and their exploitation. This is well shown in Clark's diagram illustrating the utilization of the environment by the Mesolithic hunters of Star Carr, Yorkshire (1957: 232). Clark's hunters may have an obscure culture but as consumers they are thrown into sharp relief. However, resources are what tools are made of, not what tools acquire or modify, and as such there is no interaction, no dynamic, between culture and environment.

This was to become a dominant theme in the 1960s and 1970s when the development of models, systems theory and law-like generalizations concerning human behaviour and adaptation were given special momentum by the energy of the New Archaeology movement (e.g. Binford 1972), which saw archaeology as diachronic anthropology. One of its champions, picking up Graham Clark's remarks, defines archaeology as follows (Redman 1973: 6):

> I shift the emphasis ... from the study of antiquities and the reconstruction of the past to the study of human behaviour *per se* ... The main value of artefacts is that they constitute decipherable systematic records of past human activities. When understood, these artefacts can help us understand human behaviour not only of the past, but also as it is today.

The principle underlying this approach was that human behaviour was a phenomenon which, like any other in the physical world, could be observed and measured through a rigorous scientific approach to the raw material, and subsumed within a series of laws. In this case, human behaviour – human patterning – can be predicted (or postdicted) from the material culture patterning, for the latter is a product of adaptation with the physical and social environment. Whilst offering a tempting intellectual pursuit of the past rooted directly in the tangible evidence of well-structured field work with especial appeal to the post-Rescue generation of field archaeologists, there are problems with this kind of approach. It reduces people to patterns of products, structured responses to external stimuli. Truly, products of human action are all the archaeologist has to draw upon, but these are the products of people's minds, not just their hands. All rests upon cultural attitudes – the minds that needed feeding in the past as well as the mouths – and it is the essential humanness of humanity that the archaeology of the 1970s largely failed to embrace.

Through the late 1970s and the 1980s, the search for genuinely cultural meanings to the raw material of archaeology – going for the minds not just the mouths of prehistoric people – has found particular force, drawing on a variety of theories of social behaviour (Hodder 1986). Communication theory and semiotics allow artefacts a cultural role far beyond the purely functional one of products serving practical ends. Instead, they may convey messages and meanings within and between social groups through symbol and sign (Hodder 1982; Pearce 1986c; Wobst 1977). Concepts of structuralism borrowed from the social anthropology of Lévi-Strauss (1972) and others offer insights of archaeology whereby so-called structures of meaning exist at a deep level to condition a whole range of creative acts, revealing direct links between notions of social order (gender, landscape, seasons) and material culture (hunting equipment, pottery decoration) through a series of structured differences or symmetries between notion and symbol (Hodder 1986, 45f.; Pearce 1987: 178).

The application of Marxist ideas of human progress to the interpretation of archaeological data (Spriggs 1984) presents fresh opportunities for offering genuinely cultural explanations for certain phenomena. Marxist analysis allows for hierarchical concepts relating to social stress such as the means of production (the exploited), the forces of production (technology, ecosystem, organization) and the relations of production (kinship, peer groups) to be invoked in the explanation of, for example, social and technological change in the Upper Palaeolithic (see Hodder 1986: 59 for a critique of this and other Marxist perspectives of social structure and ideology). Through such developments has the discipline of archaeology a better claim to intellectual maturity than once it had. No single application of any particular perspective will have validity if uncritically applied. It is the sheer variety of approaches which contemporary archaeology can embrace which gives it a universality to the past and to the people who inhabit it.

When H. L. R. Finberg's *Approaches to History* (1962) was published a quarter of a century ago, amidst nine approaches, 'Archaeology' could barely make it between the covers, sneaking in with 'Place names'. Today's archaeology is peripheral neither to history nor anthropology; it is neither art nor science. It studies the material manifestations of the past and the cultural or 'ideal' (relating to ideas) context to which they relate. In being mindful of ideology and its influence on people, archaeology recognizes that today's observations are as much a construct of today's context in terms of bias and belief, as they are true products of the past. As such, archaeology is truly about people – people in the past and, in turn, ourselves. Its raw material is largely material culture, to which we must now turn.

Through the 1890s, the Society of Antiquaries mounted a campaign of excavations at Silchester comprising the largest research excavation project yet seen in Britain. Regular publication within the pages of *Archaeologia* was a feature of the work, which had enormous influence on contemporary and subsequent generations of archaeologists. A typical report on the excavated artefacts reads as follows:

> The finds in bronze, iron and bone are of the usual character. Among the bronze articles are two good enamelled brooches, one of which has a cruciform device on a ground of blue and green enamel, a brooch with a sliding ring on the pin, several chains and a curious socketed object surmounted by the head of an eagle perhaps to fit in a staff. The finds in bone and glass were unimportant. The pottery too calls for no special remark. (St John Hope and Fox 1898: 22)

Paying scant regard to the detailed collection and recording of finds (Boon 1974: 20), the Silchester excavators were principally concerned with the recovery of building and street plans. A whole Romano-British town lay beneath their feet, and their perception of just what was important was conditioned accordingly. To this extent, Silchester was exceptional, for in fact the best of the mainstream archaeology in the decades before 1900 was deeply concerned with the classification and arrangement of material culture, as seen in the work of, for example, John Evans and General Pitt-Rivers.

If the work of Evans and his ilk showed the value of scrupulous assessment of a single category of artefact, 'bronze implements' for example, and its arrangement into ordered typologies for dating and other purposes, it was Pitt-Rivers more than anyone else who first underlined the importance of material culture in its totality. He believed that 'common things are of more importance than particular things because they are more prevalent' and his reports of *Excavations at Cranborne Chase* published between 1887 and 1898 set a new standard of contextual recording and presentation (Daniel 1975: 169–174).

Happily, there were other early archaeologists who shared Pitt-Rivers's view of material culture and context. None were better nor more active than J. R. Mortimer, whose collection of archaeological material, including the products of excavations into over 360 barrows on the Yorkshire Wolds, forms to this day the essential and overwhelming core of the collections at Hull City Museums. The culmination of his life's work was the publication of his *Forty Years Researches in British and Saxon Burial Mounds of East Yorkshire* (1905), which was steered through to publication by Hull's first Municipal Museum curator, Tom Sheppard, and lavishly illustrated by Mortimer's daughter, Agnes. Each barrow had been numbered and plotted onto a set of maps, each grave was given a number or letter, and all finds assigned a context, either by grave, or otherwise a general contextual description such as 'from the body of the mound'. Finds were stored in labelled trays and boxes according to site, arranged by 'barrow groups', and held in cupboards beneath sequential display cases at Mortimer's own museum at Driffield, which he opened in 1878. So scrupulous was the labelling of objects or the packages that contained them, that the recent rediscovery of hitherto unaccessioned material in the Mortimer Collection (Crowther, unpublished) yielded dozens of excavated groups of finds which could with confidence be ascribed to meaningful contexts, with a probability of subsequent mixing which was both measurable and low. The close and secure association of object with context is something we now take for granted. Indeed, it is the concept of the context of the object which is the *sine qua non* that elevates material culture studies out of antiquarianism or art history and into archaeology.

A recent model for artefact studies (Pearce 1986a: 200) provides a useful checklist of attributes a given artefact has, some of which are intrinsic (material, decoration), others relative (context, history, function), and all of which are necessary for a balanced interpretation of the object. Such interpretation, or at least a conceptualization of the object's significance, is really only the beginning of the process of using material culture for archaeological ends.

In using material culture to study people in their cultural, social and economic environment through time, archaeology looks at whole settlements or indeed whole landscapes, and deals with thousands of artefacts, each with their own qualities and attributes. With modern techniques of computerized data storage and manipulation, and higher standards of recording in field archaeology, contextual and other information relating to artefacts can be used to address a host of issues within and between sites, including function, areas of specialized activity, and the management of refuse and resources. Ultimately, material culture studies integrated with other classes of archaeological data can illuminate the whole vexed question of formation processes, or how the archaeological record was formed (Schiffer 1983).

The potential value of studying material culture in these terms is perhaps best illustrated using a specific example, in this case the Romano-British farmstead and field system at Maxey, Cambridgeshire (Crowther 1985). In this example, artefact function related to context was used to discuss the utilization of the site. It is possible to define a set of broad functional categories to which any given artefact can be assigned, though care has to be exercised to ensure that categories are selected which are meaningful and appropriate in terms of the quality and quantity of the data, and the specific questions that the exercise is designed to answer. In the case of Maxey, a site comprising houses, farmyard(s), field ditches, open (?cultivated) areas, and indeterminate structural and non-structural features – indeed in many respects a typical open, native set of rural buildings and enclosures of the Romano-British period – the question related to the distribution of material culture across these features and how it had got there. Working from the premise that artefacts enter the archaeological record either through accidental loss or by deliberate discard (including burial), are certain types of material more likely to enter the archaeological record through accidental loss, whilst others may be more likely to do so through deliberate discard, perhaps as part of rubbish management? If so, is there meaningful or exclusive patterning in the distributions of contrasting categories of artefact? If so, can anything be inferred about the behaviour of the people who generated the material in the first place?

To address such questions at Maxey, four functional categories of artefact were defined, based on a well-established hierarchical classification scheme using functional criteria that had been developed for American museums (Chenhall 1978). These categories of 'personal artefacts', 'tools and equipment', 'structural artefacts' and 'unclassifiable artefacts' (Crowther 1985: 182) produced meaningful distributions for various phases of activity across the site. Items that might be more likely to be 'stray losses', brooches for example, had a tendency to be distributed in areas where human traffic might be concentrated, such as certain building entrances and access points into yards or enclosures. This pattern contrasted with other classes of what might be termed bulk rubbish – pottery and animal bone for example – where evidence for refuse/midden heaps and their subsequent spread across cultivation areas next to the habitation areas could be inferred from finds patterning in the modern topsoil and buried features (Crowther 1983: Halstead 1985).

There is a small but growing body of case studies which illustrate locational analyses of categorized material culture across sites from both excavated contexts such as Wendens Ambo (Halstead *et al.* 1978) and Winklebury (Fisher 1985), and from topsoil surveys in the Aisne Valley and elsewhere (see Haselgrove 1985 for an overview). Much work remains to be done in determining what constitutes an appropriate sample population for analysis, and what biases are present in contexts themselves – pits, ditches, gullies – in influencing distributions. Nevertheless, such analyses, wherever they have been attempted with any rigour, have produced useful new perspectives for interpretation. Given the (hopefully) sound standard of contextual recording on modern archaeological excavations, and the professional commitment in today's archaeology museums to curate entire archives of finds and records, such locational analyses as these could be done retrospectively, after the transfer of the archive to museum, indeed after publication of the basic site report. The role of the museum in material culture studies is, or has the capacity to be, central to the interpretive development of archaeological evidence, and should now be considered.

Compared with other subject specialisms, archaeology rests very comfortably in the museum context. It uses a database which, for the most part, has undergone a change of state by virtue of its very entry into the domain of the discipline. From *in situ* and unknown, to removed and researched, before it has any impact on knowledge, the evidence has largely lost its original integrity. Its meaning rests only in the information attached to it in the form of associated records. This change of state is more than just conceptual, it is physical. Material once in a state of equilibrium with its burial environment, be it waterlogged wood or copper alloy from a dry site, will begin to deteriorate unless elaborate steps are taken to secure its welfare. Such a resource is therefore in constant jeopardy and requires long-term care and management to minimize its inevitable devaluation and decay. It is a measure of the direct social relevance of archaeology that the repositories for its raw material, semi-digested or otherwise, should be public institutions whose principle functions are the provision of a cultural service.

This service can be summarized as the collection, preservation, curation and interpretation of material culture, a set of tasks which give museums ample opportunity to develop material culture studies in a wide range of aspects. In fact, due to conflicting pressures of time and resources, it would be fair to say that little that is genuinely new or radical in theoretical approaches to material culture studies is emanating from provincial museums in Britain. However, descriptive research of the highest quality, including catalogues and appraisals of artefact types, remains a feature of museum archaeology, carried out by curators seeking to maximize the usefulness of collections (Kinnes and Longworth 1985; Leahy 1986).

Nevertheless, museums have always been more alive than many university or field archaeologists to the public need for a past, elucidated by artefacts, that is not a palimpsest of geographers' patterns, sociologists' systems or anthropologists' modes of behaviour, but which is populated by communities of individuals to which one can relate directly. This is reflected in some outstanding archaeology displays that provide an enlightening and meaningful experience for the visitor, allowing a contact with a tangible aspect of the past. A good example might be the Museum of the Iron Age at Andover, Hampshire, where the essential presentation of material culture is given greater contextual meaning by imaginative design on an appropriate scale. Public contact with their material heritage is perhaps even more meaningful outside the museum gallery. Amateur involvement in the collection and analysis of archaeological material is being taken to new levels of organization and relevance by Leicestershire Museums (Liddle 1985) and serves both a public appetite for practical involvement, and a management need for widespread data gathering.

The fact that museums operate in such a wide social context allows us to consider aspects of the meaning of objects in a contemporary sense as well as in more purely historical terms. The 'Symbols of Power' exhibition at the National Museum of Antiquities of Scotland, held in the summer of 1985, was a spectacular assembly of outstanding material from ritual contexts of the third and second millennia bc, presented to illustrate what is currently a favoured interpretation of such material in terms of the manifestation of social power and prestige in prehistory. The arguments are seductive; the language of objects as signs and symbols seems a timeless one and may offer one of the key avenues into 'reading the past' which we strive for (Clarke *et al.* 1985). One reason why it seems so plausible an approach is, of course, the astonishingly high status accorded to these very objects today. They are scrutinized and cherished, sitting in a vortex of academic and popular attention, safe behind the glass of a museum display case. We may talk about the Beaker grave group from, say, Garton Slack 37, in the context of aspects of social development in Yorkshire in the second millennium bc, or in terms of the growing importance of the individual, or as a new kind of élite, all gleaned from the funerary evidence of the period, but what kind of contexts are these? We deal in our own perceptions from our own time in our own way. It is these perceptions and trends in the way we view the past which museums can not only reflect but also monitor and record through analysis of visitor and non-visitor reaction, and through the analysis of its own housekeeping and display trends, past and present.

At Hull Museums, for example, it has been possible through the examination of parts of the Mortimer Collection, and by assessing the level of care parts have sustained or enjoyed over the last 70 years or so, to see a shift in emphasis through time from Mortimer's original approach to the ordering and presentation of all material from a given barrow, to the selective treatment of Tom Sheppard, the curator at Hull (Crowther, unpublished). Examination of old packaging materials, containers, display labels and so on can yield useful information about material culture in its post-depositional context in the museum; a reflection of past curatorial attitudes that have direct relevance to the context in which we see the material past today.

Museums hold a special place in the public consciousness as guardians and suppliers of historical knowledge, and as providing a service which even non-users can identify as being desirable (Prince and Schadla-Hall 1985: 42).

Despite a latent public interest in aspects of heritage, there is no doubt that, since Wheeler's memorable appearances with Glyn Daniel on the BBC's *Animal, Vegetable or Mineral* programmes of the 1950s and 1960s archaeology has largely failed to meet the public's expectations of science and history;

expectations which have been far more satisfactorily met on television and in popular bookshops by natural history, aspects of science and technology, and nostalgia. It has been argued elsewhere (Crowther, 1988) that archaeology is public archaeology or it is virtually nothing, and that the past failures to root archaeology in popular relevance has had a negative effect on the scope of a discipline with an unhappy tendency to answer questions no-one is asking.

With the development of post-graduate, post-Rescue field archaeology on the one hand, and the mushrooming of theoretical stances on the other, the last decade in particular had seen something of an identity crisis for archaeology as theory and practice had separated to the point of mutual incomprehension (Pryor 1983). Small wonder that there was no coherent image of archaeology for public recognition. Today, more and more, field rchaeology is being pushed into the arena of public justification through financial constraints, politics, sponsorship, developer funding, tourism and leisure. Museum services in general are witnessing similar pressures and opportunities. At the same time as this overwhelming increase in demand upon archaeology to communicate effectively, comes a new awareness of the potentialities of the material culture record for both reading the past and reading ourselves.

The process of archaeological endeavour is one of collection, preservation, research and presentation, largely of material culture. Museums are well placed not just to reflect this process but to control it. There is ample scope for a variety of approaches to material culture studies using long-held collections, and some of these have been explored here. However, there is also a real need for more and better data, which can only be gathered through field work, structured to complement the research and interpretation needs of the museum. Public archaeology and material culture interpretation begin in the field: a genuinely lively and relevant interpretive archaeology must recognize this, and will surely be found in museums in the future.

BIBLIOGRAPHY

Binford, L. R., 1972. *An Archaeological Perspective.*

Boon, G. C., 1974. *Silchester: The Roman Town of Calleva.*

Chenhall, R. G., 1978. *Nomenclature for Museum Cataloguing: A System for Classifying Man-Made Objects.*

Clark, G., 1939. *Archaeology and Society* (1st edn).

Clark, G., 1957. *Archaeology and Society* (3rd edn).

Clarke, D. V., Cowie, T. G., and Foxon, A., 1985. *Symbols of Power.*

Crowther, D. R., 1983. 'Old landsurfaces and modern ploughsoil', *Scottish Archaeological Review, 2*: 31–44.

Crowther, D. R., 1985. 'The other finds', in Pryor, F. M. M. and French, C. A. I., 'Archaeology and environment in the Lower Welland Valley, Vol.1', *East Anglian Archaeology*, *27*: 163–95.

Crowther, D. R., 1988. 'Museums are where the past is going', *The Field Archaeologist*, *8*: 120–2.

Crowther, D. R., unpublished. 'From the body of the mound; an evaluation of some rediscovered excavation finds in the Mortimer Collection at Hull City Museums.'

Crowther, D. R., French, C. A. I. and Pryor, F., 1985. 'Approaching the Fens the flexible way', in Haselgrove, C., Millett, M. and Smith, I. (eds), *Archaeology from the Ploughsoil*: 35–52.

Daniel, G., 1975. *A Hundred and Fifty Years of Archaeology*.

Finberg, H. P. R. (ed.), 1962. *Approaches to History*.

Fisher, A. R., 1985. 'Winklebury hillfort: a study of artefact distributions from subsoil features', *Procs. Prehistoric Society*, *51*: 167–80.

Foxon, A. D., 1982. 'Artefacts in society', *Scottish Archaeological Review*, *1.2*: 114–20.

Fowler, P., 1977. *Approaches to Archaeology*.

Halstead, P., 1985. 'A study of mandibular teeth from Romano-British contexts at Maxey', in Pryor, F. M. M. and French, C. A. I., 'Archaeology and environment in the Lower Welland Valley, Vol. 1', *East Anglian Archaeology*, *27*: 219–24.

Halstead, P., Hodder, I. and Jones, G., 1978. 'Behavioural archaeology and refuse patterns: a case study', *Norwegian Archaeological Review*, *11*: 118–31.

Haselgrove, C., 1985. 'Inference from ploughsoil artefact assemblages', in Haselgrove, C., Millett, M. and Smith, I. (eds), *Archaeology from the Ploughsoil*: 52–67.

Hawkes, C. F. C., 1954. 'Archaeological theory and method: some suggestions from the Old World', *American Anthropology*, *56*: 155–68.

Hawkes, J., 1982. *Mortimer Wheeler*.

Hodder, I., 1982. *Symbols in Action*.

Hodder, I., 1986. *Reading the Past*.

Kinnes, I. A. and Longworth, I. H., 1985. *Catalogue of the Excavated Prehistoric and Romano-British Material in the Greenwell Collection*.

Leahy, K., 1986. 'A dated stone axe-hammer from Cleethorpes, South Humberside', *Procs. Prehistoric Society*, *52*: 143–53.

Levi-Strauss, C., 1972. *Structural Anthropology*.

Liddle, P., 1985. *Community Archaeology*.

Pearce, S. M., 1986a. 'Thinking about things: approaches to the study of artefacts', *Museums Journal*, *85.4*: 198–201.

Pearce, S. M., 1986b. 'Objects high and low', *Museums Journal*, *86.2*: 79–82.

Pearce, S. M., 1986c. 'Objects as signs and symbols', *Museums Journal*, *86.3*: 131–5.

Pearce, S. M., 1987. 'Objects in structures', *Museums Journal*, *86.4*: 178–81.

Prince, D. R. and Schadla-Hall, R. T., 1985. 'The image of the museum: a case-study of Kingston upon Hull', *Museums Journal*, *85.1*: 39–45.

Pryor, F. M. M., 1983. 'Talking heads', *Scottish Archaeological Review*, *2.2*: 98–100.

Redman, C. L., 1973. 'Research and theory in current archaeology: an introduction', in Redman, C. L. (ed.), *Research and Theory in Current Archaeology*: 3–25.

St John Hope, W. H. and Fox, G. E., 1898. 'Excavations on the site of the Roman City of Silchester, Hants., in 1897', *Archaeologia*, *61*: 1–24.

Schiffer, M. B., 1983. 'Towards the identification of formation processes', *American Antiquity*, *48*: 675–706.

Spriggs, M. (ed.), 1984. *Marxist Perspectives in Archaeology*.

Tilley, C., 1986. 'Interpreting material culture', in *Archaeological Objectivity in Interpretation Vol 2*. World Archaeological Congress.

Wobst, M., 1977. 'Stylistic behaviour and information exchange', *University of Michigan Museum of Anthropology Anthropological Paper*, *61*: 317–42.

5 *Objects in Structures*

SUSAN M. PEARCE

For some time now fresh ideas have begun to appear in artefact studies literature (e.g. Glassie 1975; Hoffman 1977; Hodder 1982), ideas which revolve around the philosophical structures developed chiefly by European structural linguistic scholars like Ferdinand de Saussure in the early and middle part of this century. These ideas are potentially far-reaching. The traditional approaches used until the 1960s by historians and anthropologists in their interpretations of past societies tended to assume that most material culture is merely the result, or even the detritus, of communities who were thinking their thoughts and doing their living elsewhere, and that artefacts were only meaningful if they were explained from outside, because they have nothing to say for themselves; and this in spite of the fact that we know from experience that artefacts can sometimes express our innermost feelings and beliefs. Some of the ideas of the structuralists may throw light here, and an examination of them may not be out of place. I shall therefore in the first part of this paper consider the nature of the theoretical structure, and in the second part apply it to a particular range of artefacts, the material culture of the central and western Inuit; and finally, I shall endeavour to draw a few general conclusions.

The justification for applying linguistic theory to material culture is in essence extremely simple: all human communities have language and all human communities have artefacts. It is the possession of these two faculties which marks off humans from animals, or culture from nature, even though, of course, the exact time and place where the leap occurred, or the precise distinction between man and the higher mammals, have proved extremely difficult to pin down. As far as we can tell, language and artefact creation seem to begin at much the same moment in our human history and both seem to mark the moment when creatures emerged that we are ready to recognize as man-like beings. The two faculties seem to be intimately intertwined, or even, perhaps, we may be led to conclude, dual expressions of the same characteristically human ability to order the world so that human groups can live successfully within it. For various reasons, however, much more effort has been applied to the consideration of linguistics, so it is the material culture theorists who must learn, borrow and adapt.

We may take as a starting point Ferdinand de Saussure's recognition that 'language is a system of inter-dependent terms in which the value of each term results solely from the simultaneous presence of the others' (1973:4). This, transformed into material culture terms, would read: 'Material culture is a system of inter-dependent artefacts in which the value of each artefact results solely from the simultaneous presence of the others.' This seems to be convincing: a hammer is meaningless without its head and its haft, and also without its nails and the prepared wood in which to hammer them, or – but in a rather different way – the meaning of a wedding ring is involved with the simultaneous presence of a large range of gold objects. We can also say that these things and their meanings are synchronic: that is, they are true here and now, however much their individual forms and values may be a result of the accumulated history of the societies which make and use them. When we look at the material culture of a society, therefore, we are looking at a complete system, self-contained and self-maintained.

However, any given inter-dependent, synchronic system, whether of words or of things, must, it seems clear, be the result of communal choice from a wide range of possibilities, even though the moment of choice may lie far back in the history of the community, and may seem to have been determined by the then given situation: the need to develop the idea of hammers and nails must have seemed obvious at the time in Western Europe because it fitted in with the trend of social development, but of course there are other ways of doing the relevant jobs, by binding for example, and the invention of hammers and nails was a social choice from amongst a range of possibilities. In linguistic terms, the series of choices which go to make up a language, comprising its vocabulary and its grammatical system, constitute what linguists have called a *langue*, and which in English is probably best called simply 'language'. Saussure made a fundamental and very fruitful distinction between 'language' and *parole*, 'speech' or 'text', in which items of vocabulary and elements of grammar are selected out from the full *langue* in order to make up the composite but limited constructs which we call sentences, and which are our actual vehicles of communication, justifying his contention that terms have meaning only in organized relationships to other terms. Many writers have refined upon this basic idea, but the rival orthodoxies and heresies, each with their own terminology, need not concern us here, and Saussure's terms will be used. Interestingly, in order to explain what he meant about linguistics, Saussure drew upon material culture. *Langue*, he says, is the chess board, the chess men and the rules of chess, while *parole* is any individual game played with these elements.

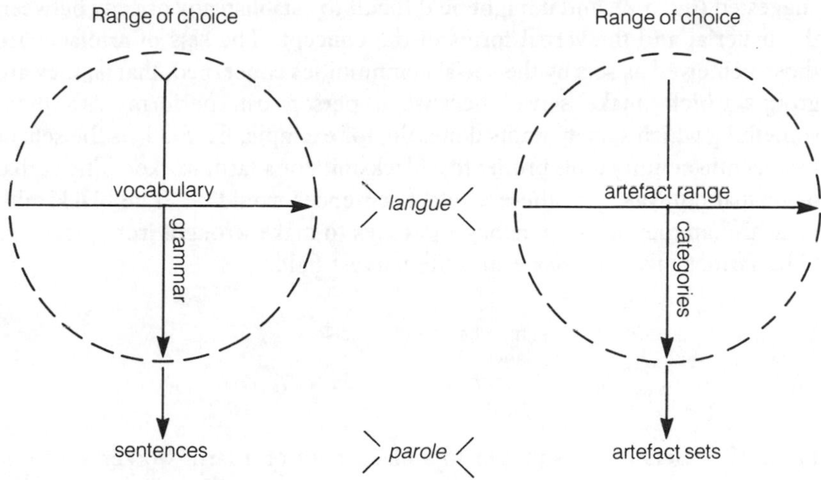

Figure 5.1 Diagram showing the relationship of choice, *langue* and *parole*, for language (*left*) and material culture (*right*)

In diagrammatic form, the linguistic analysis might look like the left-hand side of fig. 5.1 and the corresponding material culture analysis like the right-hand side of the same figure. Indeed, since the concept – of 'hammer', for example – must precede either the word 'hammer' or the artefact 'hammer', the two processes seem to be, in fact, different aspects of the same thing, dual

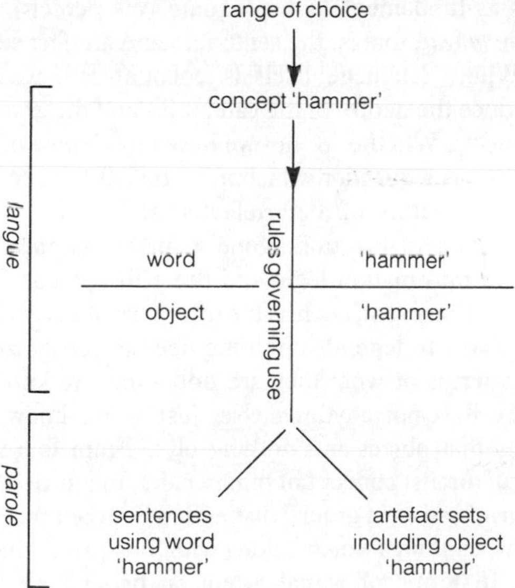

Figure 5.2 Diagram adding 'concept' to the scheme in fig. 5.1

expressions of the same human ability to organize, as has already been suggested (fig. 5.2), and it might be difficult to establish any priority between the material and the verbal forms of the concept. The sets of artefacts are those perceived as sets by the social communities concerned, that is, they are groups which 'make sense' because a person can perform with them something which society wants done. So, for example, fig. 5.3 lists the sets of nineteenth-century tools proper to a blacksmith or a farm worker. The verbal or textual equivalent of these artefact sentences would be 'The blacksmith uses his hammer, anvil, punches and tongs to make wrought iron goods', or 'The farmer takes his sickle into the harvest field.'

hammer	sickle
anvil	fork
punch	spade
tongs	

Figure 5.3 Sets of tools proper to a blacksmith or a farm worker

It is clear that the grammatical rules or categories and the words and objects which are organized by them are social constructs and as such they represent social 'decisions', for want of a better word: that is, they come from the mysterious process which produces from the range of choice for each society that society's given *langue*, where they form part of its whole vocabulary which can emerge as texts or sentences, or as artefact sets, in specific times and places, giving us the actual hammer in the blacksmith's hand. This process is influenced by functional constraints, but a purely deterministic explanation always emerges as fundamentally inadequate. We perceive only the partial expression of the *langue*, that is, the sentences and artefact sets which appear daily in use. Where language itself is encountered, we can, from this information, deduce the nature of the categories and the grammar, which the spoken word reflects. Whether or not we have any chance of doing the same for material culture is a question which must be left for a moment, while we consider further the nature of the artefact sets.

This line of argument has undergone a further important development which arises from information logic and the effort to codify what happens when a communication event, such as the utterance of a sentence or the use of artefacts, takes place. It depends upon the need to recognize that we define things mainly in terms of what they are not – that we know an object is a hammer because it is not anything else, just as we know that the sound 'hammer' means that object and nothing else. From this we arrive at the fundamental structuralist concept of binary pairs, things defined as 'this : not this'. This, in turn, leads to a crucial distinction between the difference in the relationship between things which belong with 'this', and things which belong with 'not this'. In terms of actual artefacts, fig. 5.3 sets out the list of blacksmith's tools beside that of farming equipment. Each set clearly has an internal intrinsic relationship in that the objects seem to belong together, while each set is in opposition to the other; as they stand they are equivalents, and any confusion of tools between them would seem puzzling and confusing. Many terms for these relationships are in use, but I will use those used by Leach (1976) and describe the relationship within each set as intrinsic or metonymic and the relationship between the sets as distinct or metaphorical.

These terms of relationship are capable of describing rather subtler communication events of the kind that we think of as 'symbolic' in the loosest sense. The blacksmith's hammer alone can be used to represent his trade, as it does when it figures on the sign board of The Blacksmith's Arms, or when it is paired with the sickle on the Russian flag, to represent the industrial worker and the farm worker. Here one element is picked out to stand for the whole, the relationship between it and its set is still metonymic, and it may be said to be acting as a sign. On the other hand, a harvest scene may be used to advertise a bottle of shampoo or the hammer image may be used to decorate the label of a bottle of beer; in this case the objects are being used as symbols and their relationship is metaphoric because there is no intrinsic prior relationship: hammers and beer come from different contexts and the brewer is simply trying to palm off on to us the notion that this beer will give us the strength of a blacksmith (and no doubt also some of his traditional virility) (fig. 5.4). The creation of all social categories ultimately rests upon the metonymic/metaphorical axes in every area of social activity, including kinship systems, land use or material culture, and the sign and symbol potential of categories,

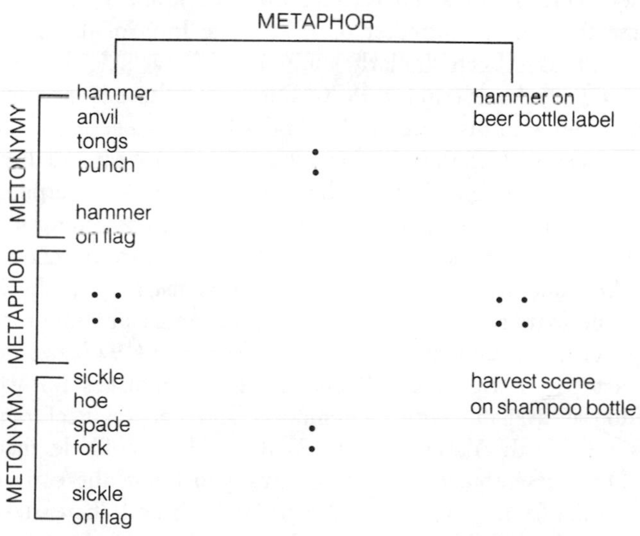

Figure 5.4 Diagram showing metaphorical and metonymic relationships

the way in which verbal language works, is the source of literary, artistic and religious creation.

The fundamental importance of all this, so the structuralists insist, is twofold. Firstly, the grid-system thinking which produces the metonymic/metaphoric ordering of the social world belongs within the *langue*, is indeed in the most basic sense the way in which our minds work. Secondly, although this working has a kind of logic of its own, it is not scientific reasoning of the sort which has been painfully developed in the Western tradition. There is no logical connection between the sickles and corn and the shampoo, just as there is no logical connection between real fertility and rites like those enacted every May Day by the dancing horses at Padstow in Cornwall, or a really happy marriage and the silver horse-shoes on a wedding cake, but we apparently instinctively behave as if there were, and this is one reason why the objects which give them expression, especially religious or 'high art' objects, can arouse some of our deepest feelings. We feel that what these objects are saying is true, although both rational thought and accumulated empirical experience indicate that it is not, and, I suppose, only the psychologists would claim to understand why this is so.

This discussion of operations within the *langue* brings us back to the main matter of this paper, the suggestion that material culture operates at this level and issues in *parole* in a way which exactly parallels other social systems like myth or kinship. This is best approached through the specific example of the Inuit of the central and western Arctic (fig. 5.5). The central Inuit, especially those of Igloolik, have been recorded by some of the greatest names in Arctic exploration and anthropology, William Parry (1824), George Lyon (1824), Franz Boas (1964) and Knud Rasmussen (1929), and I was able to spend some time there in the summer of 1975. The Inuit of the north-western Alaskan coast have been similarly studied and I was able to spend time at Barrow and Kotzebue Sound in 1976. The Inuit culture is (or was) relatively simple in material terms. Life on the tundra involves a series of artefact sets and the processes which they can carry out, which are clear and distinct to the Inuit themselves: these include caribou hunting gear, seal harpooning gear, bird hunting gear, skin-stitching implements and equipment for dealing with snow. These categories, and the artefacts themselves, are common to Inuit of the post-AD 1000 Thule tradition across an immense range of the Arctic, just as the people share a common speech, Inupik, and a common broad culture.

In a paper of fundamental significance, McGhee (1977) has taken these artefact sets from five of the larger Thule assemblages for which such information is available, over a temporal and geographical range which includes the North Alaskan coastal Walakpa Birnik/Thule material, the middle Thule assemblages from Lady Franklin Point, the early-to-middle Thule material from Nunguvik on North Baffin Island, the early-to-middle Thule material from Silumiut on the West coast of Hudson Bay, and the Cumberland Sound collections of later Thule material. McGhee has analysed

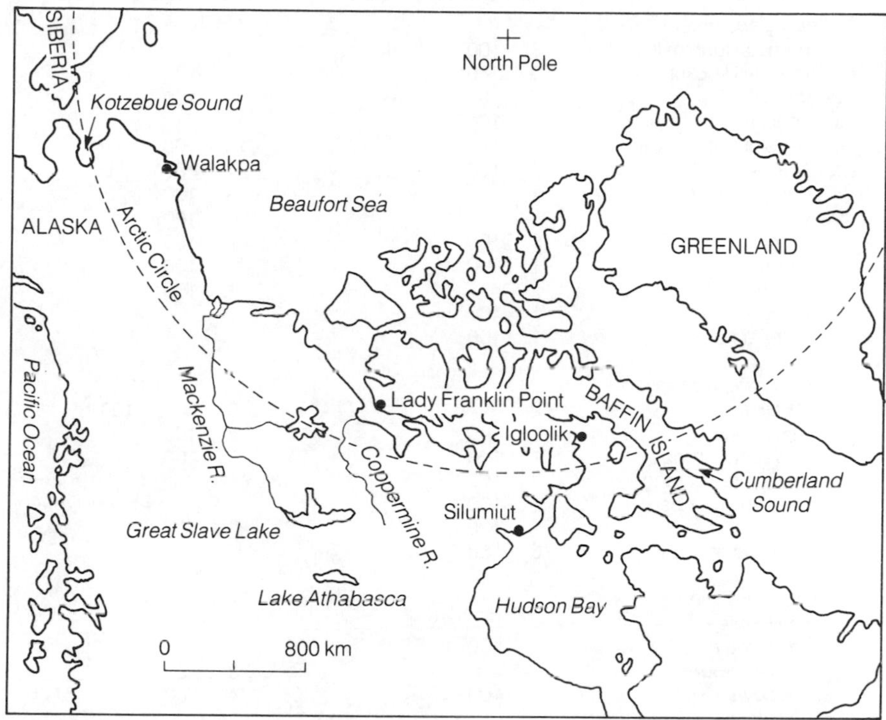

Figure 5.5 The central and western Arctic, showing places mentioned in the text

the artefacts according to the raw materials from which they are made, that is for each type of implement he has plotted the percentages of those which are made of walrus ivory/sea mammal tooth, sea mammal bone, and antler. From this a definite co-relation emerges: caribou hunting weapons are normally tipped with caribou antler, seal harpooning gear, sewing gear and snow equipment is normally made of ivory or sea bone, and bird hunting gear, too, belongs with the ivory/sea bone group.

The same picture emerges in a similar analysis of three British museum collections with reasonably tight provenances, that from Kotzebue Sound and the nearby coast of north-western Alaska collected by Lieutenant Belcher of HMS *Blossom* in 1823–5 in the Pitt Rivers Museum (Bockstoce 1977), that collected by Lieutenant Peard on the same voyage in Exeter City Museum (Pearce 1976) (fig. 5.6), and that associated with Sir John Franklin, John Richardson and John Rae, probably collected from the Coppermine and Mackenzie Delta Inuit during the course of the expeditions of 1825–7 and 1849 (Vernon 1986) in Lincoln City and County Museum (fig. 5.7). It must be

	Pitt Rivers				Exeter			
Artefact class	No.	I	B	A	No.	I	B	A
Sealing equipment								
harpoon foreshaft	3	100			3		100	
foreshaft socket	3	66	33					
ice pick	3	100			3	100		
finger rest	1	100						
line stopper	1	100			13	100		
float pieces	1	100			1	100		
harpoon head	1	100			5	100		
wound pin					6	100		
drag handles	5	100			7	100		
line toggle	1	100			1	100		
harpoon rest					1	100		
baler	1	100						
blubber hook	1	100						
Bird hunting weapons								
dart head	2		100		8		100	
dart socket	2	100			3	100		
bird spear prongs	1	100			3	100		
spear thrower tang	3	100						
spear thrower peg	1	100						
arrow head	1	100						
bolas weight sets	6	50	50					
Winter equipment								
snow knife					3	100		
snow beater	1	100						
harness hook					3	100		
drill bows	8	100			4	100		
Women's equipment								
needle case	1	100			2	100		
needles					3	100		
bag handle	1	100						
sole creaser	2	100						
awl	1		100					
thimble holder	1	100						
pendants	10	100			1	100		
scrapers	3	100			1		100	
bead					2	100		
Fishing equipment								
net gauge	1	100						
netting shuttles	1	100						
sinkers	11	100						
Caribou arrows								
arrow head	8	25		75	10			100

Figure 5.6 Analysis of Inuit material collected by officers of HMS *Blossom*

No. number in collection
I % made from walrus ivory or sea mammal tooth
B % made from sea mammal bone
A % made from caribou antler

Sealing equipment		*Fishing equipment*	
harpoon head	Iv Fe	fish hook	T Cu
harpoon head	Iv Fe	fish hook	B Fe
wound plug	Iv		
wound plug	Iv	*Caribou arrows*	
skewer	Iv	arrow	A W Cu
		arrow blade	Cu
Winter equipment		arrow blade	Cu
ice chisel	Cu	arrow blade	Cu
crampon	Iv	blade	Cu
toggle	Iv	lance	Cu B
handle	Iv	arrow head	A
		arrow head	B Cu
Women's equipment		2 sinew twisters	?A/B
thimble holder	Iv	sinew twister	?A
bodkin	B		
needle case	Iv		
pin	B/Iv?		
comb	B		
comb	B		
comb	B		
spoon	Iv		
spoon	Iv		
spoon	Iv		

Figure 5.7 Analysis of Inuit material in Lincoln Museum

A caribou antler
W wood
Cu copper
B sea mammal bone
Iv walrus ivory
Fe iron
T polar bear tooth

(after Vernon, to whom I am grateful for permission to use this unpublished material).

stressed that this is not a simple functional distinction. There is no practical reason why harpoon heads or snow knives should not be made of antler – in fact antler is much more generally available than ivory to many Inuit communities, and it is considerably easier to work, and although arrow heads must be light, small barbs of sea mammal bone would be equally effective.

This material analysis, therefore, gives us a structure for Inuit material culture which looks like that set out in fig. 5.8 where a pair of metaphorically opposed groups emerges, having internally a metonymic relationship, and where the choice of raw material operates as the organizing factor. An analysis of other systems within the broad sweep of Inuit culture suggests similar

antler	:	ivory
men's caribou hunting weapons	:	women's stitching gear
	:	men's sea mammal hunting gear
	:	winter equipment
	:	bird hunting gear

Figure 5.8 Analysis of Inuit material culture

organizing principles at work in other areas of life. In terms of food, seal meat and venison sometimes may not be eaten at the same meal, or even placed on a house floor together, with all that this involves in terms of preparation and planning and so in the *parole* of life. In terms of land use and hunting, caribou is hunted on the land in summer, from temporary camp sites, while the sea mammals are hunted on the sea and from the ice in winter, from permanent homes; caribou skins and antler gear may be smoked over a seaweed fire at the beginning of winter; seal oil may be carried into the house by one entrance and caribou meat and skins by another; and caribou skins may not be worked during the summer but only in the period between the first formation of the ice and the killing of the first sea mammals (Boas 1964: 170, 187).

The social distinction between the sexes is represented by the allotment of hunting to men and skin-stitching to women. Women are clearly identified with the sea mammals, as for example at Igloolik where they must loosen their clothing when whale is hunted because this helps the harpooning, and no work is done for three days, the normal period of mourning, after a big sea mammal has been killed. In terms of the distinction between the living and the dead, dead human bodies are treated as if they were caribou, taken to land, wrapped in caribou skin and covered with stones, just as venison is cached, and given offerings of caribou meat and fat when hunters pass the grave. Dead souls are believed to spend some time in the under-sea world of Sedna, the Sea-Woman, and then to migrate, perhaps to an upper world, rather vaguely conceived as being in the sky. Living people, on the other hand, are identified as birds. The first dress which a new-born baby receives is sometimes made from bird skin with the feathers still attached, and this dress is retained as an amulet through life and worn on the end of the hood as part of the great festival which marks the formation of the sea ice and the beginning of winter. In Cumberland Sound the community is divided into ducks (those born in the summer) and ptarmigans (those born in the winter), and the same festival features a tug of war between the men of the two groups, while bird-woman figures are sometimes made of ivory (Rasmussen 1929: 187–8; Boas 1964: 180–1, 196–7,

antler	:	ivory
caribou	:	sea mammals
men	:	women
hunting	:	stitching
land	:	sea
summer	:	winter
bodies (caribou)	:	spirits (birds)

Figure 5.9 Paired sets of categories in Inuit life

202–7). This pairing is, of course, reflected in myth and in the ritual actions of the shaman. In the story of Sedna and her father, the sea mammals are said to come from Sedna's fingers severed while she is in the sea, and this mutilation is played out by a shaman to make the game come, while, by implication at least, the caribou come from her father's feet, severed while he is on land (the cosmological aspects are further discussed in Pearce, forthcoming).

Examples could be multiplied but enough has been said to suggest that Inuit life may be organized around a paired set of categories, each set containing an element from all the main areas of life (fig. 5.9). We might say, putting all this together, that, for example, an Inuit, seeing a sealing harpoon of sea mammal ivory, sea mammal skin and wood, recognizes that here are animals being killed with their own substance, which is tantamount to saying 'with their own permission', while an arrow, tipped with antler and flighted with feathers, flies like a bird to kill both birds and caribou.

It becomes clear that a full analysis of central Inuit life according to classic structuralist principles would give us a plot like that offered in fig. 5.10, where the principle of metonymy/metaphor operates across the frame, and where the elements in fig. 5.9 are distributed across the axes of This World : The Other World, Summer : Winter, and Life : Death as we would expect (further discussed in Pearce, forthcoming). According to this line of thought, such a plot sets out the structure, the *langue* of Inuit life, from which derives the *parole*, the events of day to day as they unfold; and for the present purpose the important point is that the characteristic Inuit raw materials – ivory, antler, wood and feathers – and the material artefacts made from them – such as arrows or harpoons – are as integral and as consistent a part of the structure as are the categories from any other of the culture's systems. Material culture, that is to say, is not merely the practical reflection of cultural decisions which have been taken elsewhere, but a system in its own right comparable to those of land use, kinship or myth.

The intellectual basis of structuralist analysis has been canvassed many times, and often not very helpfully; Wylie's (1982) useful paper makes the

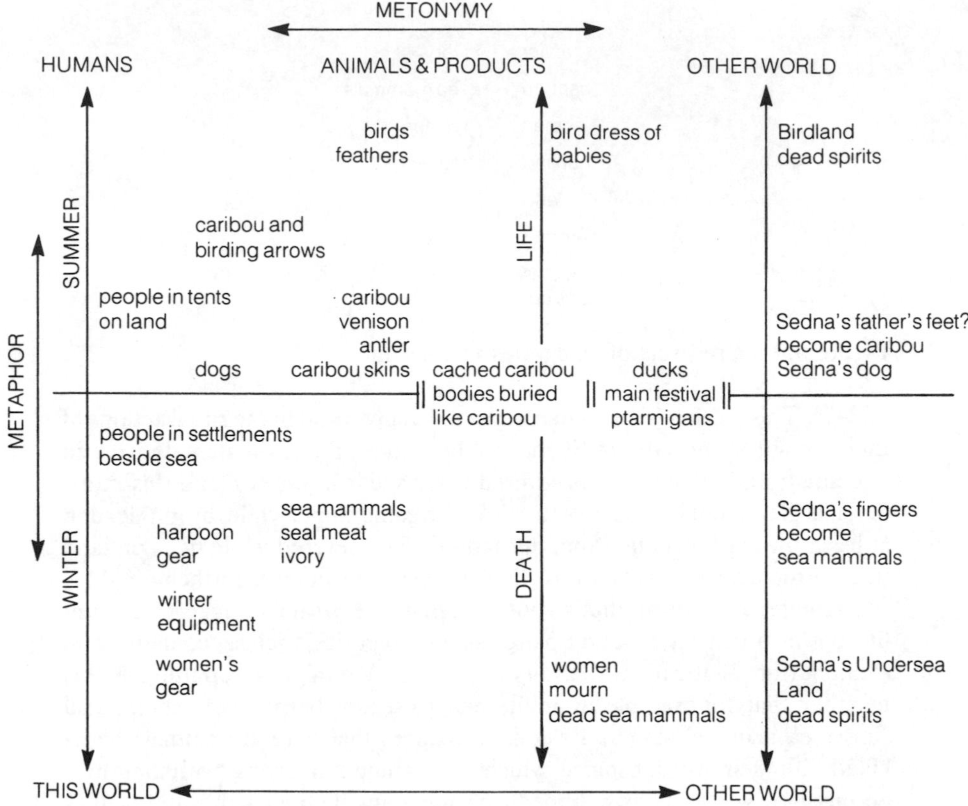

Figure 5.10 Structuralist analysis of Inuit life

fundamental point that in the final reckoning all we have to depend upon in any area of investigation are subjective hypotheses which seem for the time being to embrace, explain and illuminate what appear to be the facts, and no social analyst is likely to claim more than this. Fresh approaches to structuralism, like Giddens's (1979) concept of 'Structuration', which suggests that the actions of individuals in their ordinary lives produce and reproduce characteristic structural features so that the sum of these actions continually re-creates the social organization concerned, offer new lines of thought. These are large issues which need to be dealt with at corresponding length, and suffice it to say here that although a structuralist approach undoubtedly poses problems, it may also offer valuable perspectives, particularly if it is linked with a functionalist understanding of social organization. One of the most important of these for museum curators is the way in which structuralist analysis can show that a society's artefact system has the same standing and significance as its literature or religion. It is worth noting that the artefacts used in this particular analysis all come from museum collections, and in several cases the material concerned has been in collections of one kind or another for well over a century. This suggests that interesting and valuable analyses could be performed upon many stored collections, and clearly the potential here is very considerable.

One final thought. This paper has been devoted to discussing linguistic analysis, developed to account for our spoken and recorded word, for our languages and texts, as a framework for artefact analysis. I have treated artefacts as if they were texts, and I am reassured when I remember that the word 'text' really means 'a piece of woven cloth'.

BIBLIOGRAPHY

Boas, F., 1964. *The Central Eskimo.*

Bockstoce, J. R., 1977. *Eskimos of North West Alaska in the Early Nineteenth Century*. Pitt Rivers Museum, Oxford.

Giddens, A., 1979. *Studies in Social and Political Theory.*

Glassie, H., 1975. *Middle Virginian Folk Housing.*

Hodder, I., 1982 (ed.), *Symbolic and Structural Archaeology.*

Hoffman, H., 1977. *Sexual and Asexual Pursuit, A Structuralist Approach to Greek Vase Painting* Royal Anthropological Institute Occasional Paper No. 34.

Kleivan, I., 1962. The Swan Maiden Myth among the Eskimo. *Acta Arctica, 13*: 5–47.

Leach, E., 1976. *Culture and Communication.*

Lyon, G. F., 1824. *The Private Journal of Capt. G. F. Lyon of HMS Hecla.*

McGhee, R., 1977. 'Ivory for the Sea Woman: the symbolic attributes of a prehistoric technology', *Canadian Journal of Archaeology, 1*: 141–9.

Parry, W., 1824. *Journal of a Second Journey for the Discovery of a North-West Passage from the Atlantic to the Pacific.*

Pearce, S. M., 1976. *Towards the Pole: A Catalogue of the Eskimo Collections.* Exeter Museums Publications No. 82.

Pearce, S., forthcoming. 'Ivory, antler, feather and wood: material culture and the cosmology of the Cumberland Sound Inuit, Baffin Island, Canada', *Cosmos, 4.*

Rasmussen, K., 1929. *The Intellectual Culture of the Iglulik Eskimo: Report of the Fifth Thule Expedition 1921–4.*

Saussure, F. de, 1973. *Course in General Linguistics*, trans. Baskin Wade.

Vernon, J., 1986. *Explorers' Souvenirs: An Early Ethnographic Collection.* Unpublished typescript.

Wylie, M. A., 1982. 'Epistemological issues raised by a structuralist archaeology', in Hodder 1982: 39–46.

6 *The Museum in the Disciplinary Society*

EILEAN HOOPER-GREENHILL

This paper examines some aspects of the concept of the 'disciplinary society' as developed by Michael Foucault, and asks: what is the place and function of the museum in the disciplinary society? This is contrasted with earlier forms of 'museums'.

In *Discipline and Punish* Foucault describes the emergence of the disciplinary technologies of power during his Classical age (the seventeenth and eighteenth centuries). The disciplines – methods that divided and controlled time, space and movement – which had long been in existence in the monasteries, the armies, and in workshops, during the seventeenth and eighteenth centuries became general formulas for domination and control (Foucault 1982:137). Discipline as a technique of power operates through hierarchical observation, normalizing judgment, and examination. The concept of hierarchical observation indicates the connection between visibility and power, and introduces the idea of an apparatus designed for observation, which induces the effects of power deployed through the visibility of those subject to it.

Disciplinary technologies depend on the distribution of individuals in space and in visibility. Historically, this required the emergence of the specification of a space heterogeneous to all others and closed in upon itself (Foucault 1982:141). Schools, hospitals, military barracks, as specialized spaces, confined and controlled the inhabitants, separating and differentiating them from the mass of the population. The principle of the enclosure of space extended to individual partitioning. Each individual should have his or her own place, and each space should have its individual. This cellular arrangement of individuals in space permitted constant surveillance.

The space of the hospital – and Foucault's example is the military hospital at the port of Rochefort – acts as a filter, a mechanism that pins down and partitions the swarming mass of sailors, epidemics and goods. The medical supervision of diseases and contagions is inseperable from a whole series of other controls: military control over deserters, fiscal control over commodities, and administrative control over remedies, rations, cures and deaths. The first steps that were taken concerned things rather than people. Fiscal and economic supervision preceded medical observation. Medical technologies were put into operation later: medicines were put under lock and key, and their use recorded; a system was worked out to verify the real number of patients, their identity and the units to which they belonged; their comings and goings were regulated; they were forced to remain in their wards; to each bed was attached the name of its occupant; each individual treated was entered in a register that the doctor had to consult on his visit; later came the isolation of contagious patients and separate beds. Gradually, an administrative and political space was articulated upon a therapeutic space which individualized bodies, diseases, symptoms, lives and deaths. The space constituted a real epistemological table of juxtaposed and carefully distinct singularities. Out of discipline, a medically useful space was born (Foucault 1982: 144).

The principle of individualizing partition operated in other spaces. In the school, and the army, for example, bodies were visibly separated into ages, abilities, skills, and levels of achievement. Through separation and observation, differences became visible and thereby classifiable. The differences were judged and evaluated, entailing the production of a norm through the exercise of rewards and penalties. Normalizing judgment combined with hierarchical observation enabled the use of spaces to expose differences and to display identities.

Through the organization of 'cells', 'places' and 'ranks', the disciplines create complex spaces that are at once architectural, functional and hierarchical. Spaces fix positions and permit circulations; they mark places and assign values. They individuate things and persons in a vast table of discrimination and distinction. The division of spaces and bodies entailed the establishment of records: day-books, ledgers, inventories, filing cabinets, archives, were all required to document the spatial distribution of bodies and things. Thus in the eighteenth century the classificatory table became both a technique of power and a procedure of knowledge (Foucault 1982: 281).

Individualizing and normalizing space at the level of bodies and institutional spaces found its corollary in the division, observation and supervision of geographical space. In *The Birth of the Clinic* (Foucault 1976) Foucault describes the emergence of the French medical profession as part of the conjuncture of events during the revolutionary period. Many elements, political, military, economic and ideological, articulated to create the conditions of emergence for new medical practices. A medical network was established, a medical gaze that surveyed the entire country through the building of hospitals and the geographical deployment of staff. The new medical discourse was supported by the political ideology of the Revolution with its conception of the free citizen of the Republic as clean, pure and healthy. The theme of 'medicine in liberty' was structured in a precise historical context that enabled the definition of its institutional and scientific structures (Foucault 1976: 69). Within the space of 50 years, at the turn of the eighteenth century, a new medical discourse was established where medical space coincided with social space: 'One began to conceive of a generalised presence of doctors whose intersecting gazes form a network and exercise at every point in space, and at every moment in time, a constant, mobile, differentiated supervision' (Foucault 1976: 31).

The disciplinary society operates through technologies that survey, classify and control time, space, bodies and things. As the subject is surveyed, classified, and exposed to examination, s/he becomes her/his own self-regulator. It becomes unnecessary 'to use force to constrain the convict to good behaviour, the madman to calm, the schoolboy to application, the patient to the observation of the regulations. He who is subjected to a field of visibility, and who knows it, assumes responsibility for the constraints of power; he makes them play spontaneously upon himself; he inscribes in himself the power relation in which he simultaneously plays both roles: he becomes the principle of his own subjection' (Foucault 1982: 209). Thus human subjects, enmeshed in impersonal power relations which separate, survey and judge, become their own overseers in the ongoing process of normalization.

What is the role of the museum in the disciplinary society? How does the emergence of the museum relate to the emergence of other disciplinary technologies?

The French Revolution provided the conditions of emergence for a new programme for museums. For Foucault, a 'programme' is a set of calculated, reasoned prescriptions in terms of which institutions are meant to be reorganized, spaces arranged, behaviours regulated (Foucault 1981: 3–14). The programme grounds and enables the rationality on which 'regimes of truth' are contingently constructed (Foucault 1977: 14). The ruptures of revolution created the conditions of emergence for a new 'truth', a new rationality, out of which came a new functionality for a new institution, the public museum. The old collecting practices of the king, the aristocracy and the Church were radically revised, taken over and re-articulated in a new field of use. The collections themselves were torn out of their earlier spaces and groupings and were rearranged in other contexts as statements that proclaimed at once the tyranny of the old and the democracy of the new.

In France the museum as a public, democratic, state institution was born from the articulation of three elements: republicanism, anti-clericalism and successful aggressive war (Gould 1965: 13). The concurrent forces of these three elements, none of them new in themselves, produced an apparatus with two deeply contradictory functions: that of the elite temple of the arts, and that of a utilitarian instrument for democratic education (Nochlin 1972: 8). This new, fundamentally fragmented institution entailed the development of technologies based on existing military administrative practices. The institution that emerged was to prove decisive in the restructuring of collecting practices across Europe during the course of the nineteenth century.

During the sixteenth century the practices of collecting were limited to wealthy and powerful individuals, acting in their own interests, in order to further their own personal ambitions. There are many different articulations of the elements that make up the discursive field (Laclau and Mouffe 1985:105), but a preliminary distinction can be made between princely collections and scholarly collections. The aims of the princely collections were to recreate the world in miniature around the central figure of the prince who thus claimed dominion over the world symbolically as he in did in reality (Olmi 1985: 5; Berger 1972: 86). The wealth and knowledge of the prince represented by the private and therefore largely unseen collections justified his position as sovereign, as did other more public spectacles (Strong 1973). In addition the *Wunderkammern* played a well-defined diplomatic function in the body politic (Kaufmann 1978). Sixteenth-century scholarly collections performed similar functions, although from a different perspective. Control over the world was similarly an important element, but was understood differently by non-princely subjects. Ulisse Aldrovandi aimed through his collection of dried plants and animals to bring all of nature indoors, thereby claiming control through representation over the natural world. The accumulation of material confirmed his position as a leading medical authority (Olmi 1985: 6,8). The collections were used to establish a medical discourse through teaching, research and correspondence with other collectors and other physicians.

Collecting practices were informed by and through the Rennaissance *episteme*. Foucault describes its basic characteristics as resemblance and interpretation (Foucault 1970:2). The relationships between words and things were understood through the relations of similitude: *convenientia*, *aemulatio*, analogy and the play of sympathies. The surface appearances of things were endlessly read to discover the significance of signatures, which were then used to explain their meanings and connections (Foucault 1970: 25–30; Thorndike 1941: 294). Interpretation went hand in hand with erudition. Contemporary collections would have been assembled and understood by minds informed by a mixture of adherence to the texts of the ancients, a new more scientific interest in direct observation, and a belief in superstition and the occult (Foucault 1970: 32). The items collected were assembled in domestic spaces recoded as expository spaces. These spaces, whether palace, castle or house, were privately owned, with access being limited by invitation.

Both the accumulation of the corporeal and the method of exposition seems likely to have been organized to demonstrate the ancient hierarchies of the world and the resemblances that drew the things of the world together. The relations of *aemulatio* may be represented in the installation at Giganti's museum of repeating starfish and portraits (Laurencich-Minelli 1985: 19).

The human face emulates the sky, and the fish in the sea have their own particular stars that imbue them with particular virtues (Foucault 1970: 20). The relations of *convenientia* confuse place and similitude so that plants grow in the antlers of stags, and mosses on the outside of shells (Foucault 1970: 18). An antler enveloped within a growing tree appears in an account of the collection at Schloss Ambras at the end of the sixteenth century (Scheicher 1985: 32). Was this originally there as a sign of 'convenience'? It is still there today (Impey and MacGregor 1985: fig 12), although the original meanings of such an object were lost long ago.

The 'regime of truth' that apparatuses like the *Wunderkammern* produced was premised on hidden, complex, often secret relationships between words and things in an *episteme* that was fundamentally interpretative. The elaborate metaphysical cosmologies of the occult philosophers, organized as 'memory theatres', according to the art of memory (Kaufmann 1978; Bostrom 1985; Olmi 1985) provided a flexible and commodious programme both for collection and for exposition. It is highly likely that an investigation of these *Wunderkammern* which takes account of the epistemological character of Foucault's Renaissance *episteme* and the organizational structure of the mnemotechnical arts (Yates 1966; Godwin 1979) would begin to explain the 'truth' of these 'cabinets of curiosity', which until now have been described in the main as irrational, disordered (Taylor 1948: 122), miscellaneous and haphazard (Alexander 1979: 9).

Collecting practices up to the time of the French Revolution, and the consequent emergence of a new museological programme, were based on these Renaissance practices, although the rationality that had informed the relationship of the various diverse material elements was no longer valid. As the Renaissance *episteme* weakened, the resemblances between things were forgotten or deliberately cut away, in a new attempt to discover a more 'scientific' approach to the classification of things. The old rationality had lost its credibility and was seen as confused and disordered (Foucault 1970: 120). The classificatory table emerged as the basic structure of knowledge (Foucault 1970: 74), with the new rationality grounding itself in the identification of the differences between things, based on measurement and order. Classified and tabulated series were drawn up. Things were no longer placed in unifying categories, explained in erudite or magical ways, but began to be drawn apart from each other, placed in differentiating categories.

In relation to the compilation and ordering of collections, however, the shift to the new *episteme* was not fully achieved. The social gain achieved by the possession of the rare, the unusual, and the expensive proved a more powerful element than the cognitive reform of knowledge. The features of Renaissance collections were retained and reinscribed in new institutions, although the text of the articulation of the different elements was rewritten for a new time. The museum of the Royal Society is a specific example.

When first established in 1660, the aim of the 'Repository' of the Royal

Society was to assemble a complete representation of nature: 'the compiling of a complete system of solid philosophy for explicating all phenomena produced by nature or art, and recording a rational account of the causes of things' (Ornstein 1938: 109). The Society intended to draw up new table of knowledge, realizing that in drawing up a differentiated and identified table of specimens, they would also create a new language of description (Hunter 1985: 164). The material collections would have the revolutionary effect of defining both the units of knowledge and the units of language. This is exactly as Foucault describes the project of the Classical *episteme*; 'The fundamental task of the Classical discourse is to ascribe a name to things, and in that name to name their being' (Foucault 1970: 120). The project of the systematic collection of a complete natural series meant that common and ordinary rather than unusual things were to be assembled. In addition, things were to be seen as a series rather than as unique single items. The ordering of these things was to be related to the universal language that was the project of many of the Fellows of the Society (Hunter 1981: 118–9). These were quite new elements. But in the event elements from older collecting practices acted to subvert these new aims (Foucault 1972: 53/4).

The structures and technologies that would have provided the possibility of the emergence of a new way of knowing in the museum were lacking. The 'Repository' was institutionally weak, founded in conjunction with a voluntary society, with insecure funding, and lacking an efficient organizational structure (Hunter 1985: 166). The 'curator' of the 'Repository' combined this with his other roles within the Society (Ornstein 1938: 110). The Fellows of the Royal Society were drawn mainly from a small social group who largely subscribed to the values of the *virtuoso* (Houghton 1942), which did not encourage serious study but emphasized the 'delight' of the 'curious'. Collecting was a pleasant and easy way for these newly wealthy and leisured groups to pass their time (Houghton 1942: 60). Members of the Society gave gifts that could not be refused containing rare material that had social cachet but nothing to do with the supposed aims of the society (Hunter 1985: 165). Nehemiah Grew, employed to draw up the catalogue of tabulated knowledge, exclaimed in exasperation that it was impossible to draw up a perfect table as the collections themselves were not perfect (Hunter 1985: 166).

Renaissance collections had contained things which appear to us today as curious if insubstantial. A tree with antlers absorbed into its trunk is merely odd, and does not to us represent an aspect of the similitude of *convenientia*. In the seventeenth century it is likely that the curiousness of such objects was perceived where the Renaissance interpretation was forgotten. However, the high social position of collectors during the Renaissance encouraged emulation. A fashion for the curious was fed by the artefacts and specimens brought back from newly discovered parts of the world (Taylor 1948: 95). A collection of 'rarities' demonstrated a social sophistication (Houghton 1942), but also represented in material form, a new wealth. In bourgeois Holland the newly fashionable still-life paintings represented the desirability of material possessions for the emerging middle class (Berger 1972: 99); their cabinets displayed these possessions (MacGregor 1983: 79).

The desire for 'rarities' was often satisfied, for those who could afford it, by a purchase at one of the souvenir shops set up in the European trading centres. In Paris, for example, John Evelyn visited a shop that was called 'Noah's Ark', 'where are to be had for money all Curiosities naturall or artificial imaginable, Indian or European, for luxory or for Use, as Cabines, Shells, Ivories, Purselan, Dried fishes, rare insects, Birds, Pictures, and a thousand exotic extravagances' (MacGregor 1983: 91). The things that during the Renaissance demonstrated the ingenuity of God the creator of the world demonstrate purchasing power a hundred years later. The accumulation of wealth in the form of material things – and cabinets and collections clearly formed a part of this activity indicated the beginnings of the establishment in Europe of the resources on which the Industrial Revolution would be built (Berger 1972: 95). At this time, therefore, for many complex reasons connected with the accumulation of capital, new trade routes, and new market structures, the old script of the Renaissance collection was rewritten, remaining efficacious in a new form.

In France, however, the Revolution led to the conditions of emergence of a radically new museological programme which re-articulated collecting practices and subject positions and led to the emergence of the public museum as one of the apparatuses of the disciplinary society. In the place of intensely personal private collections housed in the palaces of princes and the homes of the scholars, public collections in spaces open to all were established. The subject in the Renaissance had accumulated collections according to their individual choice (Foucault 1986: 26) in their own private, domestic spaces. Now the gaze that had surveyed an extended geographical space initially for military purposes surveyed that same space for cultural purposes. Works of art were deployed in the same way as other strategic commodities. Modelled on the military deployment of resources, museums were established across Europe. An intersecting curatorial gaze was established that paralleled the contemporary medical gaze; a curatorial gaze that formed a network which exercised a constant, mobile, differentiated supervision. New technologies emerged to enable this large-scale spatialization. In the resulting play of dominations, collections were gathered together, filtered, redispersed, and reorganized on to the classificatory table. In the name of the newly formed Republic, the spaces and things belonging to the king, the aristocracy and the Church were appropriated and transformed, at first in France and later across Europe.

The Revolution in France marked the end of the society of the hierarchic and inegalitarian type, and at the same time of the old way of imagining the social, as a fixed order ruled by a theological-political logic (Laclau and Mouffe 1985: 155). The French Revolution was founded on the legitimacy of the people, which was something entirely new at the level of the social imaginary. An abrupt discontinuity can be identified, the invention of democratic culture. The 'museum' was created as one of the instruments that exposed both the decadence and tyranny of the old forms of control, the *ancien régime*, and the democracy and public utility of the new, the Republic.

A new discourse which legitimated and effected the articulations of the new discursive field emerged. The decision to levy war indemnities in the form of works of art was justified by the Minister of Justice in a letter to Napoleon: 'The reclamation of works of genius and their safe-keeping in the land of Freedom would accelerate the development of Reason and human happiness' (Wittlin 1949: 233). Other official statements similarly celebrated the actions of the Republic and demonstrated a new justification for museums. 'By means of courage the Republic has succeeded in obtaining what Louis XIV was unable to obtain for enormous sums of money. Vandyke and Rubens are on their way to Paris and the Flemish School *en masse* will adorn our museums . . . France will possess inexhaustible means of enlarging human knowledge and of contributing to the perfection of civilization' (quoted in Wittlin 1949: 233). The pure courage of the Republic is celebrated as both more moral and more useful than the power of the inherited wealth of the overturned sovereign. Museums are seen as apparatuses for public rather than private consumption. The education of the population through museums will contribute to the collective good of the state rather than to individual knowledge. The museum will be used to support the Republic by offering an opportunity to all citizens to share in what would previously have become the private possessions of the king. The museum is a crucial point in this articulation. It enables the triumph of 'liberty over tyranny' and 'philosophy over superstition' (Quynn 1945: 243).

The officer in charge of the convoy of Italian works of art wrote announcing their impending arrival in Paris: 'Citizens of all classes of the population ought to be aware that the Government has given them consideration and that all will have their share of the great booty. People will be able to judge what a Republican Government means if compared with the rule of a monarch who makes conquests merely for the pleasure of his courtiers and the satisfaction of his personal vanity' (Wittlin 1949: 233). The public museum was established as a means of sharing what had been private and exposing what had been concealed.

In the appropriations works confiscated from the whole of France were assembled in a few key warehouses, which were in fact often the newly vacated, newly secularized spaces of the convents (Bazin 1967: 170). The seriated spaces which had divided and controlled religious personnel were particularly useful for the task of collecting, storing and sorting works of art. These art depots acted as classifying and filtering points. New technologies were developed and new subject positions emerged. The confiscated works were assembled together, identified, catalogued, documented, repaired and assessed for their contagious potential. Works that had feudal, religious or royal connections were destroyed (Bazin 1967: 170). Special deputies were appointed for this work. Later the Commission on the Arts drew up instructions for the care and conservation of artefacts for the directors of art depots. Inventories identified the individual items, reports assessed their physical condition, and they were separated out into various groupings to enable their later dispersal to designated cultural centres. Cultural control was both enmeshed with and enabled by other forms of control: military control over confiscations and travel arrangements, and administrative and bureaucratic control over appointments of personnel. Through administrative and documentary procedures, the religious spaces were re-articulated as cultural spaces.

New technologies also emerged to facilitate the identification and removal of works from the conquered territories. It was recognized that in order to remove the works most efficiently, this should be done as soon as possible after the arrival of the shock troops. Any delay was likely to lead to difficulties (Gould 1965: 90). Artists, naturalists and other technical experts were appointed to accompany the invading forces, to carry out the task of removing material whose destination was the Louvre, the Jardins des Plantes, or the Bibliothèque Nationale (Gould 1965: 31,32,40).

In 1791 the Revolutionary Government made the decision to establish a museum in the old royal palace of the Louvre (Wittlin 1949: 119). Plans of this nature had been in existence for many years, and considerable efforts had been made during the *ancien régime* but to no conclusion (Bazin 1959: 40; Gould 1965: 22). The 'Museum Central des Arts' was opened in 1793, occupying the Grande Galerie. In appearance this was rather dark, a very long space with a continuous barrel vault, and with small windows along both walls (Gould 1965: 27). Paintings were placed between the windows, and along the centre were tables on which were arranged bronzes, busts, *objets d'art*, clocks and 'other curiosities' – 'precious spoils taken from our tyrants, or from other enemies of our country' (Bazin 1959: 47). The paintings were hung chronologically (Gould 1965: 27). At first, then, this museum was not a picture gallery as it would be understood today, but contained many of the items that had been removed from the older collections, and they were laid out as they might have been in the some of the sixteenth-century collections, with tables in the centre of the room containing mixed three-dimensional material, with paintings in multiple tiers on the walls between the windows. The museum, renamed the Musée Napoléon in 1803 (Gould 1965: 13), was soon to 'reform' its collections and methods of display.

The official historian of the Louvre describes the immense work of 'requisition, selection, distribution, installation, removals, reinstallation, classification, restoration, inventories, exhibitions, catalogues, for thousands upon thousands of works' (Bazin 1959: 52). A general archive was being created (Foucault 1986: 26). The organization of light and space played a crucial role in the re-articulation of the old palace as a new public democratic space, and the revelation to the gaze of that which had been hidden. The space was partitioned and illuminated. Plans for top lighting which had been designed during the *ancien régime* but had not been carried out were revived, and the immense perspective was divided into bays separated by great transverse arches supported on double columns (Bazin 1959: 51). New classifications were made. The work of living artists were separated out and displayed separately. Previously collections had contained both older pieces and the work of living artist/craftsmen. The tables and their contents were removed from the centre of the gallery, leaving the paintings on the walls. With the new top lighting, the windows were blocked up. At first the paintings were displayed mixed together, with the attractiveness of the painting being the only criteria of inclusion, on the grounds that: 'The museum ... is a flower-bed where we must assemble the most brilliant colours' (Gould 1965: 24). During the closing of the museum for repairs in 1796, the paintings were rehung by 'schools' of artists (Bazin 1967: 172).

This chronological method of arranging material was in marked contrast to earlier eighteenth-century display arrangements which grouped items by theme, material or size (Bazin 1967: 159). In the laying out of paintings by geographical and historical divisions into schools of artists, a 'picture-book' of art history is presented. The space constitutes a real table of juxtaposed and differentiated material objects. The viewer is able to see the panorama of history at a glance. Seeing was knowing. The subject has become the gazing subject, where the laying out of seriated ranks of things demonstrates a fundamental natural order.

Following the establishment of the Louvre as a museum in Paris, museums were established on a regional basis across France, and curators and lecturers were appointed (Bazin 1967: 180). Once museums had been set up in a regular geographical network in France, they were established in other parts of Europe. A new cultural space was articulated on the existing military space of the Empire. The museological map of Europe was superimposed onto the military map: thus Brussels, a military port, and hitherto not a centre for collections, was designated a museological centre and received 31 important paintings. Antwerp, however, seen as little more than a marginal city, a small military outpost on the outskirts of the Empire, lost many of its historic treasures (Bazin 1967: 183). Once the institutions were established with their full complement of objects, exchanges were proposed between museums, both nationally and internationally.

The overall plan for the redistribution of works to the museums was conceived on an international scale: the Louvre in Paris, capital of 130 departments of the Empire, would represent a faithful reflection of all European art, and each European city would do so on a smaller regional scale (Bazin 1967: 183). Thus a vast intersecting museological gaze was established that related collections in the regions of France and in the conquered domains to the central collections in Paris, the centre of the

Empire. Interconnections were established both in and out of the centre and across the regions.

The museum was the apparatus that articulated a new ensemble of oppositions within a new regime of truth. The oppositions included private/public, closed/open, tyranny/liberty, superstition/knowledge, inherited wealth/courage. The museum was a crucial instrument that enable the construction of a new set of values that at once discredited the *ancien régime* and celebrated the Republic. The collections, the confiscations from the tyrants and the trophies of war, accumulated together within one space, previously the property of the king and now available to all, materially demonstrated the historic shift in power.

New technologies for administering and curating the vast collections and the vast spaces had been developed. These technologies entailed the emergence of new subject positions. Subject positions within this new articulation are, for the first time, fundamentally split. Earlier, collecting and viewing were aspects of the same practice. Now, with the concept of the museum as an instrument for the democratic education of the 'masses', or the 'citizen', a division is created between knowing subjects, between producers and consumers of knowledge, expert and layman. In the public museum the producing subject is located in the hidden spaces of the museum, while the consuming subject is located in the public spaces. Power relations within the institution are skewed to privilege the 'work' of the museum, the production of knowledge through the compilation of catalogues, inventories and installations, (Hooper-Greenhill 1987; 1988). The seriated public spaces, surveyed and controlled, where knowledge is offered for passive consumption, are emblematic of the museum as one of the apparatuses that create 'docile bodies' in the disciplinary society.

Bibliography

Alexander, E. P., 1979. *Museums in Motion.*

Bazin, G., 1959. *The Louvre.*

Bazin, G., 1967. *The Museum Age.*

Berger, J., 1972. *Ways of Seeing.*

Bostrom, H. O., 1985. 'Phillipp Hainhofer and Gustavus Adolphus's *Kunstschrank* in Uppsala', in Impey and MacGregor 1985: 90–101.

Foucault, M., 1970. *The Order of Things.*

Foucault, M., 1972. *The Archaeology of Knowledge.*

Foucault, M., 1976. *The Birth of the Clinic.*

Foucault, M., 1977, 'The political function of the intellectual', *Radical Philosophy*, *17*: 12–14.

Foucault, M., 1981. 'Questions of method: an interview', *Ideology and Consciousness*, *8*: 3–14.

Foucault, M., 1982, *Discipline and Punish.*
Foucault, M., 1986. 'Of other spaces'. *Diacritics, 16.1*: 22–7.
Godwin, J., 1979. *Robert Fludd, Hermetic philosopher and surveyor of two worlds.*
Gould, C., 1965. *Trophy of Conquest.*
Hemmings, F. W. J., 1987. *Culture and Society in France 1789–1848.*
Hooper-Greenhill, E., 1987. 'Knowledge in an open prison', *New Statesman*, 13 February: 21–2.
Hooper-Greenhill, E., 1988. 'Counting visitors or visitors who count?' in Lumley, R. (ed.), *The Museum Time Machine*: 213–32.
Houghton, W. E., 1942. 'The English virtuoso in the seventeenth century', *Journal of the History of Ideas, 3*: 51–73.
Hunter, M., 1981. *Science and Society in Restoration England.*
Hunter, M., 1985. 'The cabinet institutionalized: The Royal Society's "Repository" and its background', in Impey and MacGregor 1985: 159–68.
Impey, O. and MacGregor, A. (eds), 1985. *The Origins of Museums.*
Kaufmann, T. D., 1978. 'Remarks on the collections of Rudolph II: *Kunstkammer* as a form of *Representatio*', *Art Journal, 38*: 22–8.
Laclau, E. and Mouffe, C., 1985. *Hegemony and Socialist Strategy; Towards a Radical Democratic Politics.*
Laurencich-Minelli, L., 1985. 'Museography and ethnographical collections in Bologna during the sixteenth and seventeenth centuries', in Impey and MacGregor 1985: 17–23.
MacGregor, A. 1983 (ed.). *Tradescant's Rarities.*
Nochlin, L., 1972. 'Museums and radicals; a history of emergencies', in O'Doherty. B. (ed.), *Museums in Crisis.*
Olmi, G., 1985. 'Science-honour-metaphor: Italian cabinets of the sixteenth and seventeenth centuries', in Impey and MacGregor 1985: 5–16.
Ornstein, M., 1938. *The Role of Scientific Societies in the Seventeenth Century.*
Quynn, D. M., 1945. 'The art confiscations of the Napoleonic wars', *American Historical Review, 50.3*: 430–60.
Scheicher, E., 1985. 'The collection of Archduke Ferdinand II at Schloss Ambras: its purpose, composition and evolution', in Impey and MacGregor 1985: 29–38.
Strong, R., 1973. *Splendour at Court: Renaissance Spectacle and Illusion.*
Taylor, F. H., 1948. *The Taste of Angels.*
Thorndike, L., 1941. *History of Magic and Experimental Science*, vol. VI.
Wittlin, A. S., 1949. *The Museum. Its History and Its Tasks in Education.*
Yates, F. A., 1966. *The Art of Memory.*

7 *The Fetishism of Artefacts*

PETER GATHERCOLE

> The collections of the Museum of Mankind contain over 300,000 items and are the finest of their kind in the world. As it is not possible to display all of these at any one time, this exhibition shows a selection drawn from a wide range of societies. It contains examples of sculpture, masks, clothing, items of adornment and everyday utensils.
>
> Museum of Mankind Programme Leaflet, 1987–8.

The subject of this paper is the attitude of curators towards artefacts once they are placed in museums. Do curators (in this context those of historical, archaeological or ethnographical collections) perceive artefacts *primarily* as things of themselves, rather than as things beyond themselves? To put the question more generally, are artefacts regarded by curators as basic to the existence of museums, or is it the knowledge concerning artefacts which is basic, the artefacts being merely illustrative of that knowledge? The question is not trivial. How one answers it influences, for example, collecting policies, attitudes towards display, and the ethics of museum ownership. Some of these matters are discussed later in this paper. Initially, however, it is necessary to clarify certain theoretical points.

The title of this paper should not be thought to imply that I deplore fetishism as such, or the fact that museums collect artefacts. In coining this title, I had in mind two analogies: firstly, the anthropological use of the concept of fetishism, and secondly, how Marx employed it in his discussion of commodities. To the anthropologist, fetishism is often defined, in the words of a well-known university textbook, as 'the worship of material objects supposed to have inherent power' (Mair 1965: 190). Over the years, considerable attention has been given by anthropologists to the characterization of that power, who exercises it, and to what ends. What, for example, relates the worshipped objects to the worshippers? Do the links between objects and persons actually cloak relations between persons? Such questions provide a useful introduction to my reference to Marx. In his discussion on commodities in volume I of *Capital*, Marx used a metaphor of fetishism to explain some of their characteristics:

> A commodity is therefore a mysterious thing, simply because in it the social character of men's labour appears to them as an objective character stamped upon the product of that labour; because the relation of the producers to the sum total of their own labour is presented to them as a social relation, existing not between themselves, but between the products of their labour. This is the reason why the products of labour become commodities, social things whose qualities are at the same time perceptible and imperceptible by the senses ... There, the existence of the things *qua* commodities, and the value relation between the products of labour which stamps them as commodities, have absolutely no connection with their physical properties and with the material relations arising therefrom. There it is a definite social relation between men, that assumes, in their eyes, the fantastic form of a relation between things (Marx 1906: 83).

The hypothesis here argued is that museum artefacts are analogous to commodities, in that they have properties bestowed upon them by virtue of their museum existence. They do not possess these properties intrinsic to themselves. The fetishism of artefacts, I suggest, exists when they are assumed to be what they are not. They are often regarded as evidence *per se* of cultural behaviour, but until this evidence is recognized, they remain, literally speaking, mere objects. Thus, in museum terms, the cultural status of artefacts, that is, the attribute which transforms objects into artefacts, depends upon the extent to which this attribute is perceived by curators, and is used by them in both research and display. This may appear to be a banal point, but actually the recognition of the distinction between object and artefact lies at the heart of curatorship. Although, without artefacts, curatorship could not exist, it is *knowledge* about them which is crucial to the forging of the artefact/curator relationship, not the existence of the artefacts themselves. Furthermore, the relationship that is established between curator and public is equally dependent on this curatorial knowledge.

In understanding what curatorial knowledge is, we are faced with a paradox. The indigenous cultural properties which define artefacts *sui generis* are only recognized, once the latter are placed in museums, to the extent that these properties become a part of curatorial knowledge, which is itself an expression of the museum culture to which artefacts have acceded, and to which, of course, originally they did not belong. An extreme example of this paradox is when an artefact is placed in an art museum, where its cultural properties are recognized and defined solely in terms of Western aesthetics, and its indigenous properties totally discounted or thought to coincide with Western criteria. In such an instance, and from an indigenous standpoint, the artefact does indeed revert to being a mere object. Another example, at an opposite extreme, is when the indigenous environment of an artefact is reconstructed in a museum in order to demonstrate its original meaning. Actually, however, these extremes are not necessarily far apart, because they are each contingent on the existence of curatorial knowledge. In fetishistic terms, because knowledge equals power, it is not the artefacts that have power over the curators, but vice-versa.

Curatorial knowledge, however, is much more than knowledge about artefacts; it is an aspect of museum knowledge, part of a museum culture, within which curators define, maintain, and extend their roles. This is not said cynically. Curators must know their collections, and must interpret them to outsiders, be the latter other scholars or a non-scholastic public. The measure of curatorial productivity, therefore, is one of ideas, expressed as texts of one form or another. Thus we find another paradox. Artefacts are, in the contexts of their parent cultures, indigenous instruments of production (whether they produce material things, ideas, or both, is here irrelevant). Once they are transferred to museums, however, they become some of the instruments of production which curators use to demonstrate their professional roles and to delineate their productive relations within museums. The ideas curators produce are expressions of museum ideology, and collectively are an aspect of their relations of production.

These relations of production, however, are not limited in their scope of application to within museums, since the latter exist only in so far as they have recognized roles within society. Society expects its museums to preserve artefacts, to retain and enlarge knowledge about them, and to express that knowledge in ways explicable to its members. The public expression of knowledge, therefore, is part of the productive relations of museums, as institutions, and of their curators, as servants of these institutions. Moreover, at least a part of these productive relations are what Janet Wolff has called 'the relations of consumption' (Wolff 1982: 65). As purveyors of museum knowledge, curators are as much mediators as are 'gallery owners, publishers, distributors, critics [and] administrators in determining which works will be presented, and in what way, to publics' (1982: 65). However, it could be claimed that curators have more than a mediating role in this respect because, as part of their productive relations, they are charged continually to extend and refine knowledge about artefacts. Therefore, they have a major voice in deciding which aspects of that knowledge will be brought into public gaze, and when and how this will be done. Like well-trained civil servants, curators not only service these relations of consumption, but also tune them to ensure, as far as possible, that they function as the museum requires (or is thought by the curators to require). Curators are the catalysts who determine the way relationships are established between publicly seen artefacts and consumers. They also determine much of the contents of these relationships, but, at the same time, they create opportunities for fresh knowledge, that within the consumers' heads, to be created, some of which may be added to the sum of curatorial knowledge.

Of course, the sum of curatorial knowledge is ever expanding, mainly in proportion to the amount of attention curators give to their collections. It is not surprising, therefore, that artefacts, like Marx's commodities, are such paradoxical things. On the one hand, they are at the core of museum scholarship, locked away in store-rooms, revealing their secrets only to the initiated; at the same time, some, when placed on display, act as seen specimens, representatives of alien cultures. In many respects, the two roles are quite different. Let us take, as an example, a Polynesian stone adze. As a class of artefact, a great deal is known about its method of manufacture, functions (both empirical and symbolic), typology, age-range, distribution and so on. In other words, there is readily available an enormous amount of at least potential curatorial knowledge which can be directed towards the understanding of every known specimen. Worldwide, curators are able to speak in the same language to each other about Polynesian adzes (such is the levelling-up process of scholarship), so that they can be perceived by curators as ordinary, normal, and even, one might say, domesticated items in any museum collection. But the universal language spoken by curators about these artefacts is contextual. Once one of them is taken from its store and placed on display, it is removed from its normal contextual niche and put in a novel one. Its store-room niche can be variously described as scientific, historiographic, or research-based. Once on display, the adze becomes an item for public consumption (that is, it is deemed fit for public knowledge), and its context is now sociological. Curatorial knowledge which has so carefully determined, for example, its typological refinements, might become quite irrelevant in face of the need for an apparently coarser, more contemporary knowledge. Here the curator, in order to interpret it publicly, might have to concentrate general attention on, for example, its ethnographic functions, perhaps illustrated by a reproduction of a drawing executed by one of Captain Cook's artists, and nothing more.

Thus, while forging anew, or extending, the museum's relations of consumption, the curator both extends and restricts the public's opportunities to obtain what has been, hitherto, only curatorial knowledge. What is written on the label or in the catalogue is, ideally, a distilled approximation of all that is known at present about Polynesian adzes. This necessarily involves the suppression of at least some curatorial knowledge. The usual museum response to such a criticism is, of course, that the conveying of information always has to be tailored to the means whereby this is done. True. My point, however, is that unless curatorial knowledge about our Polynesian adze is as extensive and scholastic as possible (so that the curator truly *is* perceiving the artefact as a thing beyond itself), the selection of information from that knowledge to be displayed can be made on too limited a basis; maybe even a dishonest one.

'Dishonest' may seem to be too strong a characterization. Let us consider, however, the position of an associated group of artefacts in a primary indigenous context. What sorts of information can it provide? Obviously, it can reveal much concerning technology, environmental exploitation, and other economic processes. This information can often give precision to those aspects of productive relations which refer to visibly verifiable actions. In this sense, artefacts are indeed concrete manifestations of indigenous thought in action. However, we also have to look for other expressions of social structures which are consistent with the evidence of artefacts. The latter may be excellent manifestations of social relations, which are themselves embodiments of social structures, but they cannot be the sole representations of either of these categories. A spear, for instance, is simply a spear; a caseful of them cannot be reified under a banner-like label to represent the concepts of warfare or hunting. On the other hand, if the spears possess certain common characteristics, this probably indicates the existence of indigenously endorsed patterns of thought and action. In many instances, too, it is possible to understand artefacts in symbolic terms, especially where ethnographic, historical, or even comparative information exists. The temptation to avoid, however, is always to make artefacts, as physical things, the starting point for the interpretation of cultures. Instead, they should be seen as just one form of cultural expression, however inconvenient this may be for curatorial practice, in a context where cultures are always knowable, at least in theory, by other means.

In summary, therefore: it might seem that artefacts lie at the core of curatorship. I argue, however, that this proposition is true only to the extent that, in terms of accepted conventions, museums could not exist without artefacts. It would be more accurate to say that the essence of curatorship is an understanding of the sociology of knowledge as it applies to museums, which implies an appreciation of the purpose of museums as institutions within society.

It is now appropriate to consider in more detail some examples of museum knowledge. Firstly, I shall discuss the matter of public presentation by reference to a hypothetical display; secondly, I shall raise some questions concerning the ownership of artefacts by museums, given the argument that, if artefacts should be perceived as things beyond themselves, does it actually matter which museum owns them? Let us examine a hypothetical display which, for sake of argument, has no more than the minimum number of artefacts acceptable, that is, one. To this end, I have selected an artefact which, although a part of our culture, is sufficiently historical and unusual to be considered, in display terms, exotic, namely, the famous Enigma machine, made use of so successfully by British Intelligence during the Second World War. The Government Code and Cypher School, established at Bletchley Park in Buckinghamshire, was an organization that was eventually able to decode thousands of enemy signals, sometimes within minutes of their original despatch, and distribute them to the appropriate authorities – a magnificent mathematical, cryptanalytical and Intelligence achievement. The Enigma machine, which superficially looked like a typewriter, was an electrical encoder/decoder, invented in Holland in 1919, and thereafter commercially available, which the Germans modified during the 1930s so that it could increase enormously its number of possible permutations. Therefore, to crack the German codes presented Bletchley's cryptographers with very difficult mathematical and mechanical problems.

Of course, a specimen Enigma machine could form the centre-piece of the display. But to emphasize the artefact in this rather obvious way would demonstrate precisely the technological bias that I am arguing against. The significance of Ultra (the code-name given to the material derived from breaking Enigma cyphers) was much more than this, as numerous recent books have made clear (see, for example, Calvocoressi 1980; Hodges 1985; Welchman 1982). The technology of Enigma is best understood in the context of the political, social and intellectual circumstances of the 1920s and 1930s, as much as the years of the Second World War itself. The most appropriate forms of display, therefore, would mean concentrating on these themes, and using information connected with Enigma to demonstrate their significance. For example, Polish Intelligence had been intercepting German signals with considerable success since the 1920s, and it was with its help that in July 1939 the Bletchley cryptographers eventually acquired an understanding of both the mathematical principles involved and the mechanical means to decode most of the signals themselves.

At one level, this success was due to brilliant wartime improvisation; but at another, it resulted from an understanding by the Bletchley cryptographers, who included a number of brilliant Cambridge mathematicians, that 'good cryptography lay in the creation of an entire body of rules, not in this or that message' (Hodges 1985: 165). In other words, the dominant theme of the display would be an intellectual one: that to a considerable extent the Ultra operation depended for its success on the recognition by the War Cabinet in Whitehall of the contribution made by pure mathematics. Thus an important subject would be the interaction between theory and practice, personified by the way civilian academics, as much as service personnel, found themselves playing an important part in the prosecution of the war. Related themes would concern political in-fighting between formally organized military groups and more informally established scientific advisory committees (as described so brilliantly in Nigel Balchin's novel, *The Small Back Room*, published in 1943), and the development of operational research, which, it could be stressed, had considerable influence on post-war planning.

The most exciting component in an Enigma exhibit, however, would be the emphasis it could give to the work of some of the individuals involved, notably Alan Turing, a Cambridge logician, who took a First in 1934 and seemed set for a conventional career as a King's College don. It has often been said that

Turing, whom 'even [Bletchley Park's] most brilliant cryptographers put in a class of his own' (Calvocoressi 1980: 110), was the intellectual parent of the digital computer. In 1937, before he was 25, Turing published a subsequently famous paper on computable numbers, which has been described as follows:

> In it he performed an historic thought experiment: he postulated a computer which could take its instructions from a paper tape containing a sequence of 1s and 0s, could print new sequences of 1s and 0s, which would then, if necessary, join the sequence of instructions. In this way it would modify its own programme. Turing showed that any machine which was capable of doing this much was, in a certain sense, the match of any other machine which could do this much. He called a machine of this kind a 'Universal Automaton'. (This is usually called a 'Turing Machine' today) (Ormell 1981: 528).

In our time, when the Government assesses pure research primarily in terms of its value for money, and when it is considered *chic* to characterize the Cambridge of the 1930s as a nursery of treason, an Enigma display would have a topical relevance. Indeed, Turing's later personal history also has contemporary significance, and could be noted. He was convicted for a homosexual act in 1952, at a time when such behaviour could mean extensive police harassment, and he died from cyanide poisoning in 1954, possibly accidentally. An apt title could be taken from that of Hugh Whitemore's successful play centred on Turing, called *Breaking the Code*. Indeed, why not break another code with the general proposal that, for our time, the best exhibits are those which take themes of multi-relevance, and are conceived and arranged, not to grow empirically out of a consideration of artefacts, but to be merely illustrated by them? The aim would be to go beyond relating what is displayed to visitor experience, by extending understanding through the analysis of the underlying causes of past events, and by emphasizing the degree to which we are subject to similar pressures. Controversial topics and opinions would not be buried under bland presentations.

Finally, such a display could deal in an interesting way with the principle of coherence. Generally speaking, displays are embodiments of ordered sequences; they impose rational representations on the apparent chaos of life. But one of the aims of the Enigma presentation would be to demonstrate the interrelationship between order and chaos. When Turing was working on his great paper, the problem of conceiving of computable numbers must surely have seemed to him at times chaotic (Hodges 1985: 96–106). The Second World War was very often chaotic to its participants, service personnel and civilians alike. By contrast, the Bletchley cryptanalysts and Intelligence officers could watch, though they could not divulge to many others, the unfolding of German strategies, and their translation into tactical directives to military units. To display change in museum displays is often to display paradox. An analogy would be that of a sequence of film montages, where one set of images, apparently firm, dissolves into another set, and so on. So why not mount several displays in a sequence of rooms, where the same theme is returned to several times, each with a new twist (an increasing depth of field)? Final coherence could be achieved by a portrayal of Turing's 'Universal Automaton'. Displays, as conscious arrangements, are expressions of drama. My point in this respect is that here the drama should be made very explicit, taking in the doubts, hesitations and rough edges.

To turn now to my second example: if it is accepted that the primary responsibility of curatorship is to enhance knowledge rather than to take care of artefacts, what should our attitude be towards museum ownership? Given that knowledge is ownable by everyone, does this affect our attitude to which museum owns which artefact? In considering these questions I am influenced by the fact that until recently I was much concerned with the care, documentation, study and location of Oceanic ethnographic collections. Unfortunately, the existing distribution of these collections still reflects more the history of Imperialism than present-day geopolitical and cultural realities. Despite the considerable advances made over the last 20 years in curatorial attention to Oceanic ethnography, the benefits have been stunted by the fact that the majority of important collections continue to be held outside the South Pacific itself, beyond convenient access by a growing number of indigenous scholars and by other Pacific Islanders. The increasing absurdity of this position is illustrated by the paradox created by the spectacular growth of Oceanic archaeology. This discipline has literally established an indigenous history beyond the confines of conventional written documentation, and yet the comparative ethnographic material is housed, for the most part, half a world away.

It is from this standpoint that one should assess, for example, the recent sale of the George Brown collection of some 3,000 items by the University of Newcastle, via Sotheby's, to the National Museum of Ethnology, Osaka, Japan. In scholastic as much as political and cultural terms, this collection should have been split up and repatriated to its several islands of origin, perhaps by means of an initial purchase of the whole collection by the Australian Museum, Sydney (Specht 1987: 1). The actual outcome, now that the Japanese have succeeded in using the power of the yen to emulate what European museums have done in the past, is not only a political and cultural tragedy, but also a vivid example of the present poverty of curatorial thinking concerning the ethics of artefact ownership. As Specht has said in a perceptive article on the implications of the episode, collections 'are western constructs. They have no relevance in discussions of collection disposal' (Specht 1987: 2). It is also pertinent to note his further comment that:

> some museums must rank among the most centralized bureaucratic institutions in the world. They are also expensive to maintain, as many developing countries have discovered. The days are past when the

> 'vacuum-cleaner' approach to increasing collections was possible, except for a privileged few in the western capitalist world. The promise of the National Museum of Ethnology in Osaka to establish a visiting study scheme for Pacific Islands' scholars emphasises the unequal distribution of cultural property in the world. The 'have-nots' are further away from achieving equity. Access to the material expressions of cultural heritage is well and truly dependent on being one of the wealthy nations (Specht 1987: 3).

The George Brown episode revealed, particularly in Britain, the lack of agreement within the museum profession concerning the distinction between legal ownership of artefacts by museums as institutions, and the ethical responsibilities implicit in curatorship. Curators should recognize more explicitly the power they exercise, reinforced, as it is, by the continual accretions of scholarship. The artefacts owned by their institutions are, in curatorial terms, no more than held in trust on behalf of the cultures from which the artefacts derive, or their descendants. Part of this trust means asking such questions as: is scholarship facilitated or impeded if artefacts from culture X ae held, largely unexamined and sometimes for years, in Museum Y, thousands of miles from their logical centre of research? Surely the time has now come for curators to devise schemes for the redistribution of artefacts, either immediately or in the longer term, which take into account both international museum facilities and political realities? It is by such actions, I suggest, that curators can fulfil their obligations to see artefacts as things beyond themselves, and demonstrate their own adherence to the principle of the universality of cultural knowledge, rather than to that of the universality of culture.

Bibliography

Calvocoressi, P., 1980. *Top Secret Ultra.*

Hodges, A., 1985. *Alan Turing: The Enigma of Intelligence.*

Mair, L., 1965. *An Introduction to Social Anthropology.*

Marx, K., 1906. *Capital: A Critique of Political Economy, vol. I: The Process of Capitalist Production.*

Ormell, C., 1981. 'Alan Turing 1912–54', in Wintle, J. (ed.), *Makers of Modern Culture*: 528–9.

Specht, J., 1987. 'The George Brown affair again', *Anthropology Today, 3.4*: 1–3.

Welchman, G., 1982. *The Hut Six Story: Breaking the Enigma Codes.*

Wolff, J., 1982. 'The problem of ideology in the sociology of art: a case study of Manchester in the nineteenth century', *Media, Culture and Society, 4*: 63–75.

8 *Museums of the World: Stages for the Study of Ethnohistory*

ADRIENNE L. KAEPPLER

With apologies to Shakespeare,

> All museums are stages, and all the artefacts merely players; They have their exits and their entrances; And one artefact in its time plays many parts.
>
> *As You Like It*, Act II

Depending on the artefact and its documented history, some artefacts, like some actors, are more versatile than others, playing many roles, while some, bacause of lack of documentation, are doomed forever to playing minor parts; although some talent scouts and stage managers are able to take virtually unknown artefacts and make them stars literally overnight. I remember one occasion in Edinburgh in 1969. The stage was a crowded case about Hawaii, before the exhibits had been redone in their present form. Through the gloom I looked carefully at the Hawaiian human figures standing resolutely to attention. I thought I recognized one of the figures as part of a group of drawings of objects collected during Cook's voyages, but looking through the Hawaiian section of the drawings I could not find it; I must have been mistaken. A few hours later on the train to Glasgow I pondered the problem, wondering why that Hawaiian actor/image looked familiar to me, and examined my book of drawings again – only to find what I was looking for in the North West Coast section (Force and Force 1968:171). But I could not be sure. I got off the train, caught the next one back to Edinburgh and compared their Hawaiian image to my drawing. It *was* the same object, but what was its history? Museum records noted only that it came from the Beasley collection. I then contacted Mrs Beasley and she told me it came to the Beasley Cranmore Museum without any history except that it was bought from L. Casimis of 12 Beauchamp Place, London. In 1938 Kenneth Emory had published an article about this image in which he suggested (1938:9) that it was relatively late and may have been influenced by Chinese immigrants, as shown by the Chinese pigtail carved at the back. However, as this figure was illustrated in my book of drawings completed before 1783 it had to be a Cook-voyage object.[1] My subsequent research has shown that, instead of a late image, it is an important early figure which illustrates the importance of carved backbones and their associations with Lono, god of peace and agriculture, and the visual allusions to genealogical reckoning (Kaeppler 1985a: 86–7). In 1978 the figure travelled to Bishop Museum, Honolulu, for the 'Artificial Curiosities' exhibition which marked the 200th anniversary of Cook's visit to Hawaii. Because of documentary research, this figure was able to visit its homeland as a celebrity – instead of as a Chinese-influenced carving as Emory had suggested.

Another artefact 'star' discovered through documentary research is a wooden bowl with human images from the North-West Coast of America now in the Museum of Mankind, London. This bowl was from the same collection as the Hawaiian image – the private museum of Sir Ashton Lever – but its history subsequent to the Leverian auction of 1806 is quite different. The bowl was among the collection purchased by John Rowe for his brother-in-law Richard Hall Clarke, which after several generations had lost its association with Cook and the Leverian Museum. After tracing a collection sold at auction by an anonymous owner in Torquay to the Clarke descendants, I asked them to look round the estate for any further objects depicted in the set of eighteenth century drawings. Sure enough, there was the bowl with human images and several other important pieces. The bowl was sold at another auction in 1971 and purchased by the Museum of Mankind. Had it not been for my documentary research, and especially my persistence with the auctioneer, the bowl would probably still be in the disintegrating museum outbuilding of a small estate in Devon.

Another route to stardom is to be taken from a crowded exhibition case and featured in an exhibition or on the cover of a catalogue. The now famous feather-covered temple from Hawaii, for example, was known to be from Cook's third voyage but languished without interpretation or explanation in a crowded case in the Vienna Museum für Völkerkunde until it was featured in the 'Artificial Curiosities' exhibition at Bishop Museum and illustrated on the cover of the catalogue (Kaeppler 1978). Likewise, an exquisite Fijian ivory double image was effectively hidden in the Fiji ivory case at the University Museum of Archaeology and Anthropology in Cambridge, England, until it was featured on the cover of the exhibit catalogue *The Proper Study of Mankind* (Ebin and Swallow 1984). Such objects can play many roles precisely because they are documented.

In addition to 'works of art' or 'treasures', which many objects become, they can be used in exhibitions about the history of the collections in which they are found – as at Vienna and Cambridge museums in the examples above.

Alternatively, they can be used to tell the stories of collectors or culture heroes important to the national image or history of the country in which they eventually find themselves – in the examples above, Captain Cook, culture hero *par excellence*, and Baron von Hügel, museum curator *extraordinaire*. But more importantly, if they are documented, objects can be used as important elements in the study of ethnohistory – the discipline that combines knowledge gained from research in ethnography and history. This paper is concerned with the part that museums play in that study and how they can convey that information through exhibition and publication. A museum exhibition can be considered a kind of stage in which the final product can both educate and delight. The artefacts can be considered players who intertwine their own personal histories with the stories they will tell in a particular exhibition or publication. Libraries and research offices can be considered writers' studios where information is synthesized from a particular point of view into scripts – many of which will never see the light of day but which become part of the permanent documentation of the collection. Archives and store-rooms contain the data and objects for these dramatic endeavours while we, the keepers and researchers, are the scriptwriters showing how material culture is not only illustrative material for exhibition, but is an integral part of the study of ethnohistory. Museums not only house the proscenium arches for the exits and entrances of the artefact players, but hold much of the material for piecing together the drama of ethnohistory.

Working with artefacts and associating them with their history and ethnohistory can make stars of objects overnight, and this is a proper role of museums and museum workers. Sometimes working with artefacts and their documented histories can reveal that they have not been obtained in a upright and ethical manner: in such cases artefacts can become not only famous, but infamous. Sometimes the collectors had nothing more in mind than saving objects from destruction such as Zuni war gods or Papuan Gulf bark-cloth masks; and some artefacts, such as Zuni war gods, have now been returned to the descendants of their makers in order to fulfil their original destiny of deterioration by natural causes. Anthropologists and museum workers of all disciplines, as researchers and detectives, are like stage managers and publicists who can make artefacts in their care or on which they have done research famous, infamous, and stars,[2] so that when these artefacts take their places in an exhibition or in a publication they are instantly recognizable.

'Discovery' and use by a Western artist may create an artefact's importance. Artefacts which have little to recommend them for other reasons – no documentation and poor examples of their type – may suddenly be 'found' and treated as important personages as part of Dada, Surrealist or Pop Art paintings or constructions. One of the recent incarnations of this absorption of non-Western objects into a Western aesthetic is Eduardo Paolozzi's modern art works (or conglomorations) called *Lost Magic Kingdoms*. This exhibition, which was organized and exhibited by the Museum of Mankind in London, is, in my view, a desecration rather than an enhancement of an artefact's life. It has nothing of an artefact's own culture, history, or tradition but has become subservient to the whim of a Western artist. One can only hope that the egos of the artefact/actors and, more importantly, the descendants of their makers, are not as insulted as they have the right to be. For this reason such an exhibition has no place in an *anthropology* museum. The exhibition has been the subject of some controversy (eg. Brandt 1986), but contrary to the opinion of Sir Edmund Leach (1986), in my view the Museum of Mankind should not be commended. In showing this exhibition, the museum is no longer a stage for the study of ethnohistory, but rather has become a modern art studio for the staging of an individual's one-man show.

This paper focusses on the importance of documentation of museum collections and how such documentation can be used for ethnohistoric interpretation. If objects are or can be documented, their importance multiplies and their value increases because documented objects can be used for the study of ethnohistory both for research and exhibition. Museums are stages for such study. The museums in Europe and America, with their vast collections of objects, notes, drawings, photographs and manuscripts, can be used as primary sources for the study of ethnohistory. With documented histories, objects can be used for more diverse exhibitions and are particularly important for the study of persistence and change. Objects are material manifestations of societal transformations and form a crucial part of the understanding of society and culture and their changes over time.

In an earlier paper (1985a) I demonstrated the importance of Hawaiian featherwork in understanding the societal transformations of nineteenth-century Hawaii. I showed how:

> careful study of objects, as part of socially given categories, can tell us a great deal, not only about these inanimate things themselves, but also about their owners and the society that produced them. As Hawaiian society was transformed during the late 18th and early 19th centuries, material culture not only changed by importing and adapting Western objects, but traditional Hawaiian material culture evolved as a part of these changing relationships and changing categories to meet the needs of a changed society. Objects were part of the changing social relationships between people, the gods and the environment, and were used in the service of prestige, power, authority and status (Kaeppler 1985a:109).

During the societal changes of the nineteenth century one of the fundamental Hawaiian notions, 'genealogical prestige gives power and therefore authority', changed to 'power gives authority and therefore prestige' (Kaeppler 1985a: 107). At the same time, feathered cloaks and capes evolved from sacred protective utilitarian objects into symbols of power legitimization and finally into status objects. The unique feathered temple mentioned earlier from Cook's third voyage has now been shown (Kaeppler 1985a:122–7) to have been a ritual object, a *hale waiea* used in the service of Lono, god of peace and agriculture. In the nineteenth century this artefact type was relegated to obscurity as part of a deliberately changing symbolic system induced by Kamehameha, the famous Hawaiian chief who usurped power by his own personal charisma and imported European guns.

Museums have been slow in taking up the challenge of exhibiting such concepts. They still use artefacts of no specific time period to convey romantic notions of timeless 'cultural others'. The objects have no time period, no context, and little educational value. It is time to move on. It is time to place peoples of the world in historical settings. It is time to show how a society's cultural past influences how that society operates in the modern world. It is time to show how all nations of the world are culturally and socially equal – with no implication that some societal groups are somehow the remnants of earlier stages of civilization. This is the challenge for anthropological curators/stage managers as we move into the 1990s. One of my attempts at this concept was the introductory label for my 1980 exhibition at Bishop Museum entitled 'Chiefs, Bigmen, and Mariners'. After explaining these socio-political types that were featured in the exhibition, the last paragraph of a huge exhibition label read:

> You, the viewer of this exhibition, may bring into this hall other ways of organizing society. Each, though different, is an appropriate way of looking at the world. Over the years these social, political, and religious worlds have met, clashed, and changed. In many ways, however, Pacific world views have changed only superficially. This exhibition is an invitation to examine objects and ideas of the past in order to better understand the diverse people who inhabit the Pacific world today.

While working on the Smithsonian exhibition 'Magnificent Voyagers, The U.S. Exploring Expedition 1838–1842', my interest in Fiji was renewed. Although I had spent a few months in Fiji during my years of research in the Pacific Islands, and Fijian objects were often intermixed with Tongan ones in museums in which I had studied, I had not really focussed on the Fijian objects themselves. As we started to work with the collection it quickly became apparent that the Smithsonian collection is one of the most important Fijian collections in the world outside of Fiji, and the best documented. What makes it so important is its quantity, quality, and known date and place of collection.

Let me begin with a bit of the history of the collection and its route to the Smithsonian Institution, which was founded in 1846 from the 1826 bequest of the Briton, James Smithson. The U.S. Exploring Expedition of 1838–1842 under Lieutenant Charles Wilkes was the first international hydrographic and scientific survey to be undertaken by the young U.S. Government. Its members surveyed 300 islands, drafted 200 maps and charts, mapped 800 miles of the Oregon coast, confirmed the existence of Antarctica as a continent and collected vast quantities of natural and cultural history specimens. At the time when the Expedition returned there was no U.S. National Museum and many of the objects went temporarily into the so-called National Institute located at the U.S. Patent Office. Only after 1857, when the Smithsonian Institution became a museum, did the objects move to the 'Castle' (the original building of the Institution). After the construction of the new Natural History building in 1910 they were moved across the Mall, and finally in 1962 they were moved to their present home in the East part of the building. As a result of these moves many objects had lost their labels and some were in quite bad condition. It took several years of work by Jane Walsh, a museum specialist in Smithsonian Institution documentation, to reconstruct which objects actually belonged to the collection by comparing objects, labels, photographs, various registers, the shipping lists and, most important, the original catalogue listing made by Titian Peale.

The Expedition spent three months of 1840 primarily in the coastal areas of several of the Fiji islands. In some areas the Expedition met friendly receptions but they also encountered hostilities that led to the deaths of Fijians and Expedition members. Hundreds of objects were collected in Fiji, including more than 1200 that eventually became part of the Smithsonian collection – nearly one-half of all the ethnographic objects that came to the Smithsonian from the Expedition. Because it is such a large collection, made during a known three-month period of 1840, we were able to devote most of three rooms to Fiji in the 'Magnificent Voyagers' exhibition. Particularly useful were the published and unpublished journals of the Expedition and the many drawings made by artists during the Expedition and later. Thus, because the objects were documented we could present Fiji not as a romantic timeless place, but as an operating society in 1840 focussing on ritual, everyday life and warfare.

Besides its use for exhibitions, the collection is important for research because of the large number of some artefact types collected. There are, for example, more than 80 *liku* skirts, 200 clubs, 20 baskets, 50 pieces of bark cloth, 12 nose flutes, and numerous spears and ornaments. Research can therefore be done on such questions as variation and uniformity within artefact types collected at a specific time period or the creative variations developed in types of useful artefacts. The baskets, skirts and bark cloth form a valuable study collection for analysis of Fijian design motifs and the aesthetic use of two-dimensional space, and it is not necessary to worry about time period and change in such analyses.

Having looked briefly at its history, I now want to put the Smithsonian Fijian collection into the larger perspective of Fijian collections in museums of the world – other stages for the study of Fijian ethnohistory. The Smithsonian collection itself is one of the five most important Fijian collections in the world, and probably the best documented. The other four are in Suva, Fiji; Salem, Massachusetts; Cambridge, England; and Leipzig, Germany. The Fiji Museum in Suva 'houses the most comprehensive collection of traditional

Fijian artifacts in existence' (*Domodomo*, 1983, back cover). Many of these objects came into the Museum as 'heirlooms' from Fijians and non-Fijians without precise documentation,[3] but a number of documented pieces have recently been acquired.

Some of the earliest documented Fijian pieces are in the Peabody Museum, Salem, Massachusetts. This collection includes objects from the sandalwood trade of 1804–15, the *bèche-de-mer* trade of the 1820s and 1830s, and some objects brought back by U.S. whaling ships as well as some from the U.S. Exploring Expedition. Some of the pieces can be traced to ship captains and donors, but there is little ethnographically important information associated with them.

A fourth important 'world class' Fijian collection was one of the founding (1884) collections of what is now known as the University Museum of Archaeology and Anthropology in Cambridge, England. This field collection was made primarily in the 1870s and was brought together by Anatole von Hügel, the first curator of the Museum. The objects were obtained by von Hügel himself while he was in Fiji from 1875 until 1877, and by Sir Arthur Gordon, the first British governor of Fiji (1875–80), and two members of his staff, Alfred Maudsley and Sir Arthur's nephew (also named Arthur Gordon). Other objects collected by this group were given to other museums and are now in the Museum of Mankind and in the Australian Museum, Sydney. Also in Fiji at the time was Constance Gordon Cumming, an artist who painted numerous watercolours of ethnographic importance and collected some objects which are now in Edinburgh. Sir Arthur Gordon also made several further visits after 1880. The Cambridge collection was thus made over a longer period of time than the collection from the U.S. Exploring Expedition and it also included more objects from the interior of the islands. Some of these objects are documented, such as the sculptured Janus female ivory suspension hook, for which not only is its collection data known, but one of its former Fijian owners tells of how it made squeaky sounds at night.

The fifth important Fijian collection is that made by Theodore Kleinschmidt for the Museum Godeffroy in Hamburg betweeen 1875 and 1878. After the collapse of this museum in 1879, the collection was sold to the Leipzig Museum für Völkerkunde in 1885. It includes nearly 300 Fijian objects, some of which have locality designations. The association of the objects with Kleinschmidt's notes and drawings, some of which still exist in Hamburg, has yet to be attempted.

The Smithsonian collection, then, is an intermediate collection. It forms a continuum with the collection from Salem, while the next major group of collections in Cambridge, Leipzig, and elsewhere was not started until some 27 years later. The Smithsonian collection is crucial for an understanding of these other collections and serves as a reference collection for all Fijian objects in the world, of which there are at least 25,000 pieces in known collections outside of Fiji.[4]

About 1,200 Fijian artefacts were included in the U.S. Exploring Expedition collection when it came to the Smithsonian. Nearly 400 of these were distributed to other public institutions and private individuals in the United States and abroad between 1859 and 1920 in keeping with the Smithsonian mandate of the 'increase and diffusion of knowledge'. Twenty-five 'sets of duplicates' consisting of 12 to 25 pieces were made up and prepared for distribution. These sets usually included several Fijian pieces. The largest set, consisting of 100 pieces, was sent to Denmark and included 60 pieces from Fiji. Among the 800 Fijian pieces that remain at the Smithsonian there are numerous examples of items of everyday life, warfare and ritual. Included are some unique items, the only known examples of some artefact types, and in many cases the earliest known examples in museum collections.

For example, the four carved wooden figures and the human figure carved as part of a suspension hook are the earliest figures in museum collections. Interestingly, there is a male and female pair (1817–18/2996–7), a female with bark-cloth loincloth and turban, and a male post image. The female image (1816/2998) is noted in the Peale manuscript catalogue as follows:

> Idol obtained in a consecrated grove at Sandal Bay-Island of Vanualevu, where a numerous part of natives had been slain and eaten, many stones were set up and ornamented with turbans, hair pins and the arms of the dead, around the mound where this idol or figure was placed. None of the natives of the adjoining village could be persuaded to approach the spot.

This leads one to the journals for Sandalwood Bay where there is a further explanation. Much of volume III of the *Narrative of the United States Exploring Expedition* consists of detailed accounts of the expedition's three months in Fiji. On 8 June 1840, Captain Hudson and others set out to survey Sandalwood Bay:

> On the way from Vaturua to Matainole, a piece of consecrated ground was passed, on which were mounds of stone, with a rude idol, dressed with a turban and the Feejee hair-pins. The idol was surrounded by clubs set up edgewise, and many spears, arrows, trinkets, coco-nuts, etc., lay around, which had evidently been placed there as offerings. A large party of natives, who were with our gentlemen, on seeing them approach it, deserted, excepting a man and boy, who, contrary to the others, seemed anxious for them to partake of the offerings which lay about, and offered to sell the idol, which was bought for a paper of vermilion. Neither of them, however, could be tempted to touch a single article himself, although they had no objection to our gentlemen doing so. On the next day, Mr. Peale returning from his jaunt, took his purchase and carried it on board (Wilkes 1845, III:215).

The woodcut illustrations in the *Narrative* were instrumental in finding and documenting objects. For example, the woodcut at the end of chapter V

HEAD-DRESS OF CHIEFS.

Figure 8.1 Woodcut of headdress from the *Narrative of the United States Exploring Expedition*, 1845. (Photo: Smithsonian Institution)

entitled 'headdress of chiefs' was crucial for verifying the identity of this object. It was referred to in the text in the section on the island of Somu-somu. The chief of this island, or 'the old King' as Wilkes calls him, 'was very desirous of making me presents, and among the curiosities I accepted was a huge headdress, in shape somewhat like a cocked hat. It is represented in the wood-cut at the end of this chapter' (Wilkes 1845, III 160) (figure 8.1). But where could it be? This headdress was listed at number 2483 in the original Peale list but it had no Smithsonian museum number. An object in terrible condition – having the appearance of a number of disintegrating bark-cloth cigars – was tentatively identified with the woodcut (figure 8.2). Our conservator, Kathy Valentour, was intrigued and set about to reconstruct it with reference to the woodcut. The final product is quite extraordinary and we now have an entirely unique Fijian headdress (figure 8.3).

One object that was illustrated but not acquired was an ivory and pearl shell breastplate. This was the earliest illustration of this type of ornament and it is likely that such breastplates were a new development about that time. This breastplate was acquired in the 1870s and is now in the Cambridge collection. Thanks to the detailed drawing by Expedition artist A. T. Agate, it was possible to identify the owner of this object in 1840 as Tanoa, Chief of Bau (Clunie 1983).

The woodcut of clubs was useful in locating some of the specimens which

Figure 8.2 Headdress as found in storage. (Photo: Smithsonian Institution)

Figure 8.3 Headdress as reconstructed. (Photo: Smithsonian Institution)

had lost their numbers and was also used in helping arrange the pile of clubs for a diorama illustrating a formal dance presented to Captain Wilkes and other Expedition members at Ovalau. This diorama included one of only two known examples of historic Fijian masks – both of which were acquired during the Expedition – and gave us the opportunity to dress a mannikin in a long bark-cloth loin cloth as described in the journals. Concerning the club dance itself, research carried out in 1984 on this *meke wau* suggests that it is done in much the same form now as it was in 1840. The entrance section of the *meke wau* in 1984 was the same as illustrated in the engraving after Drayton, and the recordings made in 1984 are very similar to wax cylinder recordings made at the World Columbian exposition in Chicago in 1893, now in the Library of Congress. The masked clown is no longer part of present-day ensembles but the two masks and Wilkes's description illuminates part of a tradition that has now evolved into clowning by members of the audience who might come to join the dancers. Such improvised clowning contrasts with the structured formal presentation and serves as comic interlude.

Wilkes's *Narrative* has numerous references to the use of bark cloth in Fiji. He tells how it was made from beating the inner bark of the paper mulberry and how it was decorated by placing it on a bamboo template and rubbing it with dye (III, 1845: 337–8). Although making bark cloth was the work of women, it was not worn by them. Indeed, the wearing of a bark-cloth turban and loincloth were the distinguishing marks of a male chief. A chief's loincloth or *malo* was extended to trail on the ground sometimes for 50 metres and a light bark-cloth turban was passed around the head from one to a dozen times. Numerous examples of these turbans – accordian pleated and ready for wear – were collected during the Expedition. Although Wilkes does not actually state the religious significance of bark cloth (*masi*), the varied religious contexts in which he describes its use infer its supernatural significance. Wilkes did not see a state presentation in which a chief wears hundreds of feet of *masi* and disrobes either by spinning to unravel wrapped *masi* or by dropping the looped *masi* as an aesthetic gesture in honour of the receiving chief. Expedition artist A. T. Agate, however, described the presentation of bark-cloth tribute by the people of Kandavu: 'The chiefs of Kandavu appeared, each encircled with many folds of tapa and mats ... [each of whom] after disburdening himself of the tapa in which he was enveloped, gave place to another, and so on to the last ... and the king took especial care to place the new acquisitions among his valuables' (Wilkes 1845, III:121). Theodore Kleinschmidt also described such a ceremony and his illustration of the chief of Nadrau wearing 180 metres of bark cloth for presentation was used to dress a mannikin in 100 metres of *masi*, which became the centrepiece of the 'Magnificent Voyagers' exhibition (figure 8.4).[5]

Bark cloth, along with smoked whales' teeth (*tabua*), were considered by the Fijians their most important valuables, while the art of presentation and its associated oratory formed aesthetic elements in their own right. Only chiefs

Figure 8.4 Fijian mannikin from the *Magnificent Voyagers* exhibition at the Smithsonian Institution. (Photo: Smithsonian Institution)

could make such presentations and it was considered a great honour both to give and receive. The Exploring Expedition bark cloth, when examined in conjunction with Wilkes's *Narrative*, as well as earlier and later accounts and present-day presentations, demonstrates the importance of material culture in understanding social structure, cultural categories and evaluative ways of thinking. The Fijian world view and the mental constructs with which material culture are entwined, deals with exchange and value in which valuable objects were as important as people. To understand Fijians and their society, valuables must be taken into account, for categories of people and things are tied to underlying structures and cultural philosophies: we can try to reconstruct and understand these cultural forms through ethnohistory.

And how does the Fijian of today fit into all this? Many of the rituals and presentations still exist as part of the modern world and traditional artefacts can be used to understand life in its present form. A *tabua* can no longer be exchanged for a person and women who wear *masi* are not subject to death or sanction, but locating, documenting and interpreting important artefacts is a service which all can appreciate. Establishing documentation and the history of artefacts is a first step to ethnohistory. Museums are stages for such study and can be the staging place for putting history into action. Cooperative work between museum anthropologists and indigenous peoples can move us forward with a proper study of humankind.

Notes

1. Hawaii first became known to the Western world through the visits of Captain James Cook in 1778–9. The area was not visited again until 1786.
2. Sometimes the stage managers get carried away and make unwarranted claims, such as I note in my article in the *Magnificent Voyagers* catalogue. Here I stated (1985b:143) that I knew of only two California Indian feather dresses of a certain style – the one collected on the U.S. Exploring Exhibition and one in Leningrad. In fact there are probably at least two others. One of these plays an exhibition role on a museum stage in Oakland, California, and, I understand, another plays a research role in a storage cabinet in Shoreditch in London.
3. The pedigree of many of the objects is much like the pedigree of many objects in Bishop Museum, Honolulu, or in New Zealand museums, in that they were given or purchased long after they ceased to have an active role in Fijian, Hawaiian or Maori society. Unfortunately many of them can only play an imprecise role on museum stages – they can only be 'stock characters' or 'works of art'. This is also the case with objects that sell at auction houses. Although some sellers, such as the Hooper family, attempted to document each object before their collection was sold, most objects come into sale rooms with little or no history. Why is this, one

wonders. Were they stolen? Are they fakes? Were they taken out of their homeland illegally? Or is it just malaise on the part of their owners?

4. See the UNESCO inventories of Pacific collections in the United Kingdom, Australia, New Zealand, and the United States and Canada. In addition to the 288 objects in Leipzig collected by Kleinschmidt, there are numerous other Fijian objects in Germany, some in Paris, and 144 in Leningrad.
5. The face and arms of the mannikin were cast from Navitilai Naisoro, a Fijian employee of the World Bank in Washington, D.C.

BIBLIOGRAPHY

Brandt, J., 1986, *Times Literary Supplement*, 7 February: 141.

Clunie, F., 1983. 'Ratu Tanoa Visawaqa's breastplate', *Domodomo, 1*: 123–5.

Ebin, V. and Swallow, D.A., 1984. *'The Proper Study of Mankind ...' Great Anthropological Collections in Cambridge.*

Emory, K.P., 1938. 'Hawaii: god sticks', *Ethnologia Cranmorensis, 3*: 9–10.

Force, R. W. and Force, M., 1968. *Art and Artifacts of the 18th Century.*

Kaeppler, A. L., 1978. *'Artificial Curiosities' being an Exposition of Native Manufactures collected on the three Pacific Voyages of Captain James Cook, R.N.*

Kaeppler, A. L., 1985a. 'Hawaiian art and society: traditions and transformations', in Hooper, A. and Huntsmen, J. (eds), *Transformations of Polynesian Culture*. Polynesian Society Memoir 45: 105–31.

Kaeppler, A. L., 1985b. 'Anthropology and the U.S. Exploring Expedition', in Viola, H. J. and Margolis, C. (eds), *Magnificent Voyagers. The U.S. Exploring Expedition, 1938–1842.*

Leach, E., 1986. *The Times Literary Supplement*, 21 February: 191.

Wilkes, C., 1845. *Narrative of the United States Exploring Expedition*, vol. III.

9 *Material Culture Research and the Curation Process*

HANS JÖRG FÜRST

The importance of material culture research for anthropology is that it often gives additional evidence to the written record. Ethnographies (field work based on interviews and participant observation) have the tendency to reflect a conscious formulation of the ideal by the interviewee. Material culture research, however, can give additional evidence that is not or cannot be expressed verbally or in writing – which is not to say, however, that objects are a more objective source of information (Gould 1981; McLendon 1981; Miller 1985; Silver 1979: 284). To study material culture and its actual use can provide supplementary insight into a culture and can qualify interpretative conclusions (McLendon 1981: 202). Written evidence would indicate, to take a contemporary example, that present-day Tucsonans are typical waste-makers. Continual media advertising and statistics on economic behaviour suggest that used items are not re-used but thrown away (Gould 1981). However, material culture research establishes that Tucsonans have, contrary to written sources as well as popular belief, a strong tendency to re-use objects and materials. Households 'acquire their used furniture, applicances, and other items through nonmarket exchanges which escape formal bookkeeping or other records' (Gould 1981: 58). Material culture, thus, is useful for finding out about actual behaviour that is not conformable to, or even runs contrary to, the ideal pattern – in the case above, contrary to the ideal that you have to buy brand-new goods.

Material culture research differs from other types of anthropological investigations in several ways. Objects are non-reactive, that is, they do not change in the course of research; humans, on the other hand, do react and change during the research process. The research procedure is replicable because objects are non-reactive. Objects are durable; they still exist even when their culture of origin has long since departed (Eighmy 1981: 32, 33, 49;

Rathje 1978: 51, 52). Dated material culture provides an useful diachronic record of culture in transition. Thus, objects in museums can enrich and qualify ethnohistoric data in reconstructing historical processes since ethnographies present native societies often implicitly as changeless because gradual changes 'can seldom be studied during the typical fieldwork period of one of [sic] two years' (Anderson 1979: 155, see also 36; Dark 1969: 1132; Eighmy 1981: 32, 33, 49; Fenton 1966: 78; Fenton 1974: 21; Gould 1981: 61; Graebner 1911: 14, 23; Sturtevant 1967: 3; Sturtevant 1969: 637, 639; Sturtevant 1973: 48; see also Collier and Fenton 1965: 112; Collier and Tschopik 1954: 775, 776). Turning to the training of students of anthropology, material culture (in this paper used synonymously for artefacts, objects and specimens) provides a physical and a unique access to a culture. The participants in the Conference on Museums and Anthropological Research held in Ottawa in 1963 'believed that the intimate acquaintance of a student with the material culture of a native people adds a dimension to his understanding of culture that can be gained in no other way' (Collier and Fenton 1965: 112, see also 111).

It is clear that a flexible frame for the research process offers advantages over a linear and rigid one as research interests and so the departure points of the individual researchers differ. In my belief, research has not by necessity to be inductive, that is, to start from the object (see also Pearce 1986c: 199, 200). Rather, it is equally sensible and as valid to start from either the object's curation process, or from its comparative aspects, or from its interpretation (deduction), or from its cultural context. Indeed, it is often advisable to start from the curation process as the catalogue information on the object is the crucial point of museum studies (see also McFeat 1967: 99; McLendon 1981: 225; Sturtevant 1973: 44). Independently from where in the research process you choose to start, serious research will have to look at the cultural context and the curation process of the object, and will have to compare it with others, and come to interpretative conclusions.

Documentation on museum objects is generally sparse, and information on the cultural context of the object, for example its ideological and social significance, is often even more limited (see also Bühler 1947: 229; Fenton 1974: 27). Additional contextual information on already existing collections can be obtained by ethnohistoric research and field work (see also Anderson 1979: 55; Collier and Fenton 1965: 112; Dark 1969: 1131; Feest 1968: 145; Fenton 1966: 75, 76; McFeat 1967: 91; McLendon 1981: 225; Sturtevant 1973: 42, 43; Viires 1977: 39). The curation process of a collection influences research considerably. The acquisition policy determines what comes to the museum in the first place, and restoration of objects can severely affect their research value. An object's significance, be it its artistic quality, its technological significance, or any other feature, can only be established in comparison with others of the same culture and time period (see also Lurie 1981: 187; Mathews 1981: 170, 172; Sturtevant 1969: 634–6; Sturtevant

1973: 44, 50). The goal of material culture research is to interpret and reconstruct material culture in its cultural context and to integrate the conclusions in the overall state of research (Anderson 1979: 107; Arima 1975: 26; Arima 1978; Barzun and Graff 1977: 124; Clifford 1985: 239, 244; Fenton 1966: 83; Graebner 1911: 7, 49, 55; Hodder 1982a: 219; Hodder 1982b; Leone 1977; Miller 1982; Miller 1983; Miller 1985: 201; Renfrew 1984: 254; Sturtevant 1969: 631). During the course of the four research stages already identified, information will gradually build up and mutually qualify and reinforce itself. Thus, a three-dimensional visual model of the research process would actually look like a helix (similar to the systems theoretical model of the development of science), not like the two-dimensional circle as in fig. 9.1 (see also Oeser 1976: III, 119).

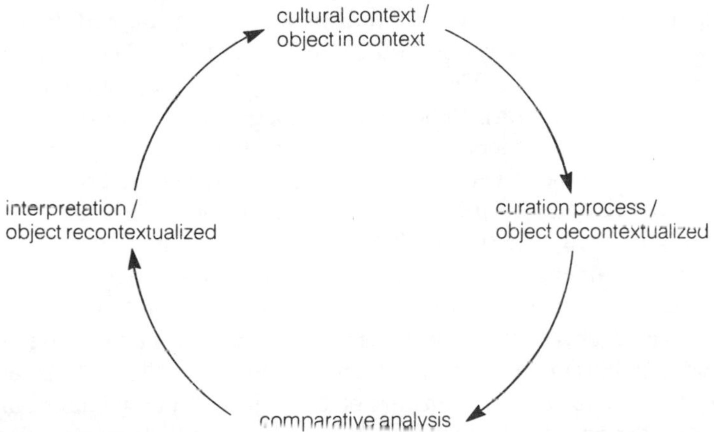

Figure 9.1 Frame for the research process

The curation process of an individual collection or of an individual artefact – acquisition, documentation, preservation measures, storage and exhibition styles – can severely limit its value for scientific research or, on the other hand, can facilitate research considerably (Rothschild and Cantwell 1981: 3). In what follows, these five parts of the curation process will be considered in detail.

The way objects are exhibited conditions research considerably because the exhibition style determines to a certain degree what the museum's acquisition policy is, 'what, from the material world, specific groups and individuals choose to preserve, value, and exchange' (Clifford 1985: 240; see also Anderson 1979: 197). Museum collections generally rather reflect exhibition styles than the complete material culture inventory of a group (see also Pearce 1986a: 134; Rothschild and Cantwell 1981: 4; Sturtevant 1967: 27). Anderson (1979) illustrates (for primitive art objects) how much collections are Western-selected and how little they represent native culture:

The items that have accumulated in ethnographic art museums in Europe and America may or may not reflect native standards of excellence. For example, after extensive fieldwork among the Bangwa, Brain and Pollock (1971) concluded that many of the Bangwa figures in western collections are 'no more distinguished than rough-hewn carvings made by youths to pass away a few minutes'. . . . Although we are better off having western-selected collections than none at all, there is ample evidence that the items we like best are not always the ones they prefer. Native artists themselves may compound the problem by regularly keeping for themselves or their patrons those works they like best, while selling to outsiders those pieces that don't quite measure up to native standards' (Anderson 1979: 197; Brain and Pollock 1971: 60).

Basically two ways to exhibit ethnographic objects dominate: the aesthetic approach and the reconstructive, with its concept of the culture area and Milwaukee style of display (Clifford 1985: 237, 241, 242; Dark 1969: 1130).

Concentrating on the object's artistic quality is by no means an approach limited to art museums alone. As exhibitions of primitive art in fine art museums had tremendous success from the 1920s on, ethnographic museums copied the style in order to remain fashionable and to increase the status of the museum (Clifford 1985: 243; Collier and Tschopik 1954: 776; Dark 1969: 1130, 1133). Primitive art, once exhibited in ethnographic museums as evidence of material culture, is now displayed in both ethnographic and fine art museums for its aesthetic value and 'objects that once went into museums of ethnography as pieces of material culture have become eligible for inclusion in museums of fine art' (Stocking 1985: 6). Art exhibits do not intend to provide information on the object's cultural background but to present the object's aesthetic qualities. The object is decontextualized, its culture of origin unimportant (Feest 1968: 145). The aesthetic approach 'concentrates upon objects claimed to have an intrinsic merit which speaks for itself' (Pearce 1986b: 79). 'Its display in isolation enhances its value. Context is not important. . . . emphasis has been given to the right of the object to stand alone, to be admired for its own sake' (Dark 1969: 1133).

The reconstructive approach presents objects as ethnographically meaningful and strives to inform about a foreign culture. The 'culture area' approach reconstructs the traditional way of life of groups with a similar culture. Traditionally, this style concentrated on the object itself and failed to provide additional information (Dark 1969: 1130; Lurie 1981: 184; Sturtevant 1969: 644; see also Fenton 1974: 21). 'These areally organized exhibits – which we now think of as open storage – were arranged with a maximum of specimens and a minimum of interpretation' (Collier and Tschopik 1954: 772; see also 778, 779). Today, the idea of the culture area is still prominent, but objects are now accompanied by sufficient information. The Milwaukee approach has a similar objective but takes the reconstruction of foreign cultures in its literal sense in transplanting half a village and its environment into the museum (see also Sturtevant 1967: 12): 'The now widely copied "Milwaukee style" features colour, light, sound effects, open dioramas ..., and exhibits the public actually enters – a Melanesian men's house, an igloo, a Japanese garden' (Lurie 1981: 184; see also 182). In a way, historic reconstructions of life-ways long past reflect a romantic, Rousseau-like, attitude towards the foreign and the past on the part of the curators and their audience, and have rightly been criticized not only for their lack of creativity but also for their lack of realism:

> Yet museum exhibits in general ..., instead of stirring the imagination of visitors, tend to perpetuate the visitors' stereotypes of 'savages' and 'quaint primitive' cultures. The anthropology exhibits keep on cultivating the romanticism of the visitor by showing exotic 'tribal' peoples in 'peculiar' attires, amidst prettily staged sentimental settings .... Museum anthropologists continue to be primarily object and tribal rather than subject or concept oriented in their exhibits (Borhegyi 1969).

The culture at 'contact point' with Western civilization is selected arbitrarily as the 'genuine' and 'true' native culture. Thus, the native history before and after is negated. Although reconstruction is certainly most insightful and interesting one should not limit oneself to just this particular task (see also Anderson 1979: 186).

These two basic types of recent exhibition styles, aesthetic and reconstructive (although this is not meant to be an exhaustive coverage) have influenced collection policies in the past and continue to do so. Objects that are 'worth' exhibition, and that are prominent in the storage area as well, either conform to the art historical approach – that is, they are works of primitive art (see also Cole 1982: 441) – or to the reconstructive approach – that is, they are old and 'uncontaminated' by culture change (Cole 1982: 441; Collier and Tschopik. 1954: 776; McLendon 1981: 217); new pieces are only acceptable if 'genuine' (Cole 1982: 441; Sturtevant 1967: 28; see also Collier and Tschopik 1954: 775; McLendon 1981: 217). However, exhibition styles that feature the contemporary state and recent history of indigenous people, and include economic aspects and human rights, are not prominent at all. Similarly, contemporary, 'acculturated', pieces are collected only seldom (see also McLendon 1981: 217). Generally, the kind of artefacts that tend to be over-represented in collections are those that have aesthetic qualities, are exotic, old, primitive and rare, while others, like fragile and less attractive pieces, tend to be under-represented. Some types tend to be omitted altogether for reasons of preservation or size, or because they are too plain (digging stick), impermanent (sand drawings), or just 'too' contemporary (Lurie 1981: 182, 185, 187; McFeat 1967: 93; McLendon 1981: 217; Pearce 1986a: 134; Stocking 1985: 12; Sturtevant 1967: 26, 27, 37–9; Sturtevant 1973: 40).

The research potential of ethnographic specimens is determined to a high degree by the quality of documentation. However, the state of documentation of most objects can only be described as just short of devastating (see also Anderson 1979: 107; Bühler 1947: 229; Feest 1968: 145; Fenton 1966: 77; Fenton 1974: 27; Kintigh 1981: 485; Lurie 1981: 186; Mathews 1981: 171; McFeat 1967: 91; Pearce 1986c: 198; Sturtevant 1967; Sturtevant 1973: 44, 45, 47; Winters 1981: 17). Documentation is so sparse and so unreliable, in fact, that research restricted to this supporting data alone would hardly be possible. This is particularly true for artefacts that were bought on the primitive art market, or came to the museum through a series of intermediaries and were collected by an amateur in the first place, but it also holds true sometimes for those collected during an organized, purposeful expedition administered by professional anthropologists and even leaders in the field (Fenton 1966: 75; Lurie 1981: 186; Sturtevant 1967: 1; see also Cole 1982: 439; Collier and Tschopik 1954: 770, 771; Dark 1969; Fenton 1974: 16). Many collectors did not bother to bring home information on the objects they acquired that went beyond the minimum of 'culture, function, and constituent materials' (see also Sturtevant 1973: 45). But even when they did, it sometimes happened that it was lost on its way to the museum. The important North American professional collector Nicholson obtained information on the specimens she bought that was comparable in quality and quantity to that of her anthropological colleagues. The information, however, did not always find its way to the museum: 'In the process the information that Nicholson had about an object . . . and she went to considerable lengths to obtain sociological background for the objects she acquired . . . often seems to have failed to accompany the object to the museum' (McLendon 1981: 214, 217).

Bills, field catalogues, notes, old tabulations, original collector's lists, reference to collection method, and other valuable documentation should be kept in the archive of the museum (Kintigh 1981: 485, 486; see also Sturtevant 1967: 36; Sturtevant 1973: 45). The problem with documentation is not only that it is sparse, but also that it is usually anonymous (Sturtevant 1973: 44, 45). Often, it is not clear what is genuine information provided by the collector and what is information added later on. Most objects are documented only in so far as their culture of origin, their function, and the year of acquisition are noted (see also Sturtevant 1973: 45). Further information in the catalogue is often added later on and needs verification (Feest 1968: 145; Sturtevant 1973: 44, 45). The less direct such documentation is, the lower its degree of reliability. 'Feest's Law of Museum Documentation holds: The uncertainty of an attribution increases with the square of the distance from the collector's statements' (Sturtevant 1973: 45; Feest 1968: 145, translated by Sturtevant 1973: 45; see also Barzun and Graff 1977: 128; Fenton 1974: 19; Graebner 1911: 33). The degree of documentation of very old collections, housed in particular in European museums, tends to be even more limited and even less reliable (see also Feest 1968: 145). 'Museums of Europe are full of what I call "Ethnological Chippendale": the specimens are what someone says they are' (Fenton 1974: 31). But it is not only European museums that, due to the age of their collections, own a legacy of more or less undocumented artefacts. North American museums have them as well, and some of these undocumented artefacts were even collected quite recently:

> This pottery, I was assured by the directors and curators, was very old, from the 17th and 18th centuries. However, there was no documentation of any kind in the catalogue, beyond the name and number of the piece. When I inquired about these pieces later, among the potters in the barrios where they are traditionally made, the potters were very amused. The elder potters remembered that the wife of a former director had come down to the barrios and purchased all pottery in the 1930s' (Kaplan 1981: 316).

Although only a few contemporary artefacts are collected (Dark 1969: 1131; Sturtevant 1969: 632, 633), one would expect that at least documentation of these newly acquired pieces would live up to scientific standards. This, however, is not the case (see also Sturtevant 1969: 632, 633). Although the opportunity is there to improve the documentation of new collections (Pearce 1986c: 199), bearing in mind the quite unsatisfactory state of documentation of already existing collections, often newly acquired collections are not documented much more fully (Fenton 1974: 16, 19; Kaplan 1981: 315; Lurie 1981: 186; Sturtevant 1969: 633).

The preservation of museum artefacts consists – in increasing order of alteration of the object – of conservation, cleaning, repair and restoration. Restoring artefacts can have serious effects on their authenticity and 'extensive restoration can create scientific confusion' (Freed 1981: 233). Restoration is when 'missing parts are replaced, either by making a substitute for the missing part or by using an existing piece from an object similar to the one being restored' (Freed 1981: 232). The goal is 'to restore an object as it was when functioning in its culture of origin' (Freed 1981: 232). The problem with reference to research is whether the object is still authentic after restoration or not, because 'the desire to improve an artifact sometimes leads, in effect, to the production of a new artifact' (Freed 1981: 232). When restorers, unaware of the needs and standards of scientific research, get loose, the desire to 'improve' the object can lead to the most grotesque results. Skinkel-Taupin (1977) illustrates this point with the case of a 'genuine' lamp, produced in the nineteenth century in the workshop of a museum:

> The basic element is the reservoir without spouts, handle-reflector, or medallion. The missing medallion was replaced by another representing Leda and the swan, which added a bit of eroticism. A new handle-reflector, which came from a larger lamp, was filed to fit the reservoir. Two clay spouts, molded, in all probability, from an original lamp, were carefully made to supply the last missing parts. Finally, the pieces were joined by

> plaster and, to conceal the joints of the diverse elements, the composition was unified by a thick layer of paint. The artifact became one of the fine pieces of the collection and was described as 'found, in 1874, on Mount Esquilin' (Skinkel-Taupin 1977: 90).

Others produce completely new artefacts or parts of artefacts altogether. The pipe bowl of a famous Blackfoot pipe, collected by Wissler in 1904, turned out to be an imitation when the exhibit where it had been on display for dozens of years was dismantled:

> The Thunder Pipe of the Blackfoot Indians ... was one of the most renowned objects on display in the old Hall of the Plains Indians at the American Museum of Natural History. ... The pipe, consisting of a decorated stem and a pipe bowl, was illustrated and described by Clark Wissler ..., the great early expert on the Blackfoot. ... Collected in the field by Wissler in 1904 and cited by Lowie in his scholarly work, the Thunder Pipe appeared to be unquestionably genuine and certainly important. ... Carefully examining the bowl, however, I observed a small chipped area which revealed the bowl as white beneath its dark surface. Apparently it was made of plaster of paris that had been painted. Some 20 years later, I can still recall my shock at the realization that the bowl of this famed Thunder Pipe was not genuine' (Freed 1981: 229).

These new 'artefacts' are, if their restoration is undocumented, 'research pitfalls' that fool even the expert (Freed 1981). As 'the kind of research pitfall represented by the Thunder Pipe is rather more common in museum collections than one might suspect' (Freed 1981: 231), the restoration of an object should not impair its authenticity for scientific research. Restoration should therefore be done in a way that shows the alterations clearly, for example, by using material of a different colour (see also Freed 1981). Also, restoration should be recorded and documented by photographs before it is done and after (Freed 1981: 243). In publications, 'restored artifacts should always be so identified' (Freed 1981: 242), and drawings or photos should show the restored areas. 'It would also be advisable to use broken lines or some other convention in the drawings of restored specimens to distinguish original from restored areas' (Freed 1981: 242).

It should be the policy of every museum to keep its collections together since the research value of the remaining pieces, as well as the research value of the objects that leave the museum, is affected by de-accessioning (Kintigh 1981: 486). Once a museum has accepted a collection it should guarantee its integrity and also maintain the museum records so that individual collections can be clearly identified (see also Salwen 1981: 567).

One of the most basic functions of a museum is to store its specimens properly – humidity control for the storage area, a dry room for metals, a safe for valuables – in such a way that minimal deterioration is allowed and the sometimes limited life of objects is extended as much as possible (see also Fenton 1974: 30; Handler 1985: 193). Research is hampered by a legacy of chaotic conditions in the storage area (Winters 1981: 17). Inevitably, some objects cannot be found any more, others are not registered:

> There are inevitably objects referred to in the literature and listed in the catalogue which cannot be found. There are also objects that are found in storage which are not in the catalogue' (Mathews 1981: 170).

> Usually some 10 to 20 percent of the specimens a visitor selects for study from the catalogue descriptions cannot be located (and in a recent visit to a national museum of anthropology in Europe, 83 percent of the specimens I identified in the working catalogue could not be found) . . . . The usual state of the storage and the catalogues and other records has to be seen to be believed' (Sturtevant 1969: 635).

The situation in most museums, however, has improved considerably since 1969 when Sturtevant concluded that 'storage area' is just another transcription for chaos.

We must now turn to the broader issue of museum collections and research. Sturtevant concluded in 1969 that anthropological collections 'seemingly have very little importance for current anthropological research' (Sturtevant 1969: 625). Although research work in museums has since then been greatly facilitated by improved storage and computerized data bases (some museums now supply print-outs of their holdings of, for example, a particular artefact type), Sturtevant's statement nevertheless still holds true. Museum studies are still peripheral to general anthropological research. The immediate reasons given for this are lack of time on the part of the curators, short staffing, and the limited budgets of the museums (Rothschild and Cantwell 1981: 2; Sturtevant 1969: 632, 633; see also Sturtevant 1973: 49). It is also true that basic museum work carries little prestige. The state of documentation and storage of collections is certainly of lesser importance for the professional standing of curators than is research generally (see also Feest 1968: 145). Museum catalogue entries, for example, were usually anonymous, and often still are (Feest 1968: 145; Fenton 1974: 19; Sturtevant 1973: 44, 45). However, it would be inconceivable to publish most research anonymously. Furthermore, research with collections is seemingly of limited significance for the professional standing of anthropologists (Sturtevant 1967: 636). Not even all curators study their own collections seriously: 'it is sad but true that even the great majority of museum ethnologists who are actively engaged in research do not study the collections under their care' (Sturtevant 1973: 41).

The reasons given, lack of money and time, and only limited scientific prestige, however, only reflect but do not account for the relative unimportance of museum studies. I believe that ethnographic objects are, primarily, not perceived as scientific evidence but are collected above all for their display value, and for their artistic quality. They are used for display or as illustration in publications, but they are not seen as evidence for scholarly research. Therefore, documentation is poor because it is regarded as less important. Also, information on museum pieces is, in fact, as often found outside the museum as inside (see also Graebner 1911: 38; Kintigh 1981: 485; McLendon 1981: 214, 217). The relative unimportance of museum studies in contemporary anthropology is also partly a legacy of the diffusionistic and evolutionistic 'misuse' of the object (Arima 1975: 25; Silver 1979: 270).

Archaeological objects, on the other hand, provide a sharp contrast. They are relatively well documented throughout. 'In recent years well over 90 percent of the archeological specimens added to the U. S. National Museum collections have come from excavations by professional archeologists.' (Sturtevant 1969: 629). Ethnographic objects, however, are less well documented: 'Yet over the last four years, nearly two-thirds of the specimens added to the ethnological collections in the U. S. National Museum were not collected by ethnologists, but were collected under non-scientific conditions by untrained people and hence lack essential documentation as to provenance, age, function, and so forth' (Sturtevant 1969: 633). Furthermore, museum studies of older archaeological collections, although not really popular, are nevertheless seen as being as useful and as valid as field work (Sturtevant 1969: 629). On the other hand, museum studies of ethnographic objects are clearly seen as inferior to field work. Also, many archaeological specimens in museums have been adequately studied, but only a minor percentage of ethnographic specimens has received scholarly attention: 'Yet I suppose at least 90 percent of museum ethnological specimens have never been studied' (Sturtevant 1969: 632; see also Fenton 1974: 21).

Quite apart from the difference between archaeological and ethnographic objects, it seems to me that objects are generally associated with a lesser degree of significance for scholarly research than written sources (see also Feest 1968: 145; Washburn 1964: 249–50). Some major museums, for example, have transferred their holdings to warehouses far from the museum and thus separated curator and documentation from the collections, clearly indicating the lesser significance of material culture: 'But if the specimens were really significant for research, it would be as inconceivable ... to separate them from the associated scientific staff ... as it is for research libraries to locate them several miles away from the researchers' (Sturtevant 1969: 633).

Although material culture has received renewed interest lately (in the shape of ethno-archaeology, historical archaeology, and museum studies programmes; see also Pearce 1986c: 198; Welsh 1981: 325), studies in museum collections have not succeeded in profiting from this development because museum research on older collections is very limited in its conclusions by a legacy of insufficient documentation (Sturtevant 1967: 29): 'The vindication of interest in material culture is gratifying, but our collections might not be equal to the questions posed' (Lurie 1981: 186). A sound basis for research in museum collections has yet to be developed. I believe that, if such studies are to go beyond their current peripheral role in anthropology, they have to learn from the 'growth trades', ethno-archaeology and historical archaeology (Deetz 1977; Eighmy 1981; Glassie 1975; Gould 1981; Hodder 1982a; Hodder 1982b; Leone 1977; Miller 1985; Rathje 1978; South 1977; see also Kaplan 1981; 315; Mannion 1979; Welsh 1981: 325). Museum studies in ethnology have also to make up for the lead in method and theory achieved by their colleagues (Pearce 1986c: 198) and ethnologists interested in museum collections should not watch inactively as ethno-archaeologists and historical archaeologists cut the ground from under their feet in terms of quality and quantity of research. To be sure, some questions can only be answered by research on old collections (Kintigh 1981: 485), but simply to collect items, and to do research on already existing collections using ethnohistoric sources, is not enough. In order to improve the quality of museum research, objects, their production, use and disposal in social life should be studied thoroughly in the field, and intensive research should precede and not follow acquisition (Kaplan 1981: 315; Welsh 1981: 325).

Acknowledgments

I am very grateful for the advice of Dr Alfred Janata, and particularly indebted to Dr Susan M. Pearce for editing this article. Both, however, have no responsibility for whatever error may be found.

Bibliography

Anderson, R., 1979. *Art in Primitive Societies.*

Arima, E., Y., 1975. *A Contextual Study of the Caribou Eskimo Kayak.* National Museums of Canada, Mercury Series, 25.

Arima, E., Y., 1978. 'Context–conscious study of material culture in anthropology', in Jimmerly, D. W. (ed.), *Contextual Studies in Material Culture*: 1–6, National Museums of Canada, Mercury Series, 43.

Barzun, J. and Graff, H. F., 1977. *The Modern Researcher.*

Borhegyi, S., 1969. 'A new role for anthropology in natural history museums', in Robbins, M. (ed.), *American Association of Museums Annual Meeting, Section Papers 1968*: 45–50.

Brain, R. and Pollock, A., 1971. *Bangwa Funerary Sculpture.*

Bühler, A., 1947. 'Ueber die Verwertbarkeit völkerkundlicher Sammlungern für kulturhistorische Forschungen', *Schweizerisches Archiv für Volkskunde, 44.* 4: 225–44.

Cantwell, A–M., Griffin J. and Rothschild, N. (eds), 1981. *The Research Potential of Anthropological Museum Collections.*

Clifford, J., 1985. 'Objects and selves: An Afterword', in Stocking, G. (ed.), *Objects and Others: Essays on Museums and Material Culture*: 236–46.

Cole, D., 1982. 'Tricks of the trade: Northwest Coast artifact collecting 1875–1925', *Canadian Historical Review, 63*. 4: 439–60.

Collier, D. and Fenton, W. F., 1965. 'Problems of ethnological research in North American museums', *Man, 65*: 111–12.

Collier, D. and Tschopik, H., 1954. 'The role of museums in American anthropology', *American Anthropologist, 56*: 768–79.

Dark, P., 1969. 'Anthropology and museums: only art?', *American Anthropologist, 71*: 1130–3.

Deetz, J., 1977. *In Small Things Forgotten: The Archaeology of Early American Life.*

Eighmy, J., 1981. 'The use of material culture in diachronic anthropology', in Gould, R. and Schiffer, M. (eds), *Modern Material Culture: The Archaeology of Us*: 31–49.

Feest, C., 1968. 'Buchbesprechung von: Benndorf, Helga, und Speyer, Arthur: Indianer Nordamerikas 1760–1860', *Archiv für Völkerkunde, 22*: 144–7.

Fenton, W., 1966. 'Fieldwork, museum studies, and ethnohistorical research', *Ethnohistory, 13*: 71–84.

Fenton, W., 1974. 'The advancement of material culture studies in modern anthropological research', in Richardson, M. (ed.), *The Human Mirror*: 15–36.

Ford, C., 1961. 'A sample comparative analysis of material culture', in Moore, F. (ed) *Readings in Cross-cultural Methodology*: 243–64.

Freed, S., 1981. 'Research pitfalls as a result of the restoration of museum specimens', in Cantwell, Griffin and Rothschild 1981: 229–45.

Glassie, H., 1975. *Folk Housing in Middle Virginia: A Structural analysis of Historical Artifacts.*

Gould, R., 1981. 'Early and late Americana', in Gould, R. and Schiffer M. (eds), *Modern Material Culture: the Archaeology of Us*: 57–65.

Graebner, F., 1911. *Methode der Ethnologie.*

Handler, R., 1985. 'On having a culture', in Stocking, G. (ed.), *Objects and Others: Essays on Museums and Material Culture*: 192–217.

Hirschberg, W., Janata, A., Feest, C. and Bauer, W., 1966. *Technologie und Ergologie in der Völkerkunde.*

Hodder, I., 1982a. *Symbols in Action.*

Hodder, I. (ed.), 1982b. *Symbolic and Structural Archaeology.*

Kaplan, F., 1981. 'The "meaning" of pottery', in Cantwell, Griffin and Rothschild 1981: 315–23.

Kintigh, K., 1981. 'An outline for a chronology of Zuni ruins, revisited', in Cantwell, Griffin and Rothschild 1981: 467–87.

Leone, M., 1977. 'The new Mormon temple in Washington, D.C.', in Ferguson, L. (ed.), *Historical Archaeology and the Importance of Material Things*: 43–56.

Lurie, N., 1981. 'Museumland revisited', *Human Organization, 40. 2*: 180–7.

McFeat, T., 1967. 'The object of research in museums', *Bulletin of the National Museum of Canada, 204*: 91–9.

McLendon, S., 1981. 'Preparing museum collections for use as primary data in ethnographic research', in Cantwell, Griffin and Rothschild 1981: 201–27.

Mannion, J., 1979. 'Multidisciplinary dimensions in material history', *Material History Bulletin, 8*: 21–6.

Mathews, Z., 1981. 'Art historical photodocumentation of Iroquoian effigy pipes', in Cantwell, Griffin and Rothschild 1981: 161–76.

Miller, D., 1982. 'Explanation and social theory in archaeological practice', in Refrew, C., Rowland, M. and Seagraves, B. (eds), *Theory and Explanation in Archaeology*: 83–95.

Miller, D., 1983. 'Introduction', *Royal Anthropological Institute News, 59*: 5–7.

Miller, D., 1985. *Artifacts as Categories.*

Murdock, P., 1967. *Outline of Cultural Materials.*

Oeser, E., 1976. *Wissenschaft und Information.*

Pearce, S., 1986a. 'Objects as signs and symbols', *Museums Journal, 86. 3*: 131–5.

Pearce, S., 1986b. 'Objects, high and low', *Museums Journal, 86. 2*: 79–82.

Pearce, S., 1986c. 'Thinking about things: approaches to the study of artefacts', *Museums Journal, 85.4*: 198–201.

Rathje, W., 1978. 'Archaeological ethnography', in Gould, R. (ed), *Explanations in Ethnoarchaeology*: 49–76.

Renfrew, C., 1984. *Approaches to Social Archaeology.*

Rothschild, N. and Cantwell, A–M., 1981. 'The research potential of anthropological museum collections', in Cantwell, Griffin and Rothschild 1981: 1–6.

Salwen, B., 1981. 'Collecting now for future research', in Cantwell, Griffin and Rothschild 1981: 567–73.

Silver, H., 1979. 'Ethnoart', *Annual Review of Anthropology, 8*: 267–307.

Skinkel-Taupin, C., 1977. 'Notes sur la restauration des lampes antiques au XIXe siecle', *Bulletin des Musées Royaux d'Art et d'Histoire, 49*: 89–101.

South, S., 1977. *Method and Theory in Historical Archaeology.*

Stocking, G., 1985. 'Essays on museums and material culture', in Stocking, G. (ed.), *Objects and Others; Essays on Museums and Material Culture*: 3–14.

Sturtevant, W., 1967. *Guide to Field Collecting of Ethnographic Specimens.*

Sturtevant, W., 1969. 'Does anthropology need museums?', *Procs. Biological Society of Washington, 82*: 619–49.

Sturtevant, W., 1973. 'Museums as anthropological data banks', in Redfield, A. (ed.), *Anthropology Beyond the University*: 40–55.

Thomas, D., 1981. 'Ethics and the contemporary museum of anthropology', in Cantwell, Griffin and Rothschild 1987: 575–8.

Viires, A., 1977. 'On the methods of studying the material culture of European peoples', *Ethnologia Europaea, 9*: 35–42.

Washburn, W., 1964. 'Manuscripts and manufacts', *American Archivist, 27*: 245–50.

Welsh, P., 1981. 'An activity system approach to material culture study', in Cantwell, Griffin and Rothschild 1981: 325–35.

Winters, H., 1981. 'Excavating in museums: notes on Mississippian hoes and Middle Woodland copper gouges and Celts', in Cantwell, Griffin and Rothschild 1981: 17–34.

10 *Museums of anthropology as centres of information*

BARRIE REYNOLDS

Museums of anthropology occupy a special place among the museums of the world. Having their origins in the early fascination of the West with the exotic cultures of other societies, they have become, for the general public, centres of information on those cultures, some of which, of course, no longer exist, while almost all have changed dramatically as a result of Western industrial influences.

Anthropology museums have a direct responsibility, not only to their visitor audiences which are drawn primarily from their own society, but also to the people whose cultural material they display. This respect for other living societies is a unique feature of museums of anthropology and places a special responsibility on the curator. In this paper I propose to examine how museums of anthropology handle their responsibilities as centres of information: responsibilities to these other societies which they seek to describe and for which so much of the material heritage is held in trust in foreign museums; to the collections, for which they have a professional responsibility, notably in their documentation and access; and to the discipline of anthropology which provides the scholarly basis for the existence of such museums.

Fenton (1974: 29) has estimated, I suspect conservatively, that the total anthropological holdings of museums throughout the world comprise some 4.5 million artefacts. Of these it would be reasonable to surmise that less than 50 per cent is used for exhibitions, educational, research or other purposes; the rest remains permanently in reserve storage. Again, it is generally recognized that for over 80 per cent and perhaps as high as 90 per cent of anthropological artefacts in museums, documentation is minimal and inadequate by contemporary professionally acceptable standards. For most the record is all too often a bald entry in a register, for example:

Spear, Yoruba, Nigeria, donated by John Smith, 8 July 1932.

Even these data, notably culture and region, can be suspect, relying as they do on the memory and assumptions of the collector. Errors in curatorial recording can compound the problem.

As centres of information, the distinctive resource of museums is their collections of what have been termed *artefactual documents*. Museums of anthropology are concerned primarily with the material aspects of cultures but are expected, particularly by the general public, to provide information on other aspects as well. In exhibitions, artefacts are used to convey this information (on belief systems, social behaviour, history and so on). The accuracy and completeness of the documentation of artefacts are therefore especially important. These standards are not always met. A common fault, arising usually from reliance on material gathered early in the century, is to imply 'This is how people live today'. Others, arising from a lack of direct curatorial field experience with the peoples concerned, are the display of secret-sacred objects and the unwitting use of pejorative terms, both of which can be highly offensive to some peoples, as well as inaccuracies in displays or accompanying texts. I have observed examples of all these in major museums in different countries during the 1980s, though, over the past two decades, there have been considerable efforts to improve exhibition standards generally in this area.

Such standards are clearly the responsibility of the curators. But if curators are to be effective they must possess, in addition to museum management skills, a solid grounding in material anthropology and also direct field experience. This is not always the case. Historical factors earlier in this century led in many countries to the separation of university departments of anthropology from their museum counterparts and to a strong shift in teaching away from material studies to social anthropology. As a result, all too few graduates were available to take up curatorial careers. This shortage, continued over decades, led to the recruitment of curators lacking post-graduate training and field experience, even basic material anthropology. Recruits were drawn from archaeology and social anthropology and even from disciplines outside the social sciences. Some of these appointments were outstandingly successful. For the most part, however, the result was the stultification of anthropological research in museums and a decline in standards. This in turn had serious effects on the quality of information provided by museums in their exhibitions and elsewhere.

Field experience is of critical importance. If curators are to communicate information about other cultures and to undertake informed research on them, they must have direct field experience. If they are to develop a general appreciation of the special concerns of societies other than their own, then exposure to another culture or cultures is vital. Unfortunately, museums, with certain notable exceptions, have given too little encouragement to systematic field work, while expecting their curators to be expert on a wide range of cultures represented in their collections. One still encounters curators who have never undertaken systematic anthropological field research. By contrast, who would take seriously an archaeology curator who had never been on a dig, a biology curator who had never observed fauna in the field?

Early in this century, the subsequently distinguished anthropologist, A. L. Kroeber, was dismissed from the California Academy of Sciences for 'excessive' fieldwork, this not being seen as part of his normal duties. There have since been many other examples of the drift of museum anthropologists to the less restrictive and more dynamic university scene. It is essential that museums accept that their anthropology staff need the time for extended fieldwork in order to maintain and advance their professional standing. At the same time, there needs to be a much closer association with university departments of anthropology. This could only be to mutual advantage, providing universities with access to rich teaching and research resources, notably on the material aspects of cultures, as well as career opportunities for their graduates. In return, museums would enjoy the stimulus of fresh ideas from mainstream anthropology and the specialist support essential to the researching of its collections and exhibitions.

As one result of this closer association, one could expect significant changes to museum exhibitions, making them more relevant to anthropology. One of the strengths of our major international museums lies in the richness of their collections from many cultural regions. This lends itself admirably to comparative exhibitions and publications. Few museums, however, adopt this, prefering the ethnographic or descriptive approach. Each exhibition usually focuses on one culture or cultural group, requiring visitors themselves to make any broader comparisons between exhibitions in separate galleries – an approach which is reflected in museum publications. Again, the opportunity is there for museums to illustrate basic general principles of the discipline of anthropology and to consider humankind on a global rather than a tribal basis, just as in biology one sees displays on food chains, ecological impact and so on. This change in approach would be invaluable to mainstream anthropology, by presenting its theoretical ideas to the public and helping to reinforce for students its teaching. The important role of informing people about particular cultures could still continue but would be integrated into this approach. The advantage would be to place such cultures in a better world perspective. To achieve all this, however, requires museums of anthropology to rethink their role. This would appear to be an exercise long overdue.

While collections form the distinctive resource for museums, they present for musems of anthropology what I see as the greatest challenge facing material anthropology today (Reynolds 1984). Looking back through the twentieth century one can see stages in the evolution of professionalism in museums. The mid-century emergence of specialized schools programmes, the dramatic improvement in exhibition presentation and, more recently, the international acceptance of the importance of conservation stand out. Expressed slightly differently, we have seen improvements in methods of *communication* of artefactual information, in methods of *preservation* of the physical form of artefactual documents. Most recently, attention has turned, perhaps belatedly, to documentation, to the information an artefact and its related records can provide. The problem may be seen as threefold: the completeness of associated documentation or cataloguing, access to documentation and to collections both from within the museum and outside and, finally, increasing the information on ill-documented artefacts.

Early in this paper I mentioned that 80 to 90 per cent of anthropology artefacts in museums are inadequately documented. This is partly due to the lack of information provided at their acquisition, for example from private collections. Partly it is also due to the absence, in so many museums, of systematic, thorough catalogues. Objects are registered – and stored away.

In a 1981 paper on 'Ethnology collections and their management in Australian museums', I sought to quantify the average workload involved in registering and cataloguing an artefact and to calculate the size of collection that would constitute a manageable workload. For the purposes of the calculation I assumed that 30 per cent of a curator's time, averaged over a five-year period, would be available for such collections management. My conclusion was that a new curator, supported by one technician, could complete the documentation of up to 5,000 artefacts within three years and could then build up to a maximum responsibility for 8,000 to 10,000. The underlying assumption was that the curator was familiar with the field concerned, in other words was not required to undertake reference research in totally unfamiliar fields or cultural regions.

In Australia at that time (fortunately things have improved in some museums), the average responsibility of artefacts per curator in nine major museums was 15,579:1, though four of those exceeded 20,000:1 and one was 27,250:1. The picture was not totally accurate, for the majority of curators were in fact archaeologists, with added responsibility for their anthropology collections. The management of these collections was often delegated in practice to juniors. I am sure that similar workloads are to be found in other countries. The result has all too often been a virtual failure to develop systematic catalogue records of anthropological value. The daunting prospect of the mass of material, often formerly in poor storage conditions, combined with the lack of proper training for anthropology curators, is enough to deter all but the most determined young curator, as I know from my own early experiences.

Curators in a museum are usually appointed on the basis of representing a discipline, rarely of actual workload, though they may be given assistants. I would suggest that there is a strong case for developing effective records of the time it takes to process an artefact and for deliberately limiting the workload – in terms both of the region for which a curator is expected to have expertise and of total numbers of artefacts. At the same time the extent of information sought in cataloguing must be carefully limited and each entry requirement challenged to determine whether it is relevant or merely a waste of cataloguing time.

Access to artefacts and to documentation is an area where there have been some encouraging developments in recent years, though within institutions there are still problems. Retrieval procedures are often slow, access areas are rarely designed efficiently and too much staff time may have to be diverted to helping the visiting researcher. Very few systems are able to cope regularly with 10 or 20 research visitors per day (paradoxically an argument perhaps for not encouraging increased collections-based research). Again, location records can be inadequate. Sturtevant (1969: 635) recorded a retrieval failure rate of 83 per cent in one European museum. My own (1981) in Australia ranged from 0 to 40 per cent. There is, of course, improvement as collections are rehoused and as support staff in increasing numbers are trained in collections management.

Major developments in the past decade have been in the form of national and regional inventories. Notable are those for Oceanian material in Australian, British, New Zealand and North American museums (Bolton 1980; Bolton and Specht 1984; Gathercole and Clarke 1979; Neich 1982; Kaeppler and Stillman 1985). These are excellent examples of what can be achieved by museums working in concert with UNESCO and ICOM. It is to be hoped that this will be extended to other cultural regions. The British inventory by Schumann (1986) and the recent surveys undertaken by Meehan (1986) and Cooper respectively, of Aboriginal collections within Australia and overseas, are also encouraging. I am sure that parallel activities are occurring in other countries.

All this survey activity is worth while. It increases curatorial awareness of the importance of their responsibilities to their collections and is a major step towards computerization on a world basis. We must, however, recognize the limitations. An inventory can be no more complete, no more accurate than the records upon which it is based. It is again a research tool, no more; it is not a substitute for material research itself. Despite these caveats these developments are most welcome.

The computerization of museum records is again of great importance, as we all recognize, and must lead to reductions in record management error, to better access and in due course to data retrieval on national and international levels. From my own university library in Australia, I have direct access to overseas, on-line, bibliographic information retrieval systems. It should not be too long before access to museum collections records will be similarly possible. But computerized records have the same limitation as do published inventories; they are dependent on the quality of the original catalogue text. The answer, for museum anthropology, must lie in joint entries of text and illustration, combined with the search facility to scan and sort, not only on the basis of words in text but also on the basis of significant elements within the illustration, just as we all do when we look at objects themselves. This, after all, is what we recognize as essential for our in-house museum catalogue entries. Such a system would enable both artefactual and photographic collections to be amalgamated in the one catalogue. With such a development the saving on painstaking curatorial cataloguing input would also be immense. How much more useful would be the sorting of material based directly on illustrations rather than on text descriptions, themselves subject to human error? With the recent rapid advancement of computer graphics and of laser technology, this facility no doubt already exists in experimental programmes for select features. It is probably but a question of developing software appropriate to museum needs.

Access is a problem that we can confidently expect to disappear in future years. But what of the quality of the information locked up inside or accompanying the artefact? This is, after all, what our efforts as curators and researchers are all about. We can see how accuracy can be improved by reducing the possibility of human error in collections and records management. We can also see how with better academic preparation of anthropology curators the quality of primary data, as well as research generally, can be improved. But we are still left with the problem of existing collections that are inadequately documented. This, as I mentioned earlier, is in my view the greatest challenge facing material anthropology today. Artefacts in themselves can be valuable sources of information. Obviously, accompanying documentation can add considerably to the range and depth of this information. Where there is no or negligible documentation, however, it is necessary to concentrate on the object itself and what it can tell us. There are essentially seven questions that need to be answered:

What is the artefact? (not always simple to answer)
What is it made of?
When was it made?
Where was it made and used (culturally and geographically)?
How was it made?
What was it used for?
What can it tell us about the people and their culture?

Researchers, of course, need to ask many other, more refined, questions of an artefact. At the curatorial level, however, these are the critical questions on which researchers can develop their own specialized searches. It is essential, therefore, that the answers are accurate and informed.

All curators have in their collections doubtful material outside their personal range of expertise and all make use of knowledgeable visitors to add to or correct the information on their records. There is the need, however, for a more systematic usage of this expertise between institutions, be they museums or universities. This is where inventories make a valuable contribution by informing specialists of the existence of particular collections. Computerized access between distant institutions, based on visual images of the artefact, would again seem to be the real answer if we are to improve our records dramatically without a huge input of manpower and considerable funding for travel and other costs. Specialists, I believe, would welcome the idea, for, with limited personal cost and effort they would gain access on a national perhaps international front, to all material, both artefactual and photographic, relevant to their specialty. Even before computer graphics enabled us to reach this state of anthropological bliss, the value of developing a more formalized method of specialist consultation between museums would seem evident. The benefits, both to museums and to the specialist advisors, would be mutual and clear, and the whole would represent a logical extension of the Oceania and other inventory projects.

With the rapid loss of traditional knowledge and skills in so many societies, it becomes increasingly difficult to obtain adequate field-based information for the cataloguing of old collections. There is, therefore, an increasing need to develop simple laboratory techniques to draw information from the artefacts themselves. These need to be non-destructive of the artefact or a significant part of it. As far as possible, they should be applicable within the curatorial laboratory. At a minimum, the skills required for the preparation of the samples should be present. Ordinary microscopy, scanning electron microscopy, X-ray, infra-red and ultra-violet photography, chromatography and many other skills common in other disciplines, notably archaeology and art history, are now being successfully applied to anthropological material. In future decades, we can expect to see a considerable expansion in this field.

We may say, in conclusion, that museums of anthropology were for too long the Cinderellas both of the museum world and of anthropology. In the past two decades, however, there have been exciting changes. Museums have begun to appreciate the need to improve documentation systems. There is a resurgence of interest in material anthropology. Non-western peoples are increasingly active in research on their own heritage and accordingly critical of information provided in museums. All this can only be of benefit and it is pleasing to observe the improvements that have resulted. At the same time, the tasks, particularly in the area of large and ill-documented collections, are considerable. To tackle these successfully and to cope with the increased demands that will be made in the future, a serious rethinking of the role of the museum of anthropology is required. Major innovative changes will need to be made to the ways collections documentation is managed and information is supplied. With the help of new technology, the results could be startling in their effectiveness and bring a new meaning to museums of anthropology as centres of information.

BIBLIOGRAPHY

American Anthropological Association, annually. *Guide to Departments of Anthropology*.

Bolton, L., 1980. *Oceanic Cultural Property in Australia.*

Bolton, L. and Specht, J., 1984. *Polynesian and Micronesian Artefacts in Australia. Vol. II: New Zealand and Eastern Polynesia.*

Fenton, W., 1974. 'The advancement of material culture studies in modern anthropological research', in Richardson, M. (ed.), *The Human Mirror: Material and Spatial Images of Man*: 15–36.

Gathercole, P. and Clarke, A., 1979. *Survey of Oceanian Collections in Museums in the United Kingdom and the Irish Republic.*

Hunter, J. E., 1968. *Inventory of Ethnological Collections in Museums of the United States and Canada* (2nd edn).

Kaeppler, A. and Stillman, A., 1985. *Pacific Islands and Australian Artifacts in Public Collections in the United States of America and Canada.*

Meehan, B., 1986. *National Inventory of Aboriginal Artefacts.*

Nason, J., 1987. 'The determination of significance: curatorial research and private collections', in Reynolds, B. and Stott, M. (eds), *Material Anthropology: Contemporary Approaches to Material Culture*: 31–67.

Neich, R., 1982. *Pacific Cultural Material in New Zealand Museums.*

Reynolds, B., 1969. *Directory of Museums of Ethnography in Africa.*

Reynolds, B., 1981. 'Ethnology collections and their management in Australia', *Coma Bulletin, 9*: 8–20.

Reynolds, B., 1984. *Material Culture: A System of Communication.* Margaret Shaw Lecture I, South African Museum, Capetown.

Reynolds, B., forthcoming. 'Artifactual documents: ethnological museum collections as an ethno-historical resource', in Wiedman, D., Williams, G. and Zamora, M. (eds), *Ethnohistory: A Researcher's Guide.*

Schumann, Y. (ed.), 1986. *Museum Ethnographers' Group Survey of Ethnographic Collections in the United Kingdom, Eire and the Channel Islands.*

Sturtevant, W., 1969. 'Does anthropology need museums?' *Procs. Biological Society of Washington, 82*: 6 19–49.

11 *The Collection of Material Objects and their Interpretation*

J. GERAINT JENKINS

In recent years, with the ever-increasing rate of technological change, there is amongst men a deep desire to preserve that which is being replaced. The last half-century or so has witnessed a spectacular growth in the business of preserving the past and there has been a proliferation of heritage centres and museums, of historic buildings open to the public and of preserved industrial sites. All these are supposedly representative of the disappearing heritage of these islands and most represent man's desire to know his roots, which can supply solidity in a world that is in a constant state of flux. In this preoccupation with the past, romance and nostalgia have their parts to play and objects ranging from children's toys to matchboxes and from radio sets to packaging labels – anything reminiscent of an almost forgotten youth – have become eminently collectable. It is questionable, though, whether the artefacts of the mass-consumerism of the twentieth century can be labelled 'material culture'.

> There is such a thing as trying to preserve too much; both man and the products of his endeavour are ephemeral indeed ... Imagine what the world, especially the western world, would look like today if past generations had been as keen on collecting and preserving as we have been during the last twenty years. Perhaps one fifth of our countries would by now be covered with museums, historic buildings, villages and towns, industries and historic harbours full of ships. A proportionate number of people would be busily occupied in administering and preserving the lot ... Considering the mad rush to preserve the past, we should think once in a while of Francis Bacon who said 'Antiquities are history defaced or some such remnants of history which have casually escaped the shipwreck of time' (Jannasch 1981: 189).

The preservation and conservation of historically important buildings, sites and artefacts is, of course, vital, but has the conservation movement gone too far? Are we attempting to preserve too much without giving much thought to the lasting value of the things preserved? Will future generations thank us for handing down to them so many historic artefacts? It is obvious that many of the material objects on view in the museums of Britain today represent only a very short span in the history of man, but it is necessary to collect material that will provide a balanced picture of man's activities throughout the centuries. As the nineteenth and twentieth centuries fade further into the past, the task of making future generations understand the past will become ever more complex. The dangers of being nothing more than purveyors of nostalgia will be with us for ever.

It is important that some coherence should be brought into our policies for collecting material objects as a matter of urgency. It is difficult now and will be even harder in the future to make the decision over what to enshrine and preserve for posterity and what to let go to the scrapyard. We can not preserve everything, and it would be far better to keep a few carefully selected examples of each category of material in which we are interested and be content with accurate plans, specifications, illustrations and histories of the remainder. The key to a coherent policy for the collection of artefacts by a museum must be selectivity and the almost ruthless discarding of irrelevant material. A meaningful collection of material objects can only be amassed as the result of in-depth research work and a full understanding of the nature of the heritage that is being preserved and presented by those who have intimate knowledge of that heritage. Without that basic research work one can never be sure that the artefacts collected are of relevance in the story that is being presented, for the days of the haphazard, random and unplanned collection of artefacts have long gone and should not be the concern of a serious ethnological institution. There is a vast difference between an enthusiastically collected miscellany of artefacts and a true ethnological collection collected as a result of deep knowledge of a particular subject. It was only as a result of two years of field work and the detailed recording of about 700 four-wheeled farm wagons that it was possible to formulate a policy of what wagons should be preserved at the Museum of English Rural Life at the University of Reading, as truly representative of the traditions of wheelwrighting in rural England. In establishing the Musem of the Welsh Woollen Industry at Dre-fach Felindre in rural West Wales, the work started by carrying out a full-scale survey of the Welsh woollen industry. All the mills in Wales were visited and examples of their products were obtained. An attempt was made to obtain details of the location of the industry in the past and, as a result of a press appeal, conversations with industrialists and with voluntary collectors, it became possible to locate nearly a thousand woollen mills in all parts of Wales. Every mill was recorded in detail and as a result of an intensive programme of research it became possible to decide where a major museum to represent the most important and widespread of Welsh rural industries could be located.

In the same way, some years ago an attempt was made to build up a representative collection of material relating to professional fishing in Welsh waters, especially that concerned with the capture of migratory salmon. The starting point of the collecting campaign was to carry out a detailed survey of methods of traditional fishing skills practised in Wales. Very early on, it was found impossible to limit the survey to Welsh rivers alone, for many methods could not be explained without reference to similar methods of fishing in rivers outside Wales. Take, for example, the use of the so-called 'compass net' used on the River Cleddau in Dyfed and nowhere else in Wales. It is a method of fishing completely alien to Wales, but it was found until recently in the Wye estuary at Chepstow and at Wellhouse Bay in the Severn estuary. Compass netting, it was found after some investigation, was introduced into Pembroke by two Gloucestershire men who came from the Forest of Dean in the early nineteenth century to work at the Landshipping anthracite mine. Two fishing stations on the eastern Cleddau still bear the names of Ormond and Edwards, the two Forest of Dean men who are said to have brought this unique method of salmon capture to a remote Welsh river. With the assistance of the river authorities a complete list of fishermen licensed to fish for salmon in Welsh rivers was obtained and over the course of four seasons in the early 1970s all those licencees – 300 of them – were visited, interviewed, photographed and filmed. Carefully selected and representative examples of the equipment used by contemporary fishermen was obtained for the Welsh Folk Museum collections. Documentary evidence, oral tradition and place-names all had their part to play in the historical interpretation of the fishing industry, and in addition to obtaining a comprehensive collection of artefacts for a national institution, a series of articles and a book (Jenkins 1974) were published. Since only a relatively small proportion of the available information was included in a publication, the museum archive was also greatly enriched with tape recordings and photographs, documents and transcripts.

A collection of material objects should similarly come into existence as the result of research work both at an extensive and intensive level. No museum, however large it may be, can ever hope to record, let alone collect, the vast variety of tools and implements, utensils and furniture, dwellings and workshops that the inventive genius of man has devised over the centuries. However large a museum may be, however plentiful its financial resources, it can nevertheless only accommodate a small proportion of the objects that may be worthy of preservation. It is a museum's duty to reflect the community that it serves and a thorough knowledge and an understanding of the life of that community is a pre-requisite before a programme of collecting is launched. To a great extent, the term 'material culture' is a misnomer, for it is never possible to consider material objects in isolation from the geographical, economic and cultural factors that are of equal importance. In the collection and presentation of material objects in a museum, those artefacts should contribute to a clearer understanding of the community that they represent; collection is not an end in itself, but merely a means of reaching the people to whom those objects had the meaning of everyday things.

As an example, let us take a broad look at the vernacular buildings of rural Wales. Those traditional dwelling-houses owe their design and layout to a complex interaction of geographical, economic and human factors. The nature of the climate, the conditions of local geology and the availability of suitable building material have all had their effect in determining the type of house found in a particular region. In the past, the countryman usually built his home from materials that occurred locally; he often designed his house and built it according to his needs and he considered primarily not architectural beauty of design but the utility of the building. In so doing, the countryman hardly ever followed a particular universal style or fashion that may have been prevalent in other regions at the time. In the Lleyn peninsula for example, much of the surface of the land is covered with coarse boulder clay and there is very little suitable building stone. From time immemorial, the peasant farmers of the region utilized earth, intermixed with straw, hair, cow dung and other materials for the construction of their cottage homes.

Wales is dominated by a high moorland plateau, dissected by deep river valleys that branch out from the central core like the spokes of a wheel. Along the valleys that run eastward many alien influences entered the Principality. Along these valleys, for example, came the English four-wheeled farm wagon, the English short-handled spade and even the English language. Along the valleys, too, came the wooden-framed, black and white vernacular buildings of Herefordshire, Shropshire and Cheshire, in valleys where the oak tree predominates. Just as the valleys of the Severn, Wye and Dee lead into the heart of Wales, so too does the southern coastal plain, the Vale of Glamorgan, act as a route into Wales. Along the southern coastal plain came the blue-coloured farm wagon of exquisite design that bears a close similarity to the wagons of Wiltshire and lowland Gloucestershire. Here too was found a technique of thatching far superior to that found in other parts of Wales. There in a Vale of trim, whitewashed villages one finds a pattern of settlement and style of vernacular building far more closely related to the West of England than to moorland Wales. There are, of course, many other regional and sub-regional types of building, such as the massive houses of Bardsey and St David's Head, with thick walls and small deeply set windows as befitted districts where the force of winter gales blowing in from the open sea could easily destroy more fragile structures. And since much of Wales consists of a vast moorland of scattered homesteads, located on windswept, rain-soaked uplands, it was important to have access to cattle and other farm animals at all times: for this reason, the long-house that accommodated man and beast under the same roof became commonplace.

It is obvious that in the intepretation of vernacular buildings, or indeed any other man-made feature in the environment, no feature can be considered in isolation. It is wrong, it is artificial, to attempt the conservation of any item of material culture without considering the other factors, natural and human, that played their part in determining human progress. This may be one of the main reasons why so many museums collecting historical artefacts are so dull and uninspiring; they show 'things' often described as 'bygones' almost as pieces of fine art, rather than as a link in man's cultural development. Too many folk life studies have become 'synonymous, not with reasoned and objective enquiry, but with a kind of prurient unearthing of the merely curious. It asks no questions – or only a passing one – of the material it uncovers and has too often been content merely to hold it up for display, making at the same time a few polite exclamations over it: "How curious! How interesting!"' (Evans 1965: 35). One could aso add 'How boring', 'How trivial'. I wonder whether we have made much progress in our museums of social history – or ethnology – or folk life? Have we gone beyond the stage of collecting 'bygones' and displaying them in forests of glass cases? Have we done more than preserve the odd site or building that takes our fancy, or than preserve a random, haphazard selection of structures in artificial parks that are nothing more than glorified glass cases? The proliferation of museums in all parts of the country is certainly worrying and the number of museums that set out to collect the artefacts of farming and domestic life, in particular, have increased spectacularly. As a result many items not worthy of preservation have been uplifted to the status of national treasures. Winnowing machines and box mangles, ploughs by Ransomes and wagons by the Bristol Carriage Works have been preserved by the dozen and many rural museums are nothing but monuments to the mass-consumerism of the 1920s and 1930s. One wonders whether these are true ethnological collections?

With the setting up of museums in chapels and warehouses, in barns and mills, there usually follows a desperate search for artefacts to fill those buildings. Attics and auction rooms disgorge all manner of useful lots that can be installed in a building; lots that may or may not be representative of the heritage that is presented, mainly for the entertainment of tourists on a wet afternoon. Many of those collections presented to the general public are merely cabinets of curiosities that have little relevance to the life of the people who visit them. More often than not, only small items can be collected, with the result that a museum collection can often provide a false picture of life within the community that it represents. Furthermore, many of the museums in Britain today possess miscellaneous collections that are not documented, and are collected not as the result of scholarly research but as the result of an acquisitive mania that seems to have afflicted many people. There is, after all, a vast difference between a 'collection of bygones' and a true ethnological collection developed as the result of scholarly research and presented with scholarly interpretation. Far too many museums in Britain today merely provide a nostalgic peepshow into a largely fictitious past.

Bibliography

Evans, G. E., 1965. 'Folk life studies in East Anglia', in Jenkins, J. G. (ed.), *Studies in Folk Life*: 36–45.

Jannasch, N., 1981. 'The maritime museums of the future', in *International Congress of Maritime Museums, 4th Conference Proceedings*: 190–1.

Jenkins, J. G., 1974. *Nets and Coracles*.

12 *Objects as Evidence, or Not?*

GAYNOR KAVANAGH

A significant proportion of museums in Britain lay claim to operating within the field of history. With various forms of self-description and qualification, from social history to folk life and local history, these museums seek to appropriate responsibility for the examination and explanation of the lives and experiences of ordinary, local people through the use of material, visual and oral evidence. In this they adopt a time period usually stretching from the middle of the last century, or thereabouts, up to the post-war years; occasionally the view stretches to the present day. The results and the achievement range from the professional to the preposterous. The central device of the history curator's practice and indeed the self-justification of the museum is the history object: the object as evidence. The centrality of the object, and the museum's responsibility to it, differentiate this institution from all others.

This paper is concerned with whether objects are evidence, or not, and with the changing role and relevance of objects in history curatorship in Britain. In this I am not dealing with the history of the realm or British political self-definition as expressed, for example, in aspects of the British Museum, or the history of power and privilege such as that expressed in the National Portrait Gallery (Hooper-Greenhill 1980). Instead my interest lies in objects as evidence of people's history and cultural experience in the last two centuries.

This field in itself is highly problematic, as 'history' and 'social history' in museums are curious affairs, with complex ranges of approaches and preconceptions. It does not necessarily follow that social history in the museum is actually addressing the history of society, or its cultural configurations and contradictions. 'Social' history in some museums is a broad-based, rigorous and astute account of people and their pasts: the work of the People's Palace in Glasgow is a case in point. However, in other museums 'social history' has come to be interpreted as all aspects of past experience, with the exception of those which in their form or content are essentially economic or technical. Therefore many museums separate scientific, industrial, transport or agricultural collections and topics from 'social history', thereby excluding the social and political view of work, travel or the land in preference for technical or construction detail (see, for example, Mansfield and Jones 1987). The problem of 'history' in the museum is further compounded by the fact that most museums designate material from the middle and upper classes, such as clothing and furniture, as fine and decorative art, thus separating it out from any consideration of cultural variation and experience. In this respect material culture in museum studies is defined and at times redefined by the curator who beholds it, and thence uses it as evidence within the bounds of that designated and operative definition.

However, my concern here is with the reality and potential of the object as evidence of ways of living and working, of self-expression and believing. In this there is a need to strip away the concerns of curators and take another look at the essence of the historian's craft, and its raw material, primary evidence. In general terms, to question whether for historians objects have value as evidence or not is perhaps as crass and vacuous as questioning whether documents have value as evidence. The plain fact is that some have and some have not. What really counts and is central to the historian's craft is the relevance of the problems posed and the questions asked (whether of two- or three-dimensional material), and the forms of criticism applied. It is from this that the value of any material as evidence emerges or is determined.

For the most part, outside museums, the study of the past would appear largely to have concerned itself with the description and interpretation of change and rupture. The sheer volume and variety of available documentary evidence, its complexity and scope, and the specific ranges of interest and enquiry have guaranteed that generations of historians have chosen to look no further than archive sources. This document-orientated approach and process has led to a set of problems that are now well recognized. Through it historians have constructed a middle-class view of the past, since not only the creation and retention of the documents, but also the development of their interpretation, has rested largely with the literate and intellectually privileged. The legitimization, in most quarters, of oral testimony as a source, yielding as it does evidence that moves beyond the scope of documentary sources revealing the ignored and forgotten, has cracked open the established mould of practice. At all levels, the study of the past has been touched if not invigorated by the acceptance that what people say and remember may be as relevant and pertinent to history as what has been committed to paper. The emergence of studies of popular culture has been partly a corollory of this, for it is but a short step from a consideration of what has been written and remembered to what has been experienced and expressed in social and material terms.

E. P. Thompson's book *The Making of the English Working Class* (1963) was a landmark in this respect. It helped to reveal a range of questions that historians should be asking about experience, activity and attitude, and the study of popular culture by historians has been greatly enriched and stiumulated as a result. Robert D. Storch has pointed out how such studies, through historians' increasing awareness of the literature of sociology and anthropology, have acquired 'a certain *cachet* and a sometimes uneasy respectability' (Storch 1982: 17). The trend is continuing, although to date *material* culture studies have not predominated, but have been subsumed into broader considerations of popular culture. In Britain, there is not a range of literature or ongoing debate that parallels material culture studies in the United States or ethnology in Sweden, both of which are arguably the product of a fusion of different disciplines (Schlereth 1982: 1–75; Klein 1985). However, this may be changing: current studies in semiotics are beginning to point out a range of new questions for historians, and there is encouragement and direction coming from a number of different quarters. For example, in a volume of essays on invented traditions edited by Eric Hobsbawm and Terence Ranger (1983), examination was made of those practices, often with the most limited of precedents, which if socially safe and ideologically suitable become rapidly enshrined as new traditions – that is, anything from the monarch's Christmas broadcast to Cup Final day. In his introduction Hobsbawm sought to justify and encourage such studies, revealing as they do 'important symptoms and indicators of problems, which might not be recognised otherwise, and developments which are otherwise difficult to identify and date' (Hobsbawm 1983: 12).

The development of such work requires a willingness to look beyond documents and oral testimony to visual indicators and records, and the expression of cultural phenomena. A number of recent research papers are clearly exploring this territory. These include Paul Pickering's very useful paper on the Chartist movement, which looked at the means through which the middle-class leadership sought to identify themselves and signify their solidarity with the movement, particularly through their choice of clothes (Pickering 1986). Another indication of how historians are beginning to look at the expression and manipulation of the material world is apparent in Asa Briggs's intention to complete his Victorian trilogy, which began with *Victorian Cities* and *Victorian People*, with a volume on *Victorian Things* (*The Times Higher Education Supplement*, 4 July 1986).

The value of material culture studies would appear to be self-evident to those already working within this sphere. The juxtaposition and manipulation of space and possessions is the physical manifestation of class and class relationships. Equally, the experience and operation of the material and social environment is as expressive as dialect in terms of delineating community and class. Moreover, through them change is graphically charted. Beyond documents, material and social surroundings offer a wealth of evidence of the means through which people were able or obliged to express themselves, their views and experiences. This is particularly so when access to literacy, authority or power was prevented or denied. Objects (or their absence) can thus be the physical indicators of ideological forces and social positions.

But what is the point of looking at an object, when a photograph, document or testimony can be far more explicit and indeed cooperative? What is the point of looking at a farm wagon if studying unionism on East Anglian farms, or a flat iron if studying women's history, or a bar of soap if studying Unilever? The answer may be 'not much', but then it all depends on the problem posed and the questions asked. The disentangling of this complex pattern depends upon the willingness to study not so much the object as the object in contexts, both as content and symbol. Thus, Sven Ek has stressed that the essential aspect in the study of the cultural complex is 'not the external cultural elements, but rather the ideologies and values that comprise the core of the culture. Not the material innovations, but the psychic changes which necessitate that these become ... the measure of the qualitative nature of cultural changes' (quoted in Christiansen 1978: 104). The importance of the object in this view is subsumed by what can be learned from its context, the ideas behind it and the forces that create change. This reverses the importance of external and internal criticism as applied to documents. It is not the form and content of the source that is paramount but its location and relationships.

Consider the use of four very ordinary blankets. Open to inspection, the quality of the material, weave and colour, and signs of wear may give certain though limited information. Markings may help disclose more. From this the quality and type of uses might be suggested, perhaps little else, unless forensic science was applied. The same four blankets may have very different tales to tell. The first, from South Wales, was used pricipally to carry a child. In the eastern valleys of Wales, as in many working-class, industrial and upland areas, women carried their babies in a blanket. This would be carefully pulled around themselves to allow one hand free for a toddler to grasp or for a shopping bag, more likely both. Young girls learnt how to bind themselves in this way to carry younger siblings. This use of the blanket was common throughout the nineteenth century and carried on certainly until the 1960s. However, this is no quaint survival, no last vestige of a Welsh national peasant garb (any suggestion of which is the romantic and imposed creation of an English aristocrat, Lady Llanover). Instead it is a practical expression of the social and physical environment. Women carried babies in this way over such a long period for a number of reasons. Besides holding the child snugly, the blanket gave both child and mother extra warmth. This was particularly important, since the expense of child-rearing often meant that overcoats were a luxury item, hence many had to do without. Prams and pushchairs were only available to the more wealthy, who were not in the majority in these areas. Even when second-hand prams started to become available there was some resistance to change; the steep hillsides made pushing a cumbersome pram, from the towns on the valley floor to the homes above, a difficult procedure. It was easier to carry baby in a blanket 'the Welsh way', especially if there was a chance of catching a bus home. There was no way that a bus would accommodate a pantechnicon of a pram. In the eastern valleys the advent of folding pushchairs, the Maclaren buggy, the family car (no matter how rough), and eventually the duvet, has at last put paid to the use of blankets in this way, except of course for grannies well schooled in this method of child care. Yet at the end of the day it is just a blanket.

The second blanket is from the Lincolnshire Wolds (Museum of Lincolnshire Life collections). This blanket is from a farm in Wilton-on-the-Cliff that regularly sold its wool to a local wool merchant whose outlet was a Yorkshire woollen mill. One year the dealer brought back to the farm a blanket from the mill, one that theoretically might have been made from wool on that farm. The relationship of raw material to manufacture held an importance to the farmer who through the blanket held a record of the relevance of that farm to manufactured goods. The production of the fleeces was not an isolated act terminating with payment from the wool merchant but had a connection to the world beyond the farm. Through it the farmer had a very different and tangible expression of the farm's work and it was retained as a token of this.

The third blanket could be one from Glasgow. In the East End of the city a significant proportion of the population was employed through proverty in hawking and in the rag and second-hand clothes trade. This gave rise to institutions known as Paddy's Market and the Barrows, which were superbly recorded in photographs at the turn of the century by Glasgow's Chief Sanitary Inspector, Peter Fyfe (King 1985: 65). These trading activities had early precedents. For example, in an official report on pawnbrokers in the 1870s, it was recorded as being not uncommon for blankets to be pawned in the morning and the money used to buy a basket of fish or fruit. This was then sold at a profit which bought the day's food and left enough over for the blanket to be redemmed before the pawn-shop closed at 10 p.m.; the risk of course lay in failing to sell the produce (Fraser 1981: 19–20). The blanket's potential function of giving warmth was matched by one that might produce enough income to feed a family for the day.

The fourth blanket had a totally different use and was an instrument and symbol of resistance and protest. In September 1976 Ciaron Nugent, a convicted Provisional IRA prisoner at the Maze Prison outside Belfast in Northern Ireland, in protest at being denied political status began what was to be called the 'dirty protest'. He was joined by other prisoners who like him refused to wear prison clothes, wash, shave, or use lavatory facilities. The press were not allowed access to the prison; therefore descriptions of the conditions of self-imposed squalor came primarily from the priests who were allowed pastoral access. In 1978 Father Murray described the men 'clutching at their blankets or blue towel to cover their nakedness'. The protests lasted for two and a half years. They were halted by the IRA in March 1981 because some concessions had been given, but also reportedly to ensure that attention was focussed on the hunger strikes which began with Bobby Sands on 1 March 1981, and ultimately led to his death and the deaths of others. At the time the protest was called off, 411 men at the Maze and 28 women in Armagh gaol were involved in the protest and were 'on the blanket'. Even after the protests ended some prisoners continued to cover themselves with blankets as a symbol of the protest (*The Times*, 14 December 1978; 5 and 30 January 1981; 3 March 1981).

In each of these cases the fact of the individual blanket is greatly outweighed by what it was and what it represents. Each has some relevance, culturally, socially or politically, to the communities that produced and used it. Measuring or handling the blankets would hardly reveal their historical place or importance. This would have to be attempted or reached through studies on or questions about women, farmers, poverty or protest. To pursue research further the historian would have to employ a wide range of sources, other than the blankets themselves. The object, in this case the blankets, indicates rather than determines or concludes the direction of enquiry.

Only one of these blankets exists within a museum collection. With the latter two examples, it seems unlikely that they woud survive to be retained for other purposes, that is to become a museum object. However, each obviously has something important to say and record. Determination of what this is lies at the centre of curatorial practice. The difficult and crucial process of determining areas for study, questions to raise, and the social and economic relevance and symbolism of objects, is the intellectual core of professional museum activity. The results of this process reveal and differentiate astute and relevant history curatorship from the rest, for it is upon grounds of relevance and symbolism that decisions have to be taken regarding recording, acquisition, preservation and interpretation – the basic components of any museum's functions. This is a complicated process because the decisions and views adopted are inevitably made on grounds that are not static, but change over time and have a specific kind of dynamism.

An object in its own right may be a signal or symbol, a trigger to emotion or memory. Thus a swastika, a kissing shuttle, the Jarrow March banner (re-used in 1986) and a range of like material, to certain sectors of society, need little introduction. The object in this sense behaves as a kind of visual shorthand which we may or may not be able to read, according to our level of experience. Such readings and responses may depend upon the social or personal memory the object can unlock and reveal. In this there will also be some dependence upon relevance. Thus objects may only be of real significance as long as the things they symbolize have some meaning and currency. Furthermore, the environment in which the object is encountered may add to, or detract from, the reading of it and the conclusions drawn. The field here is loaded with preconceptions and with emotions, and is re-ordered according to time, experience and environment. So, depending on the arrangement or place of the object, the viewer in certain circumstances can be called to experience empathy or sympathy, pride or revulsion with the material to hand. Because of this, the view becomes subject to and dependent on firm influences from external sources, in particular personal experiences.

As a result, the meaning of an object will undergo a number of different shifts of meaning and reading, from its creation to its ultimate destruction or loss, and even beyond. For example, one museum observer commented that a stuffed tiger in a case was not a tiger: it was just a museum object. Here is one simple change of position in meaning: from live animal to dead museum object. However, the likelihood is that this is just one in a whole range of changes that have transformed such a tiger, given that, as in the case of so many 'museum objects' of this kind, it is a process that may well have been going on since the last decades of the nineteenth century. In its natural environment the tiger has meant cub and sibling, perhaps it also meant mate and mother. Most probably it had been predator and hunter, an object of fear. Its ultimate demise may have transformed it into a prize, evidence of accomplishment, the gratification and confirmation of the perceived socially superior status of the big game hunter. For others involved in the event, it may have simply represented the means by which meagre incomes were supplemented through the service of a self-indulgent sport. The carcase as economic device would have been maintained as a trained taxidermist transformed it, fixed it in shape and altered its substance. For the museum that acquired it, it may have been a prime acquisition, connecting the museum to the donor and thus indirectly in his class and class values. As times change the tiger becomes evidence and symbol of imperialists at play, disrupting and wasting wild life and natural resources. The quality of natural history programmes on television deflect the public gaze from the tiger, and it is transformed from evidence of the exotic wildlife of other lands to a kind of community cuddly toy, a source of popular affection, as is the case with the tiger at King's Lynn Museum, the brown bear at Sheffield City Museum, and the polar bear at Paisley Museum (Blackburn 1987). The chances are that with the current pressure on museum space, the tiger may now be read quite differently by curators and may simply be a 'flaming nuisance', a symbol of folly in acquisition. The tiger can change in meaning yet further; for example, it might become a convenient device in multi-cultural museum teaching. In sum, it is and has been much more than simply a tiger or a museum object and the way in which it can be read will continue to change throughout its existence, and maybe beyond.

The curator then has to pin and place the object and its various readings. But in this, the levels of communication move beyond the craft of label-writing. The much broader social and cultural contexts of the museum overlay, even reframe, the object and its meaning. Unless there is a conscious attempt to jolt its reading either by revealing the object in real or personal terms, such as at the John Hodge Gallery at the Somerset Rural Life Museum, or by the startling juxtaposition of images, such as in the Paolozzi exhibition at the Museum of Mankind in London in 1987, the museum may contribute, no matter how well meaning it is, to a broader mythologizing process about the past. This is well illustrated by research undertaken by Edward L. Hawes in Springfield, Illinois (Hawes 1986). Hawes sought to test his hypothesis that there are certain objects or ranges of objects that gain symbolic content when placed in a museum. Taking as an example the American Mid-West, settled by Europeans in the nineteenth century, Hawes selected a group of material that included axes, open-hearth cooking pots, rifles, wool-cards, spinning wheels, looms and prairie ploughs. The tests revealed that certain groups of material, particularly the pot and the axe, repeatedly generated responses based in the web of myths about 'colonial' and 'pioneer' days, woven no doubt for strong social purposes in the home and in schools. Those objects from the test groups which failed to conform or find a place within the established myth structure, for example a photocopy of an 1850 newspaper, a table cloth or a Wedgwood plate, were ignored or seen as not relevant. The responses took no note of the real significance of the objects to hand or of any real connections the objects might have had.

Hawes's research would seem to confirm the degree to which our lives are coded by the objects around us and how these objects can be re-encoded according to different social needs and pressures. As Hawes points out, there is a definite 'politics to certain museum artefacts and the tales and myths associated with them'. This reading of objects according to a previously encoded pattern is not confined exclusively to the museum. But as a legitimizing institution, the causes and effects hold strong significance. The role of the museum as either the purveyor of myths or the responsible recorder of social change is open to question in the light of this research.

The view of the object as evidence not only changes according to social readings. Within the field of history curatorship, it has also been subject to considerable shifts in professional practice and attitude which relate to a range of influences and needs, some well considered, others pragmatic. In this, the position of history museum activity outside the direct influence of academic and intellectual developments in its discipline, unlike archaeology, art and anthropology in museums, has to be remembered.

At the end of the last century, museum interest in objects from a more recent British past had no parallel with the all-consuming passion and drive for a meticulous record that fuelled the work of Artur Hazelius and the romantic museum movement in Scandinavia he inspired (Alexander 1983: 241–75). Connections between museum interest in recent, local material and the evolutionary school of anthropologists seeking to provide an explanation of continual human progress has been drawn (Skinner 1986: 392–5), and certainly the folk lore movement took inspiration from anthropology (for example, Burne 1913); but the depth and extent of this influence in museum work has to be seriously questioned, for much evidence from acquisition records would seem to suggest that although there were a number of thoughtful commentators on the potential of museum activity, in practice much that was undertaken was random, even accidental. Horn lanterns, tinder boxes, scold's bridles, man-traps and rush lights were not uncommon acquisitions for museum collections at this time, more often than not simply added to registers with just the name of the object, rarely with the study of context or even field notes to add to our knowledge or understanding. Whereas there may have been some museums whose frame of reference sprang from an anthropological view, for a larger number a more casual reasoning was applied. For these, objects were evidence of the odd and incidental, the safe and the unchallenging.

During the First World War another, quite radical approach to the object as evidence was adopted. In March 1917, the National (later Imperial) War Museum was founded. The Museum's Committee decided that the purpose of the museum was to provide as complete a record as possible of the experience of the war. This it did through a network of specialist sub-committees and field-workers, using a process that would now be described as contemporary documentation (Kavanagh 1985). For a brief period the Imperial War Museum sowed the seeds of the idea that objects could be evidence if taken as part of a comprehensive and informed programme of recording, but these seeds fell on barren land. The initiative was not taken up by other museums and in the post-war years was largely forgotten.

The mid-war years saw the last major fling of the private, sometimes eccentric collector. Men and women such as Dr John Kirk (Brears 1980: 90–2) and Dr I. F. Grant (Cheape 1986) brought together collections of astonishing richness yet varied importance. Arguably there was a strong relationship between their personal experiences and expectations and the material collected, a rejection of the industrial present and the changes wrought by mass-produced goods. The objects they amassed perhaps were as much, if not more than, evidence of selective memory as they were of the life and times they sought to represent. Their activities stand out not only because of the range of their collections (upon which the Castle Museum, York, and the Highlands Museum, Kingussie, were founded), but also because they were conducting their activities at the time against a background of very limited activity and interest coming from museums (a notable exception being, as ever, Thomas Sheppard at Hull Museum).

From the years just before the war and up to perhaps the late 1960s or thereabouts another shift occurred. During this period there was a staggering growth of folk life, later 'social history', museums. This would appear to coincide with a rejuvenated profession, at long last taking over from the generation of curators that held sway from the final decades of the nineteenth century (Miers, 1928: 19–22). Perhaps of more practical significance, it coincided with a period of tremendous social and technological change which rendered redundant a wide range of objects and practices. It was as important to record these with depth and discernment as were the changes themselves; but it appears that this responsibility was not always followed through (Higgs 1963: 28). A tremendous variety of material suddenly became available to museums, and a massive influx of objects to museum collections resulted, with or without documentation. Thus museums became well blessed with craft and agricultural tools, sometimes regardless of their true social and economic relevance locally, while other practices that were continuing and developing, like midwifery or the legal profession, or new, like car manufacture or cinema-going, were rarely represented. This became not necessarily 'objects as evidence' so much as 'objects as ease'. They were there to be collected and were particularly suitable if they obligingly did not confront or disrupt images of a safe, secure and essentially rural past (for example, see Wheeler 1934: 191–6).

In contrast to this situation, and of importance to history curatorship in Britain, there emerged the first generation of specialist curators whose ability, training and perspectives actively prevented history museums from becoming merely warehouses for bygones and the *ad hoc* – particularly Dr I. Peate (see, for example, 1948 and 1976), and later John Higgs (1963), Ann Buck (see, for example, 1976: 5–26), Dr George Thompson (see, for example, 1982), Dr Alexander Fenton (1985), Dr Geraint Jenkins (see, for example, 1972: 497–516 and 1974: 7–11) and Dr Alan Gailey (see, for example, 1982). Their work and philosophies have a variety of influences which might include not only Scandinavian and Middle European approaches to ethnology, but also the ideas of historical geography that emerged from Wales, Scotland and Ireland in the inter-war and immediately post-war years. With them came a group identity as regional ethnologists, which in turn has sustained the Society for Folk Life Studies, founded in 1961. In terms of research, acquisition and interpretation, the object became centrally placed as evidence, alongside a wide range of other source material, of which film, oral testimony, song and story were of prime importance.

The emphasis has now moved yet again. Curators today are self-styled social historians. The approach adopted has theoretically moved to the diachronic, with the museum responsible for explaining change over time rather than predominantly in-depth, local, synchronic studies. This imposes a major set of problems in that the museum's role must now be to explain changes and the inconstant flux that is life, past and present, with the physically unchanging and constant that is objects. Arguably this has brought with it a crisis of confidence in the object and its role in museum activities. For example, Stuart Davies has argued that historians have used objects as primary sources when dealing with periods that lead up to and include the Renaissance world. Thereafter other sources proliferate and the object gradually ceases to be of value. By the twentieth century, the range of source materials is such that 'the object has no value as evidence'. He maintains that the main point in favour of history collections is that they 'materially assist in the presentation of the past to the public' (Davies 1985: 28). For some curators objects have become, at the very best, useful as illustration to a story-line drawn from other sources, and at worst a drain on resources and energy. For them, objects have become increasingly qustionable as evidence, as has their relevance to museum activity.

However, many curators continue to work imaginatively and with great flair through objects, using them as an integral part of the evidence of ways of living and working, ways of believing and self-expression. Recent exhibitions at Slough Museum, on life in Slough during the 1930s; at the Museum of London, on the popular use of cosmetics in London, at the People's Palace, Glasgow, on the Easterhouse and Barrowfield housing estates; and at Bishop's House Museum, Sheffield, on Tudor and Stuart Sheffield, afford firm and clear indication of the high level of skill and sensitivity to people, their pasts and presents, and objects as evidence of these, currently to be found in history museums in Britain.

Largely in the absence of university interest, the use of objects as evidence of a more recent British past has for several decades remained principally the preserve of history museums. Clearly this is beginning to change as more and more historians begin to raise questions about popular culture and the operation and importance of material things within it. This may have a beneficial affect upon museums, stimulating, or even repositioning the directions taken. The risk, however, is that, apart from a central core of concerned curators, history museum practice in general will ignore this stimulus, in the ways in which the potential influences of anthropology, ethnology and specifically, of late, structuralism have been overlooked. This would intellectually isolate history museum practice even further, arguably leaving it with a rump of activities and intentions operated solely within short term leisure interests. The longer-term social commitment of museums as data banks or community archives would suffer if this were taken to extremes.

The dialogue about objects as evidence and the changing role of the museum in conveying knowledge about the past and present has largely been coming from outside the United Kingdom, from SAMDOK and Nordiska Museet in Sweden (for example, Rosander 1980; Szabó 1986) and from America (Schlereth 1982). This is beginning to change, as is indicated by the papers collected in this volume and by such seminars as that at the Wellcome Institute on 'Classification and Knowledge' held in May 1987, which have grappled with the boundaries, configurations and constructions of the object as evidence within museum contexts. The need for a firm intellectual base for curatorial activity is as urgently required now as it ever has been. Artur Hazelius, over a hundred years ago, was convinced that museums could be both fun and educational, but only if they had a sound and developing research base and a continuing archive function, in which objects had a definite and integral part. The role of theory must have its place too. Otherwise 'objects as evidence' becomes not a searching area of intellectual and professional debate, but simply an odd title for a paper.

BIBLIOGRAPHY

Alexander, E. P., 1983. *Museum Masters*.

Blackburn, M., 1987. 'Polar bears in the community – a new role for a traditional museum', *Museum Professional Group News, 25*: 1–3.

Brears, P. C. D., 1980. 'Kirk of the Castle', *Museums Journal, 80–2* 90–2.

Buck, A., 1976. 'Costume as a social record', *Folk Life, 14*: 5–26.

Burne, S., 1913. *The Handbook of Folk-Lore*.

Cheape, H., 1986. 'Dr I F Grant (1887–1983): the Highland Folk Museum and a bibliography of her written works', *The Review of Scottish Culture, 2*: 113–25.

Christiansen, P. O., 1978. In 'Peasant adaptation to bourgeois culture? Class formation and cultural redefinition in the Danish countryside', *Ethnologea Scandinavia*: 98–152.

Davies, S., 1985. 'Collecting and recalling the twentieth century', *Museums Journal, 85, 1*; 27–9.

Fenton, A., 1985. *The Shape of the Past. Essays in Scottish Ethnology*.

Fraser, W. H., 1981. *The Coming of the Mass Market 1850–1914*.

Gailey, A., [1982]. 'Folk-life study and the Ordnance Survey memoirs', in Gailey, A. and O'Logain, D. (eds), *Gold under the Furze*: 150–64.

Hawes, E. L., 1986. 'Artifacts, myth, and identity in American history museums', in Sofka, V. (ed.), *Museology and Identity, ICOFOM Study Series, 10*: 135–9.

Higgs, J. W. Y., 1963. *Folk Life Collection and Classification*.

Hobsbawm, E., 1983. 'Introduction: inventing traditions', in Hobsbawm, E. and Ranger, T. (eds), *The Invention of Tradition*: 1–14.

Hooper-Greenhill, E., 1980. 'The National Portrait Gallery. A Case Study in Cultural Reproduction'. (Unpublished MA dissertation, University of London.)

Jenkins, J. G., 1972. 'The use of artifacts and folk art in the folk museum', in Dorson, R. M. (ed.), *Folklore and Folklore. An Introduction*: 497–516.

Jenkins, J. G., 1974. 'The collection of ethnological material', *Museums Journal, 74.1*: 7–11.

Kavanagh, G., 1985. 'Museums and the Great War'. (Unpublished M Phil. thesis, University of Leicester).

King, E., 1985. *The People's Palace and Glasgow Green*.

Klein, B., 1985. 'Swedish ethnology in the 1980's.' Unpublished paper presented at the annual meeting of the American Folklore Society, Cincinnati, Ohio, 16–20 October 1985.

Mansfield, N. and Jones, B., 1987. 'Win some, lose some – industrial history in museums', *Social History Group News, 14*: 4.

Miers, Sir H., 1928. *Report on the Museums of the British Isles, other than the National Museums*. Prepared for the Carnegie United Kingdom Trust.

Peate, I., C., 1948. *Folk Museums*.

Peate, I., C., 1976. 'Some thoughts on the study of folk life', in Danaghar, C. . (ed.), *Folk ad Farm*: 229–34.

Pickering, P. 1986. 'Class without words: symbolic communication in the Chartist movement', *Past and Present, 112*: 144–62.

Rosander, G., 1980. *Today for Tomorrow. Museum Documentation of Contemporary Society in Sweden by the Acquisition of Objects*.

Schlereth, T. J., 1982. 'Material culture studies in America', in Schlereth, T.J. (ed.), *Material Culture Studies in America*: 1–75.

Skinner, G. M., 1986. 'Sir Henry Wellcome's museum for the history of science', *Medical History, 30*: 383–418.

Storch, R. D., 1982. 'Introduction: persistence and change in nineteenth-century popular culture', in Storch R. D. (ed.), *Popular Culture and Custom in Nineteenth Century England*: 1–19.

Szabó, M., 1986. *Some Aspects of Museum Documentation*.

Thompson, E. P., 1963. *The Making of the English Working Class*.

Thompson, G. B., 1982. 'Some considerations concerning the significance of open-air museums in present day society', *Report of Conference, Association of European Open-Air Museums*: 122–9.

Wheeler, R. E. M. 1934. 'Folk museums', *Museums Journal, 34*: 191–6.

13 *Material Culture, People's History and Populism: Where Do We Go From Here?*

PETER JENKINSON

The experience of recent years has shown that there is a need to share views and experiences of material culture studies, both from within this country and from further afield, and to consider new theoretical approaches to artefact study. In this paper I should like to address some of the basic problems associated with the study of material culture that I have encountered in my short experience of working in museums, and in particular the problems attaching to the use of material culture by museums in the production of histories. I will then propose some possible new approaches to history production, and briefly describe a project to illustrate using such approaches.

The basic problem that frustrates all our efforts to create effective and socially useful museum institutions seems to be not so much a lack of methodology in the study, use and interpretation of the vast accumulations of objects that constitute our museum collections as a more generalized poverty of theory, a poverty of theory made all the more surprising given that the collection, conservation and use of objects is still held to be the primary function and legitimation of museums. Collecting objects, inheriting the debris of past, and sometimes present, societies, is what all museums have in common; and yet in the absence of theory, there are no common approaches to material culture amongst museum workers, but instead a bewildering range of approaches that constitutes not so much a charming diversity of cultural expression as a form of sanctioned professional anarchy. We become qualified, in the formal sense of acquiring paper qualifications, and once qualified we can do almost whatever we like in the museums that we come to regard as belonging to us – 'my museum'.

We must recognize therefore that the question of new theoretical approaches to material culture is also the question of precisely what kind of museum we would like to see, of where we see the museum, as cultural institution, fitting into society. We have to ask not only what we are doing but also why we are doing it. What functions can, or should, museums perform in our rapidly changing societies in the West? As the nature of society changes, from one controlled by consumer capitalism to one controlled by a capitalism founded in information and information technology, questions about public cultures, and museums in particular, will be posited with even greater urgency (Elliott 1982).

It is now three years since I left the Department of Museum Studies at Leicester to start working in museums. In that short time, in meeting and talking to other curators, it has become clear to me that there are almost as many approaches to material culture as there are curators themselves. There are those, particularly amongst the younger generation of museum workers, who believe that objects have outlived their usefulness and should be abandoned if museums are to overcome the atrophying, necrophiliac tendencies that afflict them. At the other end of the scale there are those museum workers, the 'object worshippers', who believe that objects are paramount and are the one resource that no other cultural institution can offer or exploit. Other material, written, visual or verbal, is to them of mere secondary or contextual importance.

Between these two poles, of those who loathe objects and those who love them, is a vast world of differing, and often conflicting, attitudes and practices in the ways that museums both collect and use objects. Despite the increasing implementation of collecting policies in museums, curators are ultimately free to collect whatever they feel like acquiring. Even within the terms of collecting policies there is immense scope for the free reign of a curator's whim, conceit or adherence to currently prevalent collecting fashions. Within the field of social history today there are thus certain objects that are fashionable: bakelite and other early plastics, gas and electric domestic appliances, indeed almost anything with a plug, 1950s kitsch, 1960s furniture, 1970s clothing, 1980s packaging.

Undoubtedly, in a museum context, such objects could be used to produce a whole range of interpretations of immense social historical interest: the implementation of domestic technologies and the implications of this for women perhaps, the genesis of youth culture, the impact of advertising in contemporary society. But the point here is that all too often such objects are collected not because they are found necessary for the mobilization of a particular analysis or interpretation of social history or of material culture, but simply because they happen to be in vogue and every museum should therefore have one. They are objects collected for objects' sake, and, of course, whilst these cultish objects are being collected others, it is clear, are ignored, making explicit the gaps, the silences, the eccentricities in collections that are being created today. There is no compulsion for us as curators to provide fully developed criteria or justifications for our collecting activities. It is up to us and, in the absence of a theory that maps out and structures the role that material culture should take in the production of meaning in museums, such professionalized collections anarchy can only continue.

This collecting mania takes place in a position of splendid isolation. Museums are isolated both from the main cultural theory discourses that have informed, and transformed, other areas of cultural practice in the last two decades, most notably structuralism and semiotics, and from other cultural and educational/historical institutions. In comparison with the United States, Canada, Sweden and many other countries, there are in Britain very few formal or informal links between museums and higher education or research institutions. This isolated position of museums within the world of cultural and intellectual endeavour is compounded by the failure of history museums to connect effectively with the development of a new, populist, radical and intentionally anti-academic social history in this country, as represented by the initiatives in people's history, community history and popular memory, which collectively has done so much to change the directions and assumptions of conventional historical enquiry since the 1960s (Samuel 1981: Popular Memory Group 1982).

Whilst many curators are aware of, and sympathetic to, the aims of these movements, there has been less success in incorporating the approaches practised by these 'history from below' movements into everyday, object-worshipping museum practice. Oral history work in particular is generally recognized as a legitimate and rewarding practice, but is still seen to be of subsidiary importance to the main task of collection care and interpretation, rather than as a critical element in the production of histories in museums. We would do more, the argument runs, if only we had more time, money, staffing and so on. Were if not for the dubious merits of the Manpower Services Commisson, one of the cornerstones of the Thatcher regime, it is doubtful whether many museums would have undertaken any oral history work, or any other community or outreach work, at all.

To summarize so far, then, we now face a situation where museums in Britain continue to pursue the collection of objects as their main function but do not have any theory to inform this, their major legitimating practice. Museum workers have failed to connect with, and be invigorated by, the leading trends in cultural theory of the last two decades, or with the aggressively iconoclastic, anti-elitist people's history movements. Yet the need for a theory, or theories, is obvious and urgent and if theory is to emerge then there are several fundamental questions that need to be asked.

Firstly, there is the question of the professionalization of museum work and thereby of historical production in museums. Basically, it is in the interests of professionals to control not simply the objects of their work, the material culture, but also the subjects of their work, 'the public'; yet this undermines the project of democratization of museums in which many museum workers believe.

Museums have been under the sway of a broadly populist impulse in the liberal-democratic period since 1945 – an impulse to break down the elitism that had characterized museums in the past and to open up museums to everyone, to all classes, all interest groups. There are very few other cultural institutions that interpret their potential audience so broadly and attempt to provide for the whole population. Nevertheless we in museums believe that museums are for the people, all the people, and not just the culturally literate bourgeoisie, and we have all worked therefore to extend the range and quality of the services available to the people. Professional training has been an essential element in this populist project of serving the general population more effectively. A very disparate group of museum workers, a very motley crew of women and men arriving in museums from all directions with differing skills and competencies, has been pressganged into taking 'professional qualifications', into conforming to 'professional standards' and, perhaps most importantly, into considering themselves to be part of a profession – the 'museum profession' – will all that that entails.

The creation of the professional, as opposed to the amateur or antiquarian, curator has been one of the most marked developments within museums in the last 40 years, and is a trend that is likely to continue. We are now in a situation where our current President of the Museums Association, the body that acts as the primary focus and instigator of this professionalization project, is suggesting that by the year 2000 the great majority of people working in museums will have achieved a museum qualification – the Museums Diploma – and that those without the Diploma should find it difficult to obtain employment (Robertson 1986). All curators then will also have to be diploma-bearing professionals. But what does this mean? We can all of course question whether or not acquiring these pieces of paper actually makes us into better curators. I am sure that every curator could think of at least one colleague in this 'profession' of ours who has all the proper qualifications and yet still has difficulty in dealing with even the most basic museum practice. Undoubtedly, however, the general result of this increasing professionalism has been an improvement in the standards of the storage, conservation and general care of our museum collections. Whilst this is very commendable, my concern here is that in this project we are marginalizing the needs of the people museums are intended to serve, and in many cases suppressing those needs.

We have to remember that, as with all forms of professionalization, important questions of power, of authority, are raised (Berger 1967). Professionalism distances museum workers from precisely those people that museums are delegated to serve. Professionalism intentionally creates institutional barriers, endowing museum workers with a special status, so that museums, operated by professionals, can be said to be for the people but definitely not of the people. Only curators are qualified to make use of the resources that are available in museums in the production of histories, or any other cultural construct, for public consumption. Professionalization has served to create a relatively autonomous institutional core of salaried museum workers, generally educated to degree level at least and middle-or upper middle-class in origin, who, operating as experts, specialists, connoisseurs and the policers of style and taste, act as the gatekeepers, often quite literally, to the knowledge within their exclusive ownership. Hiding behind the guise of the expert, and speaking a special professional language developed during the process of professionalization, the museum worker is able to guard against any criticism or demand from someone excluded from the rarefied confines of the profession. Like daddy, the professional always knows best.

This gatekeeping function that we all perform with varying degrees of rigour aligns museums unmistakably with the forces of high culture and against the forces of a radical popular cultural democracy with which many of us have great sympathy. Ironically, our aim of a populist museum practice, informed by notions of cultural enfranchisement for 'ordinary' people, is confounded by our very position within the process of cultural production. It can come as no surprise in this context that the late, and much lamented, Greater London Council (GLC) in its development of a popular cultural policy for London, a policy widely recognized as one of the most original and radical solutions to the endemic crises of municipal cultural practice, placed museums firmly in the camp of elitist institutions, along with opera and ballet, precisely because of the perceived lack of popular involvement and participation in the process of production (Mulgan and Worpole 1986: 74–90). It was the fields of community theatre, community film and video, community publishing and newspaper workshops, writing and music workshops, in which people were able to have some direct involvement, that were seen as the areas of cultural production that should be encouraged, and as the indicators of the ways in which cultural practice should develop in the future (GLC 1985; 1986).

It appears, however, that the consciousness of the dilemmas of professionalism is not an issue that concerns museum workers greatly. In these post-encyclopaedic days all scholarly work, research work, historical endeavour, requires some specialization, some particularity, but does it always have to be the so-called professionals undertaking this work? Why, in considering theoretical approaches to material culture, are the demands of the user, the consumer of museums, likely not to be considered? We have, as professionalized workers, to be conscious of our considerable power within the process of production and must ensure that the further exploration and theorization of material culture does not become an elaborate form of academic work-creation scheme remote from the needs of the museum's publics, and serving no social purpose.

This brings me to a second concern: the lack of political critique within material culture studies, which serves to align museums once again with high culture, with the powerful, with the winners in our society. Analyses of power relations, of oppressions, resistances and popular autonomies, of contradictions and betrayals are avoided. Our material culture is left to 'speak for itself'. But what do we hear? The lack of political critique in museums is rooted in the commitment of many museum workers to avoiding controversy and debate and maintaining balance and fair play in the best tradition of English cricketing ethics. The museum is seen, not as a place where the competing claims for history, on the rollercoaster between reality and myth, can be played out, but as a bias-free institution, concerned with objectivity and the production of a single authoritative narrative for public enlightenment. There is no sense of the cultural fragmentation and crisis of legitimation that has affected other, more theoretically alert, areas of cultural production, no recognition that we now live in 'a society in which difference and discontinuity rightly challenge ideas of totality and continuity' (Foster 1984). Peculiarly, in museums the truth is still felt to be achievable. In the absence of theory museum work is still considered to be non-intellectual, practical work, the practical creation of taxonomies and the practical arrangement of the evidence – the objects – to produce master narratives. In this world where empirical practice reigns supreme, the 'evidence' – the material culture – is treated as anodyne, unproblematic, as fact, so that interpretations are created, as in boy culture where a child builds a monolith out of Lego brick by brick, object by object and fact by fact. Even in situations where the evidence is not real, not genuine, as in copies and reproductions, the aim remains the same, to provide the 'real' truth (Eco 1986).

Inevitably this failure of museums to face and interrogate ideas of truth, reality and ideology situates them in a position of conformity with dominant, conservative political forces and the values of a British national culture characterized by Perry Anderson in his vintage critique as 'mediocre and inert' (Anderson 1968). Far from being apolitical, museums tend to reflect the beliefs of the right in a tamed and proud past, without conflict. This is what museum objectivity really means, and it is because of this that museums rarely come under the scrutiny of ruling groups. Museums have rarely induced the kind of moral panics that have been witnessed both in the past and the present, especially in the present, in other areas of cultural activity such as cinema, theatre and television, pop music and literature. Apart from the occasional policing of metropolitan art galleries in the late nineteenth century, museums have in general been left alone.

We are constantly being reminded that we are living in post-modern times. I do not feel confident enough to try to define here exactly what post-modernism is, and indeed, definitions have not yet been settled upon (Lyotard 1986). However, one of the main themes emerging in the discourse around post-modernism is that of the crisis of values and beliefs in which the major legitimating narratives that have informed and underpinned development in the modernist period have disappeared, leaving us to search for a new political and cultural agenda to replace the devalued, failed theories and practices of the past. All is confusion and doubt (Burgin 1986). Interestingly it is museums, as institutions, that are being used increasingly as illustrations of sites where the crises and confusions of the post-modern age are being played out. Museums represent the discredited past but give no guidance for the future (Horne 1984; Hewison 1987). Where do we go from here?

I have sketched out briefly some of the problems resulting from the pre-eminence of the object in museums. It is now time to undertake a major re-evaluation of the role of material culture in our museums. I believe that we have come to a dead end: we cannot simply carry on collecting objects religiously, mindlessly. I am not suggesting here that objects are of no use in museums but that their use should be put into perspective. In the field of social history objects represent only part of the story, and we therefore have to consider other, more effective, ways of representing both the past and the present. There are many aspects of social history that are not revealed, or that are very inadequately revealed, through the mobilization of objects. These include many of the most intimate life experiences: birth, sexuality, death and the infinite range of tastes, emotions, ideas and psychological states that punctuate and enliven those life experiences. Feminist social historians have shown how many fundamental experiences in the lives of women, such as menstruation, are not and cannot be represented by objects. Objects have only limited value for social historians. Beckow has argued that the idea of the artefact is the idea of culture: 'We are all', he suggests, 'students of human culture and our source of information is almost exclusively the human artifact ... When the dances all are danced and the problems all are pondered, we enter to gather up the artifactual traces of human activity and preserve the memory of what we did and how we did it in other ages' (Beckow 1982). For Beckow, then, the artefact can tell us all that we want to know. Yet how, we might ask, would we even begin to document, using objects, the most dramatic threat to world health in generations – AIDS? Would just one condom be sufficient? In this context Beckow's notion of objects being used in the performance of an autopsy on past civilizations 'when the dances all are danced' takes on a particularly morbid and ironic significance. If AIDS is difficult to document or represent through objects, then how many other social disasters in the past are now forgotten because they are not represented in our material culture inheritance?

It soon becomes clear that our museum collections are pitted with yawning gaps, gaps that represent major historical silences. Our material culture inheritance is fundamentally flawed as a primary resource for the production of histories and we will therefore have to look beyond objects for the solution to this problem. And so I return to the question 'Where do we go from here?' What should replace or supplement material culture in history production?

To this question I would answer simply 'experience'. It is people's experience, revealed in oral history and reminiscence, in film, video and photography, in writing, in performance, in painting and so on, that is the essential feature of an effective, relevant and responsive social history in museums. Museums have to connect more directly with the people whose lives and experience they are charged to represent. Connection through the fetishized medium of objects is unsatisfactory and, as we have seen, leaves enormous gaps, gaping silences. We can all go around collecting people's objects, emptying out their 'interesting' garbage bins, rummaging through their laundry. But this can never be a substitute for the process of talking and listening to people. The cultural practice of museums has to become more closely enmeshed in the society in which museums are unavoidably situated. Many years ago now, Raymond Williams considered the relations of culture and society, these being two forces in a relation of constant tension and sometime opposition, of culture versus society (Williams 1958). Perhaps we might add material culture versus society. Williams has recently returned to the problematic of culture and society (Williams 1986). Since the first raising of this fundamental issue the battlefield of culture has been taken up by two opposing theoretical discourses – very crudely, a structuralist model on the one hand and on the other a sociologistic model. Williams has suggested that the problem of theorizing culture, or in our case material culture, is the problem of theorising (away) the gap between culture and society. I would suggest that, in the context of museums and their current dilemma, it is the recovery and representation of experience, requiring significantly transformed cultural assumptions and practices, that would assist musems in negotiating this gap between culture and society, material culture and society.

Nevertheless, we should not assume that just by involving people in our museums and employing their experience in social histories we have somehow resolved the problems caused by object fetishism, or indeed by professionalization. The recovery of experience is not a simple matter. It is fraught with just as many difficulties, of use and interpretation, as a museum practice based on material culture in isolation. But the main point here is that the recovery of experience is, potentially at least, a strategy for articulating the silences represented in our museum collections, and most importantly, a strategy for radically altering the relation between the producers of knowledge – the curators – and the consumers of that knowledge – the public at large. In oral history in particular it is the lay person who becomes the 'expert', the lay person who is giving knowledge to the museum professional. The relations within cultural production are thus altered.

Even in people-centred museum work, however, the museum worker continues to exert considerable power. It is the professional who sets the agenda, who selects just whose experience will be useful, structures the encounter, who asks the questions, decides on the usefulness of the answer, and who finally edits out (of history) the material not required (White 1981). We cannot pretend, therefore, that we have totally escaped the problem of the professional through people-centred work. We cannot claim that we have suddenly surrendered our gatekeeping role, that we are 'allowing' self-representation. There is an interaction, an inter-relatedness of interest and purpose, between the museum worker and the subject of investigation, but it is the museum worker who remains very firmly in control. The mediating or enabling function is not really very far removed from the original gatekeeping function, no matter how much we hide behind a liberal-democratic discourse of emancipatory practices. Did not colonial missionary workers, working amongst the 'natives', believe that they were liberating people too? Terry Eagleton, parodying reception theory, has illustrated the ways in which we, as professionals, imagine that, just because we allow access to our sacred inner temples, our encyclopaedias of knowledge, we somehow surrender power and allow production from the outside (Eagleton 1986). He cites the Readers Liberation Movement, whose slogan was 'The authors need us: we don't need the authors', and which believed that everyone was capable of producing literature. Thus writers, such as Roman Ingarden, supplied texts to the reader with certain gaps which the reader could then fill in, thus creating an original 'work of art'! In other words the reader/writer fleshed out the literary skeleton. Eagleton sees this not as an emancipatory activity but as a 'shabby authorial plot to permit readers the fantasy of participation while reserving power squarely in the hands of the authorial class', equivalent to allowing 'a medieval craftsman to doodle the odd gargoyle'. We in museums have to recognize that anything short of handing musems over to the people will be allowing the people the fantasy of participation and nothing more. This is the foundation upon which we must base our theories and practices.

I very much doubt that there are many museums workers today who see the aim of curatorship to be the establishment of the conditions in which curators are no longer needed – that is the ultimate withdrawal of the professional – after all, and, especially under the present economic order, nobody wants to talk themselves out of a job. We therefore have to talk of, and negotiate, 'stages' in the withdrawal from power, which may not include the most radical solution, the final utopian stage, of the creation, or release, of the autonomous, truly popular and professional-free museum. In this context the development of a museum practice making direct use of the resources of human experience is infinitely preferable to our current object-centred representations being imposed from above on a public that has had no direct participation in the creation of those representations.

In order to illustrate some of the benefits of a people-centred approach to social history in museums, and by implication the inadequacy of the object-centred approach, I will now describe briefly a research project in inner city Birmingham which I undertook, on first leaving the Department of Museum Studies, with Karen Hull, a colleague on the Museum Studies course. The project, *Change in the Inner City*, was sponsored jointly by Birmingham City Museum (Department of Local History) and Birmingham Reference Library (Department of Local Studies) and aimed, as its title suggests, to document the immense social, economic and cultural changes in Birmingham's core inner city areas in the period since 1900, primarily through the media of photography and the tape recording of oral history. Whilst in the initial brief the collecting of objects was, potentially at least, a constituent element of the project, the collection of artefacts was not to be the major legitimation or purpose of the project; rather the project was intended to uncover areas of the social, economic and cultural history of the inner city that had not received the attention of the museum or library services in the past, and to make the project results available in as many ways as possible, including exhibition, publication, education and a publicly accessible sound archive.

The existing representation of the inner city in the collections of the City Museum and the City Library was patchy. Some areas of the city – where there were particular industries, for example – were well documented, whereas other areas had no representation at all in the city's material culture collections. The gaps in the collections extended from places in the inner city to the people who lived there, most obviously the almost complete lack of representation of the multi-racial nature of the inner city. Birmingham has large Afro-Caribbean, Asian, Chinese and other minority ethnic communities, many of whom were originally seduced to Birmingham in its macho, post-war heyday by fulsome promises of employment and prosperity, and were now condemned to live in some of the most multiply-deprived urban areas in this country. Yet, according to the 'evidence' of the collections, these people did not exist. Their immense contribution to the city was unrecognized. The project thus had to tackle the historical silences relating to both place and people.

As the *Change in the Inner City* project was concerned primarily with photographic and oral history work, we were liberated from the necessity to base the project around the existing 'official' city collections, and were therefore free to consider themes in social history which are generally poorly represented, or unrepresented, by objects and which could be tackled on a city-wide basis. Our ideas for themes included Crime, Death, Housing, Women's Lives, Education, Religion, Immigration and Rural-Urban Migrations, Sport, Leisure and Popular Culture, Hospitals and Healthcare, Friendly Societies, Pawnbroking and Banking. Clearly there were objects that could begin to illustrate some of these aspects of social history, a football for Sport, for example, or a coffin for Death, but the main feature of all of these proposals was that these were areas of human experience that could be recreated only by people who had experienced these things. There was a great deal of soul-searching in attempting to decide a theme for the project. We were conscious that our freedom of choice over the project theme, and the resources available to us, was a luxury that few of us ever enjoy. We eventually selected the theme of Food and Drink, and specifically of changes in the public, as opposed to private or home-based, consumption of food since the Second World War, and including a considerable degree of contemporary documentation work.

The project covered a very broad area of food provision and public consumption of food, tracing the growth in the habit of eating out in public, the development of catering by ethnic minority groups, and the transformations of catering generally from a haphazard conglomeration of individual efforts, sited firmly in Birmingham's 'traditional' vernacular food culture, into an increasingly highly-capitalized service industry run by national and international companies (Hull and Jenkinson 1985).

Post-war service industries have received very little attention in museums, precisely because the development of services, whether of the Welfare State or of capitalist industries more generally, cannot be dealt with through objects. Yet these developments have had, and continue to have, an extraordinary influence on our lives, not least in the provision of employment. Thus with 13,500 people employed in catering, on a full-time basis alone, in Birmingham's inner city in the early 1980s (as many as in the 'traditional' metal industries for which the city was once famous), it seemed important for a project to examine how this situation had come about and to consider the morphology of a service industry. This aspect of recent social history was especially suitable for a photographic and oral history project, as Kenneth Hudson has suggested:

> The archaeology of restaurants and cafes is a sadly neglected field of research. More than any other type of commercial premises they have been obliterated, concealed or transformed by mergers, bankruptcies and closures ... The social historian in search of source material has particularly difficult problems with the catering industry, and it is for this reason that personal reminiscences are so important (Hudson 1980).

Starting at the Second World War with the breakdown in a time of crisis of 'traditional' food patterns through the imposition of rationing, the disruption of home life and the massive growth of wartime public feeding centres – the 'British Restaurants' – the project went on to examine the immense diversification of catering provision in the inner city in the last 40 years. This included cafés and restaurants, tearooms, espresso bars, milk and sundae bars, take-aways and the most recent fast food outlets. It looked at changes in the supply of food in the city's markets and beyond, including a bean sprout factory and a halal slaughterhouse. It also looked at pub, hotel and chain store catering; industrial catering and the development of 'welfare catering', in particular the school meals service; at catering by the city's diverse communities including Afro-Caribbean, Asian, Chinese, Greek-Cypriot and Italian; and at areas of catering provision, such as oyster bars, cow heel shops, cooked meat stalls and Italian street hawkers, that have declined, or disappeared, since the Second World War.

We had no idea when we began the project of the enormous scale and diversity of this developing service industry. It was almost totally undocumented in the city's museum and library collections beyond a few sepia turn-of-the-century photographs. Had we started the project in the conventional manner of museum historical enquiry, that is by working outwards from the evidence of the collections, we would not have discovered this rich and suggestive area of recent social history. We would not have discovered, for example, the development of the British Restaurants, largely demolished in the post-war redevelopment and thereby made invisible to the object-centred historian; yet these restaurants played a major role in feeding the population of war-torn Birmingham, serving 11 million meals in 1944 alone, and provided many people's first experience not only of the labour-saving cafeteria service that was pioneered in the 'BRs' as they became known, but also of eating out in a public space. We would not have discovered the critical role that catering played in the economic and cultural lives of the first and later generations of minority ethnic communities, particularly the Asian and Hong Kong Chinese communities.

Food is part of the fabric of our lives. There is hardly anything that is closer to people, more intimate, more necessary, than food. We all have to eat. Yet we do not all eat the same things. Food is above all else culturally and ideologically coded and the study of its production and consumption can, I believe, throw light upon the changing values and attitudes and the transforming class allegiances of post-war British society. It is therefore surprising to find that historians, in musems and beyond, have remained silent on this area of human experience that can be employed, as can other areas of consumption and service provision, as a key to the major transformations in social, economic and cultural conditions under consumer capitalism. This silence among historians extends beyond the enormous changes in food consumption and in the food industry since 1945 to the thousands of women and men, mainly women, working in the catering industry, made invisible because they are, often quite literally, behind the scenes providing the service. Whilst the decline and virtual disappearance of the servant class up to the Second World War is currently enjoying something of a vogue amongst social history curators, the rise of the service class that replaced it has received virtually no attention.

Along with cleaning, check-out operating and hairdressing, catering is one of the poorest occupations in Britain, employing the most marginalized groups in society – women and first- or second-generation immigrants – who have been, and are, weakened by their lack of recognized skills, poor working conditions, unsocial hours, and very low pay, and often forbidden access to trade union organization. There is an assumption in Britain today that poverty has been obliterated, that no-one goes without any longer. Yet it is painfully clear that these metropolitan myths are confounded within the context of the service society where one person's pleasure is bought at the expense of another's invisible and extremely ill-rewarded labour. It is ironic that museums, whilst happy to represent the safe, distanced, romanticized poverty of Victorian England, choose not to be concerned with representing the very real, and 'dangerous', poverty created under the tyranny of advancing consumerism in the last 40 years and, more particularly, in the last decade.

In studying food and public catering we are not seeing simply the choice of one individual leading to the exploitation of another. Food is now also extremely big business. In the 1980s agriculture has become a highly-capitalized industry, food production is controlled by six major corporations, food retailing is controlled by ever larger supermarket chains and multiples and food catering is increasingly controlled by rapidly expanding hotel, contract catering and fast food companies. Whilst we all harbour the illusion of choice – the keyword of the consumer society – all too often what we eat is being decided for us by a food industry worth £30 billion a year. In the battleground of food the cynical manipulation of taste, most spectacularly through advertising, and the short cuts to profitability, as in the new forms of food adulteration but most importantly through the exploitation of labour both in this country and in the Third World, means that the poorest in society inevitably get the poorest deal.

I have described this project at some length in order to illustrate how the parameters of our social history have markedly shifted in the post-war period. We can no longer speak of a distinctly local history but have to look beyond to the forces that structure our society if we are to arrive at analytical, socially responsive social histories. To put it crudely, we have to start thinking big. It involves looking at structures of an immensely complex nature and being prepared to adopt a political perspective rather than pretending to objectivity. We have to involve people in our museums and be prepared to release some of our professional power by giving space for people to represent their perpectives in 'our museums.'

In conclusion, then, it is clear that, in the field of social history, there has to be a major shift in emphasis for museums to serve their function in society more fully and more effectively. We have to take a very critical and imaginative look at our material culture inheritance and seek out the many gaps, the many historical silences. We have to tackle the recreation and representation of social histories not by building from material culture upwards but by the interrogation of historical themes, issues, structures and analyses, drawing reference or illustration from whichever media, or combination of media, is appropriate. We have to begin using the media of the twentieth century – sound recording, photography, film and video – to record and interpret the twentieth century, and in this project we have to work in closer cooperation with people of all classes, all interest groups, all backgrounds, whilst maintaining a political perspective. We have to be able to accommodate the competing claims for history and provide a space for controversy, for the sorting out of disputes, in the very public forum of the museum. We have to become fully conscious of our own role as musem professionals in the process of cultural production, and prepare for the surrender of all, or some, of our power, in the project of creating socially useful museums.

If some of this change comes about, and we move confidently beyond material culture rather than being contained by it, then we shall have discovered a new world of possibilities for history museums previously undreamt of, and, in 50 years time a solitary condom will not be the only thing in our museums to represent and commemorate the major social disaster of the late twentieth century.

BIBLIOGRAPHY

Anderson, P., 1968. 'Components of the national culture', *New Left Review*, 50: 10–21.

Beckow, S., 1982. 'Culture, history, artifact', in Schlereth, T. J. (ed.), *Material Culture Studies in America*: 123–45.

Berger, J., 1967. *A Fortunate Man.*

Burgin, V., 1986. 'The end of art theory', in *Criticism and Postmodernity*: 140–204.

Eagleton, T., 1986. 'The revolt of the reader', in *Against The Grain. Selected Essays*: 181–4.

Eco, U., 1986. 'Travels in hyper-reality', in *Faith in Fakes: Essays*: 1–58.

Elliott, P., 1982. 'Intellectuals, the information society and the disappearance of the public sphere', *Media, Culture and Society, 4*: 243–53.

Foster, H., 1984. 'For a concept of the political in art', in *Art in America*: 114–23.

GLC, 1985. *The State of the Art or Art of the State. Strategies for the Cultural Industries in London:* 131–66.

GLC, 1986. *Campaign for a Popular Culture.*

Hewison, R., 1987. *The Heritage Industry.*

Horne, D., 1984. *The Great Museum.*

Hudson, K., 1980. *The Way We Used To Work.*

Hull, K. and Jenkinson, P., 1985. *A Taste of Change. Some Aspects of Eating in the Inner City, Birmingham 1939–1985.*

Lyotard, F–F., 1986. 'Defining the postmodern', *ICA Documents*, 4: 6–7.

Mulgan, G. and Worpole, K., 1986. 'Saturday night or Sunday morning?', in *From Arts to Industry – New Forms of Cultural Policy:* 74–90.

Popular Memory Group, 1982. 'Popular Memory: theory, politics, method' in Johnson, R., McClennan, G., Schwarz, B. and Sutton, D. (eds), *Making Histories. Studies in History Writing and Politics*: 205–52.

Robertson, I., 1986. Speech at South East Federation of Museums and Art Galleries Meeting, Beaulieu.

Samuel, R., 1981. 'People's history', in *People's History and Socialist Theory*, xiv–xl.

White, G., 1981. 'Beyond autobiography', in Samuel, R. (ed.), *People's History and Socialist Theory*: 33–41.

Williams, R., 1958. *Culture and Society 1780–1950.*

Williams, R., 1986. 'The uses of cultural theory', *New Left Review, 158*, 19–31.

14 *The Social Basis of Museum and Heritage Visiting*

NICK MERRIMAN

According to the Museums Association Database Project, there are now 2,134 museums in Britain (Prince and Higgins-McLoughlin 1987: 12), compared with 217 a hundred years ago (British Association 1887), and they are still opening at the rate of 30 a year (Museums and Galleries Commission 1984: 46), although it should be noted that no figures on closures are at present available. These museums have recorded visits of c.70 million per year, with total visits likely to be much higher, as many museums do not record their visitor figures. In 1985 it was a museum (the British Museum) that was the most visited tourist attraction in Britain (3.8 million visits), and the Tower of London was the most visited attraction at which an entrance charge was levied (British Tourist Authority/English Tourist Board 1986).

In view of these developments, it is surprising that we still know so little about the general role of the past in contemporary society, and specifically the role that museum visiting plays in British culture. Museum visitor surveys, although useful for each individual museum, have largely resulted in the continued replication of the same findings (Cruickshank 1972; Greene 1978; Heady 1984; Klein 1974; Mason 1974). They have rarely advanced the overall understanding of what motivates museum visiting and non-visiting, because they have lacked a theoretical framework within which to interpret their results. If we wish to understand why some people visit museums and others do not, we must understand the nature of the museum itself, which entails comprehending its place first within the scope of leisure activities and second within the wider society, and this naturally involves confronting theories of leisure, culture and society.

In this paper a first step will be made in this direction, using the interim results of a survey which does try to place museum[1] visiting in its context within the wider culture of British society. Underlying the whole work are two basic assumptions. The first is that museums are interesting and worthwhile places to visit and potentially do offer something to everyone in the community. The second is that it should be the aim of general 'public' museums to provide for all of the community. This aim is enshrined in the founding charters of many museums, and is an obligation for those that are funded to a large extent by taxpayers' money. Museums have always had the potential to be 'people's universities', offering a second chance for self-education, especially for those who did not take full advantage of the educational system first time round (Chadwick 1980: 101–2; Millas 1973), although this potential has rarely been realized.

It is not suggested here that museum curators will be failing in their purpose if they do not persuade every person in Britain to visit a museum at least once a year. It is rather argued that there are various cultural factors which make museum visiting a daunting and difficult experience for some members of the community who are otherwise interested in the past, and that it is the dismantling of these barriers which must be a first step towards achieving a wider public for museums. Consequently this paper will concentrate more on the non-visitor to museums, in an attempt to understand the nature of deterrents to visiting, and to see if museums can learn anything from the sort of past-related activities that non-visitors do choose to participate in. The characteristics of museum visitors and non-visitors will be established and compared with those of visitors to other heritage presentations. It is argued that participation in heritage activities is dominated by the better educated and more affluent groups in society because these are the people who are socialized into participating.

The work presented here is the interim result of a nationwide survey carried out in 1985 of 1,500 people selected randomly from the electoral registers of Great Britain, who were sent a questionnaire by post which gauged museum visiting patterns, attitudes to the past, and other heritage-related questions. The survey was carried out using an American technique known as the 'Total Design Method'. The method was effective enough to achieve a final response rate of 66 per cent, which is above average for a postal survey, and around the average that could be expected for a personal interview survey on the same subject Kviz 1977: 266). A discussion of the method, the problem of non-response, and the variables used, will be found in the Appendix.

Surveys all vary to such an extent in their wording, presentation, sampling, weighting and analytical method that absolute comparisons are difficult to make; comparisons are better made within the dataset between, in this case, contrasting groups such as museum visitors and non-visitors. The problem of comparing different surveys is shown by a consideration of how much of the population actually goes to museums (table 14.1). The figures of the survey under current consideration suggest that 58 per cent of the British population visit a museum or gallery at least once a year, and even if all non-respondents are taken as non-visitors (which the follow-ups indicated was not the case), then the minimum figure for museum participation is 40 per cent.

Table 14.1 Incidence of museum visiting in Britain

	Visitors percentage	[number]
The current survey	58	[930]
The ETB survey	24	[4,142]
Henley Time-Use survey	47	[523]
Minimum figure for current survey	40	[930]
Likely 'true' figure	47	[930]

This conflicts with the figure of 24 per cent participation per year reported in a nationwide survey carried out for the English Tourist Board (1982). This was, however, carried out in a different way, with a different sampling strategy, and it asked slightly different questions. For example, the figure of 24 per cent covers museums only; 13 per cent of respondents also visited art galleries at least once a year.[2] Another questionnaire on leisure activities, the Time Use Survey, carried out regularly over a number of years for the Henley Centre for Forecasting (e.g. Henley Centre 1985), shows an average museum participation of around 47 per cent. Lewis (1975) summarizes visitor participation for a number of other countries, quoting figures of 48 per cent per year for Canada, 55 per cent for West Germany and 68 per cent for France. The total picture does therefore suggest that the ETB figure is too low, and that the figure for the current survey may be too high. In order to check this, a small sample of non-respondents were contacted by telephone and it was established that 80 per cent of them had not visited a museum in the previous twelve months. If 80 per cent of all non-respondents to the survey are assumed not to visit museums, then the likely actual figure for museum participation in Britain is 47 per cent.[3]

Table 14.2 shows that most visitors go to a museum once or twice a year. However, it should be borne in mind that the term 'museum visitor' as used in most surveys is an arbitrary definition, denoting at least one museum visit per year.

Table 14.2 Frequency of museum visiting in 1985

	%	
None	42	
1–2 times	40	
3–10 times	17	
11+ times	2	[number=930]

It is therefore important to understand what the term 'non-visitor' really means in the context of this survey. For example, the survey in fact shows that most people have visited a museum in the last four years, with a very sharp fall-off after that, the next largest group being those who have never visited a museum. There seem to be three major clusters in museum visiting: 68 per cent who have visited a museum in the last four years, 18 per cent who have never visited, and the rest (13 per cent) who are very occasional visitors.

As noted above, a large number of surveys carried out within museums have shown the characteristics of the museum visitor to be fairly uniform, and those of the non-visitor, where discussed at all, have been inferred as the inverse of those of visitors. It is only possible to compare the characteristics of museum visitors with those of non-visitors in a systematic way by taking a sample of the general population, not just of museum visitors. This has been done with useful results by two local surveys in Britain (Erwin 1971; Prince and Schadla-Hall 1985), and on a national scale in Canada (Dixon *et al.* 1974). The current survey was constructed to provide such information on a national scale for Britain.

As the characteristics of museum visitors are well known, they will not be dwelt upon at length: a summary chart of the main demographic tendencies of both museum visitors and non-visitors as revealed by the current survey is given as a guide (table 14.3).

Table 14.3 Tendencies of typical museum visitors and non-visitors[4]

Visitors	*Non-visitors*
'Middle' age group (35–59)	The over-60s
Owner-occupiers	Council house tenants
Car owners	Non-owners of car
Students or those in employment	Retired, unemployed or part-time work
Attended selective school	Attended non-selective school
Stayed on at school	Left school at minimum age

Demographic profiles of visitors to museums do not reflect profiles of the general population. The sort of people who are more likely to visit them are the better-educated and the better-off, and those who are less likely to do so are the less well-off, particularly the retired and the unemployed.

This last point implies that museums are visited least by those with ostensibly the most time to do so. This throws into doubt the arguments of those who foresee the coming of a society increasingly oriented towards leisure, in which museums would fulfil a vital role by providing meaningful entertainment and education for people with increased leisure time (Dumazedier 1967; 1974). This viewpoint arises from a misunderstanding of the nature of leisure and, as David Prince has pointed out in another paper (1985), there is in fact no relationship between unemployment and museum visiting; it appears not to be part of the perception of the range of leisure choices that are open to most unemployed people, or indeed to those in retirement.

It is important to distinguish between those reasons for non-visiting that are physical (due for example to lack of mobility), and those that are cultural, because the simplest explanation of the behaviour of non-visitors would be that they do not visit museums because they are physically unable to do so. The distribution of museums nationally might also be thought to have an effect on museum visiting patterns. As an experiment, respondents' participation in museums was weighted according to the number of museums available in their county, as a rough guide to museum provision in the area. This showed that in some areas the paucity of museums was reflected in lower-than-average visiting. However, in some metropolitan areas, most notably London, where there is a great concentration of museums, visiting is also less than the national average, whilst in other areas with few museums visiting might be above average. In short, the geographical provision of museums does not necessarily have an effect on the level of visiting. A further physical constraint is access to a vehicle. As might be anticipated, those with no transport of their own are much less likely to visit a museum (51 per cent visit) than those who do (62–67 per cent).

Those past retirement age are the only group who are more likely to be non-visitors than visitors (table 14.4). This may be a product of genuine decreased mobility in old age; however, 42 per cent of all over-60s are in fact visitors, and similarly, 51 per cent of all those people who do not have access to a car are still able to visit a museum at least once a year. As the elderly are those who are least likely to have access to a car, then physical factors can explain the behaviour of only a small proportion of non-visitors. The answer for much of the non-visiting must thus lie elsewhere, in cultural factors which make museums a less attractive leisure choice.

Indeed, cultural factors may explain the behaviour of elderly non-visitors more accurately than physical factors (not all of the 58 per cent of elderly non-visitors can be housebound). The work of Robert and Rhona Rapoport (1975), for example, looks at the sort of leisure activities that different age groups are likely to do, given the expectations appropriate to their particular stage in the life-cycle. In the case of those approaching retirement an approach based on analysis of the life-cycle would argue that this group is less likely to visit attractions such as museums not primarily on grounds of physical immobility, but because the consensus of research suggests that retirement is a phase of gradual disengagement from public activity, when leisure is likely to be increasingly centred round the home (Roberts 1981: 79). The withdrawal of older people from museum visiting is not thus necessarily purely for physical reasons: it is a cultural factor seen over the whole of the social arena (Clarke and Critcher 1985: 153–5).

Table 14.4 Museum visiting crosstabulated by age

Age	*Visitor* %	*Non-visitor* %	[number]
17–19	58	42	[19]
20–24	59	41	[102]
25–34	64	36	[177]
35–49	67	33	[235]
50–59	67	33	[135]
60–64	42	58	[78]
65+	42	58	[180]

The major cultural factor which would explain the lack of museum visiting amongst certain sections of the population might simply be that they are not interested in the past. However, answers to one of the survey questions establish that there is in fact a high degree of interest in the past in Britain, with 91 per cent believing it worthwhile to know about the past to some extent (table 14.5). But, as fig. 14.1 shows, only 58 per cent express this interest in the past by museum visiting. Although non-visitors are more likely than visitors to question the value of knowing about the past, only a small percentage of non-visiting can be explained by lack of interest – only 19 per cent of non-visitors are seriously doubtful about the value of knowing about the past.

Table 14.5 Basic interest in the past:
'Do you think it is worth knowing about the past?'

	Definitely %	*Probably* %	*Perhaps* %	*No* %	[number]
Visitors	89	9	2	1	[543]
Non-visitors	65	17	11	8	[386]
All	79	12	6	4	[934]

Respondents were also questioned on their visiting of castles and historic houses. A typology of 'heritage visitors' was then built up by dividing respondents into four categories: those who visited none of the attractions, those who visited one out of three, those who visited two, and those who visited all of them. The demographic profiles for these types of visitor are similar, but more accentuated, to those for museum visitors and non-visitors, with those who do not visit any heritage attractions significantly more likely to be retired or unemployed, of low status and to have received minimum education, and those who visit everything being significantly of higher status (table 14.6).

Table 14.6 Heritage visitors crosstabulated by status

Status	*Visits nothing* %	*Visits one attraction* %	*Visits two attractions* %	*Visits all attractions* %	[number]
High	13	38	10	40	[148]
Intermediate	23	37	14	26	[597]
Low	46	31	2	20	[161]

When these groups are crosstabulated with visits to certain other activities, specifically chosen because they are of a 'higher culture' nature, the patterns of heritage visiting are carried through into patterns of visits to these activities. For example, those who visit no heritage attractions are least likely to visit the theatre, classical concerts and ballet, and there is increasing participation in these activities the more the respondent is involved in heritage visiting. The culmination of this is the group who comprise 27 per cent of the sample. These are the people who go to museums, castles and historic houses, and they are far more likely than other groups to go to the theatre at least once a year (74 per cent), to go to classical concerts (38 per cent) and to go to the ballet (18 per cent) (table 14.7).

Table 14.7 Heritage visiting crosstabulated with visits to other cultural activities (percentage of each group visiting at least once a year)

	Visits nothing %	*Visits one attraction* %	*Visits two attractions* %	*Visits all attractions* %
Theatre	20	38	48	74
Classical concerts	5	9	14	38
Ballet	2	2	9	18

Two explanations for the continuation of heritage visiting patterns into other 'high culture' activities immediately suggest themselves: the first is that heritage visiting is itself a high culture activity and thus appeals to those who participate in other high culture activities. The second is that visits to the two types of activity (heritage and high culture) are unrelated and are just part of a very wide range of activities participated in by people who lead very active leisure lives and who participate in both high culture and popular culture activities. The truth probably lies in an amalgam of both explanations: part of the explanation for museum visiting patterns lies in the fact that museums still have the legacy of an elitist high culture image that certain groups find intimidating, and partly in the fact that some people participate in a much wider range of activities in their leisure time than others.

When respondents were asked to indicate from a list of institutions which one of them a museum reminded them most of, clear-cut distinctions between visitors and non-visitors were evident (table 14.8).

Table 14.8 The image of the museum crosstabulated by museum-visiting

	Visitor %	*Non-visitor* %
Monument to the dead	25	46
Library	40	27
Church or temple	8	12
School	12	9
Community centre	4	1
Department store	1	0
Other	9	5
	[number=529]	[number=369]

While the largest category of visitors (40 per cent) thought a museum most similar to a library, the largest category of non-visitors (46 per cent) saw it as being most like a monument to the dead. An image redolent of monumentality and of deathliness seems a curiously Victorian one, and indeed to some extent the explanation for it can be sought in the great municipal museum movement of the mid to late nineteenth century (Lewis 1984). Although the movement was largely inspired by a genuine desire to improve the cultural provision of the population, especially of working people, it did tend to present museums as Temples of Culture, with primarily a didactic purpose of instilling correct moral thinking and feeling (Cunliffe 1981: 192; Lewis 1980: 152). This is not, however, enough to explain the current strength of the image: it must still partly be true in the minds of certain groups in order to survive. There is evidence from other questions to supplement the negative image of the museum amongst non-visitors. For example, they are much less likely than visitors to agre that museums have a pleasant atmosphere and they are more likely to agree that they are too middle-class (Table 14.9).

Table 14.9 The atmosphere of museums:
'They have a pleasant atmosphere'

	Strongly agree %	*Agree* %	*Neither* %	*Disagree* %	*Strongly disagree*	[number]
Museum visitors	14	61	16	9	–	[516]
Museum non-visitors	8	43	29	18	1	[339]

Table 14.9 cont.
'They are too middle class'

	Strongly agree %	*Agree* %	*Neither* %	*Disagree* %	*Strongly disagree* %	[number]
Museum visitor	2	9	16	56	16	[532]
Museum non-visitor	5	18	23	47	7	[363]

There does therefore seem to be a strong impression amongst non-visitors that museums are rather unwelcoming in their atmosphere and only aimed at a specific group. In other words, the museum is still socially divisive, or at least visiting patterns to it reflect social divisions. The reason for this is to be sought in the way in which people are socialized into museum use (or non-use).

One of the most wide-ranging approaches to the place of museum-visiting in contemporary culture is provided by a consideration of the work of Pierre Bourdieu, who is rare amongst sociologists in that some of his work has been directly, or indirectly, concerned with museums and galleries (Bourdieu and Darbel 1966; Bourdieu and Passeron 1977; Bourdieu 1984). A concept of central importance is that of the 'habitus'. This is defined as 'a system of dispositions', which are themselves defined as:

> the result of an organising action, with a meaning close to that of words such as structure. It also designates a way of being, a habitual state (especially of the body) and, in particular, a *predisposition, tendency, propensity* or *inclination* (Bourdieu 1984: 2; his emphasis).

Bourdieu argues that individuals are socialized in the first instance by their family into various ways of thinking and feeling, which he terms 'the habitus'. The family habitus exerts a strong influence on achievement in the educational system (Bourdieu and Passeron 1977: 43). School culture is seen to be strongly couched in terms familiar to the middle class, who construct the syllabus and comprise the teaching staff. As a result the middle-class child is predisposed to higher achievement at school than the working-class child, because he or she will feel more at home in the school environment and will better be able to grasp the concepts used, or, in Bourdieu's terms, he/she will be better able to decipher the code of the school (1971: 192). If this argument is extended to museums, museum displays can be seen as a code, a special form of communication which has to be correctly decoded in order to be understood. As in schools, the language of museums is one spoken only by certain groups of people who possess sufficient educational background (similar to that of the curators) to understand the message of the museum: 'A work of art has meaning and interest only for someone who possesses the cultural competence, that is, the code, into which it is encoded' (Bourdieu 1984: 2).

Lack of training in the conceptual method needed to make decontextualized objects assume a historical meaning can lead to an assessment of all museum objects in similar terms which are familiar within the visitor's range of experience. Objects may be assessed purely in terms of their size, colour, workmanship or exoticism, with the result that boredom can easily set in and inadequacy can be felt in the face of a failure to make the objects mean anything else (Bourdieu and Darbel 1966: 68). Possession of this code is described as a form of 'cultural capital' which acts as an adjunct to economic capital. Bourdieu sees it as increasingly necessary for economic power to conceal and legitimate itself in symbolic terms in order to be effective. An investment in the cultivation of 'cultural capital' has a subsequent return in school, university, social contacts, on the 'marriage market' and on the job market (Brubaker 1985: 757). For some people, then, possession of the cultural capital necessary to understand the museum is an adjunct to the economic power they already possess (or wish to possess), part of a general cultivated lifestyle appropriate to it (Dimaggio and Useem 1978: 152).

The survey data used here show that in general it is the better-educated and more affluent who feel most at home in the culture of the museum. This, it can be argued, is a product of two interlinked strands, both of the historical associations of the museum with high culture, and because it is the better-educated who, through the cultivated lifestyle encouraged by the 'habitus' inculcated by family, school and peers, possess the perceptual apparatus necessary to decode the message of the museum. For those who do not possess the relevant cultural capital, the museum can seem imposing and uninviting. Thus, despite great improvements effected on the museum's image since the nineteenth-century citadels of culture, the museum still seems in general terms to divide society into those who have the culture to understand it and those who do not.

If museum workers wish to remove the cultural barriers to museum visiting, a useful starting point is to examine other ways of experiencing the past. Attractions popular with those who choose not to visit museums can be isolated and studied to see if there is anything in the experience they provide that museums can learn from.

Table 14.10 The most enjoyable way of finding out about the past

	Frequencies (%)
Visiting the site/area	20
Guided tour of site/area	19
Watching a TV programme	16
Reading a book about it	13
Listening to a talk by an expert	12
Enquiring in a library	7
Visiting a museum	7
Going to evening classes	6
	[number=942]

Museums in fact came equal seventh out of eight choices given in a question concerning the most enjoyable way of finding out about some local site (table 14.10). The most preferred categories were to visit the site by oneself or to be given a guided tour of it, with 'watching a TV programme about it' third choice. This immediately suggests, first, that museums are relatively unenjoyable, and, second, that seeing something in context on site, or even in the context provided by television, is the best way to make it understandable and hence enjoyable.

Those who visit neither museums, castles, nor historic houses – that is, those who seem not interested in conventional heritage presentations – are most likely to prefer finding out about the past by watching television, and those who just visit one of these attractions are likely to prefer reading a book. Those who visit two or all of them are significantly much more likely to want to visit the site or area by themselves or as part of a guided tour (table 14.11).

Table 14.11 The most enjoyable way of finding out about the past crosstabulated with heritage visiting

	Visit museum %	*Read book* %	*Visit area* %	*Tour site* %	*Ask in library* %	*Evening classes* %	*Watch TV* %	*Talk by expert* %	[number]
Visits nothing	5	16	16	14	12	2	25	12	[222]
Visits one attraction	8	18	13	15	6	8	16	16	[187]
Visits two attractions	7	12	23	22	6	3	16	10	[232]
Visits three attractions	9	9	25	25	4	10	8	11	[236]

Thus, those who participate least in visits to conventional heritage presentations are most attracted to ways of finding out about the past that are centred around the home, such as T.V. viewing or reading. With increased participation in conventional heritage, the likelihood increases of wanting to get out of the home and view the remains of the past in their context. This distinction between appreciation of the past based around the home and that outside the home is one that has important implications for presentation and will be discussed more fully below.

Table 14.12 shows figures for participation in other heritage-related activities. While 4 per cent of respondents are, or have been, members of a local history or archaeology club, 7 per cent have used a metal detector for 'treasure hunting'. The figure of 10 per cent for participation in an archaeological dig or fieldwalking may seem encouraging, but it may be slightly high due to the phrasing of the question, which meant that anyone who

Table 14.12 Participation in 'heritage' activities:

'Have you ever done any of the following things?'
(% of respondents participating)

	%
Been a member of a local history or archaeology club	4
Been a member of a local collectors' club	3
Used a metal detector for 'treasure hunting'	7
Gone on an archaeological dig or gone fieldwalking for pottery	10
Researched your family tree	15

had wandered across a field and found some pottery would answer affirmatively. The figures are, however, enough to suggest that finding the physical remains of the past is more popular than organized clubs (which may, however, include a substantial fieldwork component as part of their activities). The social basis of club membership and individual treasure hunting remains to be explored, but it is possible that treasure hunting owes at least part of its popularity to the fact that, once the metal detector is bought, it can be practised with minimum effort by one person alone, it usually achieves some interesting results, and it avoids the social conventions and commitments of club membership. It is also noteworthy that, of all these past-related activities listed here, researching the family tree is the one most frequently indulged in. This is perhaps because it exerts a unique interest for every individual, and is a personal link to the past, a way of peopling history and making it come alive: this is the reason family tree research is a frequent topic for school projects, which may account for some of the instances here.

Participation in all of these 'extra-museum' ways of experiencing the past also varies with status (table 14.13). No respondents defined as 'low status' have ever belonged to a history or archaeology club, and only 2 per cent have belonged to a collectors' club: it is the higher-status people who are more likely to belong to these sorts of organizations, and to research their family tree. By contrast, it is the lower-status people who are most likely to have used a metal detector. Practical archaeology and fieldwalking have a slightly more even spread of participation, which might suggest that practical archaeology has the potential to be a genuinely popular subject.

The relative popularity of metal detecting amongst lower-status individuals has been seen (Gregory 1983; 1986) as evidence that it is a way of finding out about the past amongst those who feel alienated from formal archaeology. However, when participation in these various activities is crosstabulated with the classification of 'heritage visitors' already used, the results are remarkably uniform: again, it is the people who do not visit museums, castles or historic houses who are least likely to participate in metal detecting, and those who visit all of them who are most likely to participate in all these other activities, including treasure hunting with a metal detector (table 14.14).

Table 14.13 Participation in past-related activities crosstabulated by status

Status	*History/ archaeology club* %	*Collectors' club* %	*Metal detector* %	*Dig/Field-walking* %	*Family tree* %
High	6	6	6	8	20
Intermediate	5	3	7	11	15
Low	–	2	10	10	10

Treasure hunters thus do not seem necessarily to be alienated by museums. It seems more likely that they are people who are very interested in many aspects of the past, but who may feel excluded by the decline of amateur field-work in archaeology. The experience of treasure hunting may be a different, perhaps more fulfilling, adjunct to the sense of the past offered by museums. It is notable that, besides researching the family tree, which has a direct personal interest, the most popular activities here are those which are out of doors, 'on site' (finding pottery, going on excavations, going treasure hunting). The emphasis again is on discovery of objects in context. This, it would seem, is where for many people a sense of the past is best gained, and it is just this that has been lost by the decline of amateur fieldwork in archaeology and has been taken up by metal detector enthusiasts.

Table 14.14 Participation in heritage activities crosstabulated by type of heritage visitor

	History/ archaeology club %	*Collectors' club* %	*Metal detector* %	*Dig/field-walking* %	*Family tree* %
Visits nothing	2	2	3	3	8
Visits one attraction	2	2	6	7	14
Visits two attractions	3	3	8	10	17
Visits three attractions	9	5	12	21	20

It could be argued, then, that all manifestations of the past are areas that are appropriated by the better-educated and the more affluent, and that those of lower status are really not motivated to learn about the past. However, it is important to draw a distinction between 'the Heritage' and 'the Past'. 'The

Past' I would define as the total range of human past activities, whether real or imaginary, whereas 'the Heritage' is the physical representations of the past, or conventional activities associated with it, known through such media as museums, historic buildings, archaeological excavations, town trails, countryside interpretation, and activities such as genealogy and collecting antiques.

The survey has shown that museum visiting lies within a wider pattern of participation in 'the Heritage', and that visiting patterns to all of them are broadly similar. The reasons for the heritage visiting patterns demonstrated in the survey are to be sought in the social basis of the use of the heritage. First, certain groups are socialized through family, school and peer groups to place a higher overt value on 'the Heritage' (as distinct from 'the Past') than others. Heritage visiting is encouraged as a habit, and it becomes, along with visits to other attractions such as the theatre, a symptom of a particular lifestyle, such that participation in the heritage can be seen as an emblem of affiliation to a certain group, usually of the better educated and the well-off. As a result, heritage presentations have become largely associated with this group, and couched in terms most readily understandable to them.

There are elements of the survey data that suggest that there is an underlying substratum of less 'tangible' ways of gaining a sense of the Past, which do not come under the purview of conventional 'Heritage'. These are hardly touched on by this work because they consist of the sort of things that are difficult to approach with a questionnaire survey. This aspect is suggested by answers to a question on the importance of different types of history. Respondents were given a list of different kinds of history, from world history to family history, and asked to rank them according to their importance so far as they were concerned. When these answers were crosstabulated with status, the following clear distinctions were evident (table 14.15).

Table 14.15 Importance of different types of history crosstabulated by status

High status	*Intermediate status*	*Low status*
1. World history	1. Family history	1. Family history
2. British history	2. British history/ local history	2. Local history/ history of homeland
3. History of homeland[5]	3. History of homeland	3. British history
4. Local history	4. World history	4. World history
5. Family history		

The high-status respondents showed a clear hierarchy from the global approach of world history being the most important, down to family history being the least. In contrast, the low-status people's choices were almost the reverse, with family history being the most important, as it was with those of intermediate status. This might suggest that, amongst those who are less likely to go to museums and other conventional historical presentations, a sense of the past is really found within the family and perhaps within the local area. Although this needs to be tested by further work, I would predict that this experience of the past is largely intangible because it can take the form of private memories, nostalgic chats with contemporaries or younger people, perhaps supplemented by family photographs, souvenirs or simply walks in the local area. This means of thinking about the past may be far more meaningful than any visit to the museum, but it would be rather difficult for the museum to draw on it to provide a better experience for a wider range of people. Indeed, such approaches to the past might be popular precisely because they escape the artificial atmosphere of the museum. It remains to be seen whether the development of such things as 'reminiscence centres' will encourage this way of experiencing the past, or will simply appropriate it as another area of conventional heritage.

The survey shows that museum visiting reflects social divisions in British society, and that cultural barriers which deter certain groups from participating in them lie deep within our socialization processes. It has been argued that such processes also lead certain groups to place a more overt value on the conventional heritage and tend to dominate visiting to it or involvement in it. The sort of elements that people find most interesting and rewarding in giving a sense of the past are contextual: objects and sites, seen in their setting, preferably out of doors; usually with an element of self-discovery, and ideally with some form of personal link, whether it be to the family or to the local area. This suggests that on the one hand the way forward for museums is decentralization and the creation of a number of site museums and full-scale reconstructions (if in accessible areas) where objects can be seen in a fuller context. The desire for personal discovery of the past can be aided by the promotion of self-directed trails, and by a general encouragement of participation by non-professionals in the recovery of the past, such as helping in documentary research or the fostering of amateur fieldwork in archaeology.

On the other hand, these changes would be those that appeal most to people who are already committed to heritage visiting. Therefore these improvements might attract more visitors, but not necessarily of a wider social group. It has been demonstrated above that, for those people who are least likely to visit heritage presentations, the past is preferably experienced via the television, at home. In these cases, the museum curator will again have to venture outside the museum itself and meet the expectations of the public. Contributions to local television or radio programmes are possible if the curator is willing to put in the effort to approach the producers; there might even conceivably be a market for home videos on the history of the area, produced by the museum. Advice might be given on family tree research or displaying family history in a photograph album. Efforts need not be confined to the media alone: taking the museum to areas of everyday activity is an oft-suggested, but rarely practised, way of making people aware of local history, and of the existence of the museum. The use of building society windows, the mounting of temporary exhibitions in shops, even the use of mobile musems which tour shopping centres, are all possible; they just require effort. In all of these approaches (which are just a few among many that are possible) the museum object is of paramount importance: a small collection of authentic objects in a prominent High Street window will attract far more interest than a series of maps and photographs. However, it is only by going out of the museum and attempting to use a display language familiar to the 18–20 per cent of people who never visit museums that museums can hope to attract a range of visitors that is representative of the total population.

Acknowledgments

Greatest thanks are due to my supervisor Cathie Marsh for her invaluable advice, and to Ian Hodder for initially suggesting the project. Encouragement and useful advice has also been received from Colin Renfrew, Nicholas James, Chris Tilley, Patrick Wright, Kate Pretty and Caroline Beattie.

Notes

1. Thoughout this paper, the term 'museum' also covers art galleries.
2. Information kindly supplied by the English Tourist Board and NOP Market Research Inc. It is not known to how much of the 24 per cent of museum visitors accounts for the 13 per cent who visit art galleries.
3. In experiments it was found that weighting the sample figures to produce these visiting proportions had the effect of skewing the demographic profile so that it was unrepresentative of the total population. In view of this, and the fact that the main interest of the work is comparative, the original weighting structure is retained.
4. In assessing the characteristics of museum visitors and non-visitors it should be stressed that these are tendencies only: the greater number of characteristics in a list a person possesses, the more they are likely to be a visitor or non-visitor.
5. By 'homeland' is meant country of origin. This was included to cover those people who were not born in Britain and do not feel that their roots lie there.

Appendix

The survey method

The Total Design Method (Dillman 1978) essentially relies on a high response rate being achieved by easy-to-answer format, relevant covering letter, careful attention to personalization of the survey package, and the use of reminders and follow-up mailings to achieve higher response. Questions were formulated on the basis of unstructured interviews around themes at an early stage, and by a pilot survey of 100 people using open-ended questions to establish the most common topics.

Non-response

In such a survey the problem of non-response is likely to be critical, because the 34 per cent who did not reply to the survey may be completely different from those who did. They can be expected, for example, by the very fact that they did not reply to the questionnaire, to be less interested in museums than those who did reply, and probably to visit them less. In order for the survey to be representative of the general population, the probable answers of those who did not reply must be estimated and appropriate weighting factors added to the survey results. Estimation was done in two ways. First, the answers of those who required two follow-up mailings before they answered were used as an approximation for non-respondents on the basis that, because they took the longest to reply, their answers were the most like those of non-respondents. Second, a small sample of actual non-respondents were contacted by telephone to try to ascertain reasons for non-reply. These varied from lack of interest to physical disability. When all of these elements had been taken into consideration, weighting factors were added to the survey results which gave the closest approximation to the likely answers of the non-respondents, while still retaining the demographic structure of the total population. This is standard practice in survey analysis (Moser and Kalton 1971: 183–6). All figures given here are weighted figures, and all differences are statistically significant.

Demographic variables used

The commonest explanatory variables used have been the basic ones of age and length of formal education. The 'status' variable was calculated by combining the results of questions on education, housing tenure and car ownership, such that those who are house-owners, car-owners and stayed on at school are high status, and those who rent their accommodation, have no car and left school at the minimum age are low status. Intermediate status covers those who have various combinations of these characteristics.

BIBLIOGRAPHY

Bourdieu, P., 1971. 'Systems of education and systems of thought', in Young, M. (ed.), *Knowledge and Control*: 189–207.

Bourdieu, P., 1984. *Distinction.*
Bourdieu, P. and Darbel, A., 1966. *L'amour de l'art: les musées et leur public.*
Bourdieu, P. and Passeron, J–C., 1977. *Reproduction in Education, Society and Culture.*
British Association, 1887. 'Report of the Committee on the Provincial Museums of the United Kingdom', in *Report of the British Association for the Advancement of Science 1887*: 97–130.
British Tourist Authority/English Tourist Board, 1986. *Heritage and Leisure Attendances, 1985.* BTA/ETB Research Services.
Brubaker, R., 1985. 'Rethinking classical theory: the sociological vision of Pierre Bourdieu', *Theory and Society, 14*: 745–75.
Chadwick, A., 1980. *The Role of the Museum and Art Gallery in Community Education.*
Clarke, J. and Critcher, C., 1985. *The Devil Makes Work: Leisure in Capitalist Britain.*
Cruikshank, G., 1972. 'Jewry Wall Museum, Leicester: trial by questionnaire', *Museums Journal, 72. 2*: 65–7.
Cunliffe, B., 1981. 'The public face of the past', in Evans, J., Cunliffe, B. and Renfrew, A. C. (eds), *Antiquity and Man: Essays in Honour of Glyn Daniel*: 192–4.
Dillman, D., 1978. *Mail and Telephone Surveys: The Total Design Method.*
Dimaggio, P. and Useem, M., 1978. 'Social class and art consumption', *Theory and Society, 5*: 141–61.
Dixon, B., Courtney, A. and Bailey, R., 1974. *The Museum and the Canadian Public.*
Dumazedier, J., 1967, *Towards A Society of Leisure.*
Dumazedier, J., 1974. *Sociology of Leisure.*
English Tourist Board, 1982. *Visitors to Museums Survey*, 1982.
Erwin, D., 1971. 'The Belfast public and the Ulster Museum: a statistical survey', *Museums Journal, 70. 4*: 175–9.
Greene, P., 1978. 'A visitor survey at Norton Priory Museum', *Museums Journal, 78. 1*: 7–9.
Gregory, T., 1983. 'The impact of metal detecting on archaeology and the public', *Archaeological Review from Cambridge, 2. 1*: 5–8.
Gregory, T., 1986. 'Whose fault is treasure-hunting?' in Dobinson, C. and Gilchrist, R. (eds), *Archaeology, Politics and the Public.* York University Archaeological Publications: 25–7.
Heady, P., 1984. *Visiting Museums, A Report of a Survey of Visitors to the Victoria and Albert, Science and National Railway Museums for the Office of Arts and Libraries.* Office of Population and Census Surveys, HMSO.
Henley Centre, 1985. *Leisure Futures.*
Klein, R., 1974. 'Who goes to museums?' *Illustrated London News*, April 1974: 27–9.
Kviz, F., 1977. 'Towards a standard definition of response rate', *Public Opinion Quarterly, 41. 2*: 265–7.

Lewis, B., 1980. 'The museum as an educational facility', *Museums Journal, 80. 3*: 151–5.

Lewis, G., 1975. 'The museum and its public', in *Museums as an Influence on the Quality of Life*. Group for Educational Studies in Museums, Conference Proceedings.

Lewis, G., 1984. 'Collections, collectors and museums in Britain to 1920', in Thompson, J. *et al.* (eds), *Manual of Curatorship*: 23–37.

Mason, T., 1974. 'The visitors to the Manchester Museum: a questionnaire survey', *Museums Journal, 73. 4*: 153–7.

Millas, J., 1973. 'Museums and lifelong education', *Museum, 25. 3*: 157–64.

Moser, C. and Kalton, G., 1971. *Survey Research Methods in Social Investigation*.

Museums and Galleries Commission, 1984. *Eleventh Report 1978–1983*. HMSO.

Prince, D., 1985. 'Museum visiting and employment', *Museums Journal, 85. 3*: 85–90.

Prince, D. and Higgins-McLoughlin, B., 1987. *Museums UK: The Findings of the Museums Data Base Project*. Museums Association.

Prince, D. and Schadla-Hall, T., 1985. 'The image of the museum: a case-study of Kingston-upon-Hull', *Museums Journal, 85. 2*: 39–45.

Rapoport, R. and Rapoport, R., 1975. *Leisure and the Family Life-Cycle*.

Roberts, K., 1981. *Leisure*.

Index